Pentecostal Preaching and Ministry
in Multicultural and Post-Christian Canada

McMaster Divinity College Press
**McMaster Ministry Studies Series,
Volume 4**

Pentecostal Preaching and Ministry in Multicultural and Post-Christian Canada

EDITED BY
STEVEN M. STUDEBAKER

◆PICKWICK *Publications* • Eugene, Oregon

PENTECOSTAL PREACHING AND MINISTRY IN MULTICULTURAL AND POST-CHRISTIAN CANADA

McMaster Ministry Studies Series, Volume 4
McMaster Divinity College Press

Copyright © 2019 Wipf and Stock Publishers. All rights reserved. Except for brief quotations in critical publications or reviews, no part of this book may be reproduced in any manner without prior written permission from the publisher. Write: Permissions, Wipf and Stock Publishers, 199 W. 8th Ave., Suite 3, Eugene, OR 97401.

Pickwick Publications
An Imprint of Wipf and Stock Publishers
199 W. 8th Ave., Suite 3
Eugene, OR 97401

McMaster Divinity College Press
1280 Main Street West
Hamilton, Ontario, Canada
L8S 4K1

www.wipfandstock.com

PAPERBACK ISBN: 978-1-5326-5563-0
HARDCOVER ISBN: 978-1-5326-5564-7
EBOOK ISBN: 978-1-5326-5565-4

Cataloguing-in-Publication data:

Names: Studebaker, Steven M., editor.

Title: Pentecostal preaching and ministry in multicultural and post-Christian Canada / edited by Steven M. Studebaker.

Description: Eugene, OR: Pickwick Publications, 2019 | McMaster Ministry Studies Series 4. | Includes bibliographical references and index.

Identifiers: ISBN 978-1-5326-5563-0 (paperback). | ISBN 978-1-5326-5564-7 (hardcover).| ISBN 978-1-5326-5565-4 (ebook).

Subjects: LCSH: Pentecostal churches. | Preaching. | Christianity—Canada—21st century. | Pentecostalism—Canada.

Classification: BR1644 P4556 2019 (print). | BR1644 (ebook).

Manufactured in the U.S.A.   11/04/19

Contents

Acknowledgments / vii
Contributors / ix

1. Partners in (the) Spirit: Introduction / 1
   TAYLOR MURRAY AND STEVEN M. STUDEBAKER

2. The Decline of Religion and the Future of Christianity in Canada / 10
   MICHAEL WILKINSON AND BRADLEY TRUMAN NOEL

3. Even Pentecostals Need More of the Spirit: The Spirit and the Three-Fold Faithfulness Required to Reach this Generation for Christ / 30
   GARY TYRA

4. Missional Pentecostalism: What it is, why it is Needed, how to Unleash it in your Church / 54
   GARY TYRA

5. What does Brussels Have to do with Toronto? Insights from the European Edge of the Post-Christian Frontier / 78
   DAVID COUREY

6. The End of Pentecostal Preaching / 103
   VAN JOHNSON

7. Samosas at the Pentecostal Potluck: Pentecostal Hospitality for Multicultural Ministry / 125
   JOSH P. S. SAMUEL

8 Spirit Baptism, Exclusion, and Emerging Adults: An Ecclesiological Approach to a Present Challenge / 149
   PETER D. NEUMANN

9 Pentecostal Spirituality amidst Other Spiritualities: Religious and Secular / 186
   LYMAN KULATHUNGAM

Index of Subjects / 209
Index of Modern Authors / 211
Index of Ancient Sources / 215

Acknowledgments

This book is the result of the third conference dedicated to Pentecostal theology and ministry sponsored by McMaster Divinity College (29 January 2016). The conference theme was "Pentecostal Preaching and Ministry in Multicultural and Post-Christian Canada." The event brought together a large group of Pentecostal theologians and ministry leaders. I would like to extend my thanks to our speakers who presented in plenary and parallel sessions. I appreciate your contribution to this event and your willingness to be part of casting a vision for the way Pentecostal ministry can adapt to the changing context of Canadian culture.

Gary Empey (who works with the Pentecostal Assemblies of Canada International Missions in Cuba, Latin America, and the Caribbean) and Mike Middlebrook (Lead Pastor, Bethel Gospel Tabernacle, Hamilton, ON) played key roles in planning the vision and direction of this conference.

I want to recognize several faculty, staff, and graduate assistants at McMaster Divinity College for helping make this conference a success. Nina Thomas (Vice President Enrollment Management and Marketing, and Registrar) supported the vision for the conference and provided important leadership for planning and taking care of the logistical aspects of the conference. Vital in this respect was the support of Nina's staff members—Melissa West (Advancement and Marketing Assistant) and Virginia Wolfe (Finance Assistant). This conference was also the inaugural event of the Centre for Post-Christendom Studies at McMaster Divinity College. I am grateful for my collaborative work with Gordon L.

Acknowledgments

Heath (Professor of Christian History) and Lee Beach (Associate Professor of Christian Ministry) on this conference in particular and the Centre more generally. Bonghyun Yoo and Gerry Mielke were my graduate assistants and helped with the myriad of logistical details and chores before and during the conference. Taylor Murray, the graduate assistant for the Centre for Post-Christendom Studies, was indispensable in the transformation of the conference papers into a book, and he also co-wrote with me the introduction chapter.

Stanley E. Porter (President and Dean, Professor of New Testament, Roy A. Hope Chair in Christian Worldview) and Phil Zylla (Vice President Academics, Associate Professor of Pastoral Theology, J. Gordon and Margaret Warnock Jones Chair in Church Ministry) of McMaster Divinity College deserve gratitude for their continued support of Pentecostal theology and ministry by making McMaster Divinity College and its resources available to host these conferences.

I am most grateful for all those who attended and participated in the discussions at the conference and trust that they found the presentations on Pentecostal theology and ministry in post-Christendom Canada encouraging and helpful for their ministries.

Finally, I would like to thank McMaster Divinity College Press and Wipf & Stock for recognizing the value of publishing the essays presented in this volume. In this respect, David Fuller (Managing Editor, MDC Press) provided necessary editorial assistance in the final stages of the preparation of the manuscript.

Contributors

EDITOR

Steven M. Studebaker (PhD, Marquette University) is the Howard and Shirley Bentall Chair in Evangelical Thought and Professor of Systematic and Historical Theology at McMaster Divinity College. He is the author of *A Pentecostal Political Theology for American Renewal* (Palgrave, 2016) and *From Pentecost to the Triune God* (Eerdmans, 2012), as well as several other books on Jonathan Edwards' Trinitarian theology and Pentecostal theology.

CONTRIBUTORS

David Courey (PhD, McMaster Divinity College) is Guest Lecturer at Evangelical Theological Faculty in Leuven, Belgium, and Lecturer at Continental Theological Seminary in Brussels. He is author of *What Has Wittenberg to Do with Azusa? Luther's Theology of the Cross and Pentecostal Triumphalism* (T. & T. Clark, 2015).

Van Johnson is the Dean of Master's Pentecostal Seminary in Toronto, the Director of the MTS in Pentecostal Studies at Tyndale Seminary, and part of the pastoral team at Agincourt Pentecostal Church in Toronto, a large multicultural and multi-generational congregation. His most recent publication is a chapter on eschatology in a textbook designed for a growing Slovenian Pentecostal community: *Pentecostals in the 21st Century* (Wipf & Stock, 2018).

Contributors

Lyman Kulathungam (PhD, McMaster University) is Dean Emeritus (Intercultural) of Master's College and Seminary in Peterborough. He has published in the areas of Logic, Philosophy, and Religion in scholarly journals, and is the author of *The Quest: Christ Amidst the Quest* (Wipf & Stock, 2012).

Taylor Murray is a PhD student in Theology (Church History) at McMaster Divinity College. He has contributed to several encyclopedias, books, and journals, writing primarily on Baptists in Canada and the history of fundamentalism in North America.

Peter Neumann (PhD, University of St. Michael's College) is the Academic Dean and instructor in theology at Master's College and Seminary in Peterborough, and serves as an adjunct instructor, teaching Pentecostal Theology at Tyndale Seminary in Toronto. He has also served on the pastoral staffs of two churches in the greater Toronto area. He is the author of *Pentecostal Experience: An Ecumenical Encounter* (Pickwick, 2012).

Bradley Truman Noel (DTh, University of South Africa; DMin, Acadia University) is currently on faculty at Tyndale University College where he is the Director of Pentecostal Studies, and Associate Professor of Christian Ministries. He is the author of *Pentecostal and Postmodern Hermeneutics* (Wipf & Stock, 2010) and *Pentecostalism, Secularism, and Post-Christendom* (Wipf & Stock, 2015).

Josh P. S. Samuel (PhD, McMaster Divinity College) is Professor of Bible and Theology and Director of Worship and Creative Arts Ministry at Master's College and Seminary in Peterborough. He is the author of *The Holy Spirit in Worship Music, Preaching, and the Altar: Renewing Pentecostal Corporate Worship* (CPT Press, 2018).

Gary Tyra (DMin, Fuller Seminary) is Professor of Biblical and Practical Theology at Vanguard University of Southern California. His most recent publications include *Pursuing Moral Faithfulness: Ethics and Christian Discipleship* (IVP Academic, 2015) and *Getting Real: Pneumatological Realism and the Spiritual, Moral, and Ministry Formation of Contemporary Christians* (Cascade, 2018).

Michael Wilkinson (PhD, University of Ottawa) is Professor of Sociology and Director of the Religion in Canada Institute at Trinity Western University. He is the author of numerous articles and books including *Canadian Pentecostalism: Transition and Transformation* (MQUP, 2010) and *A Culture of Faith: Evangelical Congregations in Canada* (with Sam Reimer, MQUP, 2015).

1

Partners in (the) Spirit
Introduction

TAYLOR MURRAY AND STEVEN M. STUDEBAKER

THE PAST FORTY YEARS witnessed the rise of both the post-Christian West and global Christianity. As Canada and other Western nations became less Christian, the rest of the world became more Christian. In one generation, Canada became a secular, multicultural, and religiously plural society. Canadian society has become a place of declining and, in many cases, of closing churches. Though a majority of Canadians still self-identify as Christians, Christianity no longer enjoys the cultural privileges of the Christendom era.[1] Mainstream culture has marginalized Christianity.[2] Indeed, many cultural and political elites regard it as an embarrassing heritage hanger-on that is best left in the dustbin of pre-multicultural Canadian history.[3] Yet, while Canada became less Christian

---

1. For the history of Christianity in Canada and its decline, see Bibby, *The Emerging Millennials*, 165, table 9.1; Bowen, *Christians in a Secular World*, 28, table 2.3; Bramadat and Seljak, "Charting the New Terrain," 6–11.

2. Joel Thiessen attributes religious decline to falling demand for religion among Canadians—see *The Meaning of Sunday*.

3. E.g., Governor General of Canada, Julie Payette, compared people who believe that God took part in the creation of life to those who think sugar pills can cure cancer (see Wood, "Science v. Religion") and the controversy over the pro-choice/reproductive rights attestation required by the federal government to qualify for the Summer Jobs Program, which jeopardized funding for many religious organizations (see

and more secular, it also became more multicultural and religiously plural.

Indeed, since the 1970s the percentage of people who never attend religious services doubled (from 20 per cent to 40 per cent). Even bleaker is the statistic that only 13 per cent of the post-boomer generation attends religious services on a weekly basis.[4] As David E. Eagle points out, "Canada has transitioned from a country where less than one-fifth of the population would not set foot in the door of a church or other religious venue in a given year to one where this is the norm for almost half of the population. This change occurred over a mere 22 years . . . these changes signal major societal shifts."[5] Eagle believes this transition reflects the process of secularization. Sociologist Reginald Bibby argues that the decline narrative is overblown and that a renaissance of involvement with organized religion and a polarization of society into religious and non-religious groups is underway. Although scholars differ on the meaning and extent of these changes, they all agree that religious participation among Canadians is in decline and the only categories that show any meaningful growth are non-attendance and no religious affiliation.[6]

And yet without discounting the well-documented decline narrative, the outlook is not all doom and gloom. The overall wane of participation in Christian religious activities seemed to reach a bottom at just under one in three Canadians in the late 1990s.[7] Statistics from 2010 show that while only 28 per cent of Canadians attend religious services on a monthly basis, 65 per cent say that spirituality and religious issues are important to their everyday life.[8] Moreover, Sam Reimer and Michael Wilkinson document that Canadian evangelical Protestant churches, if not mainline Protestant and Catholic churches, have retained institutional vitality.[9]

Reimer, "Canadians Split").

4. Bowen, *Christians in a Secular World*, 31.

5. Eagle, "The Loosening Bond of Religion," 838–39.

6. Bibby, "Continuing the Conversation," 831–37; Bibby, *Beyond the Gods and Back*, 133–35; Eagle, "Changing Patterns of Attendance," 187–200; Eagle, "The Loosening Bond of Religion," 838–39; and Thiessen and Dawson, "Is There a 'Renaissance' of Religion?" 389–415. The chapter in this volume by Michael Wilkinson and Bradley Noel Truman dives deeper into these issues.

7. Bibby, "Continuing the Conversation on Canada," 835, table 2.

8. Bibby, "Continuing the Conversation on Canada," 835, table 2.

9. Reimer and Wilkinson, *A Culture of Faith*. David Millard Haskell, Kevin N.

At the same time that Christianity declined in Canada (and across the Western world), it grew rapidly in the rest of the world. The past decades saw the face of Christianity change from being a religion of primarily White Europeans and North Americans, to a religion of the majority world. As Philip Jenkins states, "The era of Western Christianity has passed within our lifetimes, and the day of Southern Christianity is dawning. The fact of change itself is undeniable: it has happened, and will continue to happen."[10] Consider the example of China. Just a few years ago, Christianity in China was no more than a few beleaguered bands of house churches behind the bamboo curtain. The previous official number of Chinese Christians was 100 million; however, a government-sponsored poll by East China Normal University in 2007 revised that estimate to 300 million. (For context, today, according to the Pew Forum, the United States has 173 million adult Christians, which is 71 per cent of its adult population of 245 million.)[11] Other estimates are smaller. They range from 67 million to 130 million and even go as high as 147 million. The numbers, nevertheless, are massive.[12] Consider that the number of Christians in China, by the lowest estimate, is twice the entire population of Canada, which until a generation ago was one of the leading "Christian" nations in the world. A recent headline even declared, "China on course to become 'world's most Christian nation' within 15 years."[13] We may quibble over numbers here and there, but one thing is clear: The church in the West, and Canada in particular, is in hospice care; but in the rest of the world, it is just leaving the maternity ward.

What is important for Pentecostal ministry going forward is that the two stories—the rise of the post-Christian West and Christianity in the rest of the world—intersect. Immigration out of the global south to Western European countries, to Britain and, for the interests of the conference that was the foundation of this book, to Canada, has brought

---

Flatt, and Stephanie Burgoyne argue that slumping religious activity is not emblematic of dropping demand for religion, but rather, is a reflection of the declining supply of the theologically conservative religion to which people respond. Haskell et al., "Theology Matters," 515–41.

10. Philip Jenkins, *The Next Christendom*, 3.

11. Pew Research Center, "America's Changing Religious Landscape," 20–32. For the history of Christianity in China, see Bays, *A New History*.

12. Pew Research Center, "Global Christianity," Appendix C, and Center for the Study of Global Christianity, "Christianity in Its Global Context, 1970–2020," 36.

13. Phillips and Liushi, "China on Course."

global Christianity to Toronto, Calgary, and Vancouver. Ironically, while Canada became post-Christian, secular, multicultural, and religiously plural, it also became more Christian. Global Christianity and its new vitality has come to Canada. But it has become "Christian" in way that people enculturated to White middle-class and upper-middle class suburban style churches may find uncomfortable.

The church in Canada and Pentecostals in particular face a challenging context for responding to the call to bear witness to Christ in the power of the Holy Spirit. In this situation, traditional Christendom Christianity is in decline; secularism, multiculturalism, religious pluralism, along with Global South Christianities, are on the rise. How should we respond? Not with fear. Paul encouraged Timothy that "God did not give us a spirit of timidity, but a spirit of power, of love and of self-discipline" (2 Tim 1:7). But the power is not the vain triumphalism of human hubris. Like the disciples on the Day of Pentecost, we need the Holy Spirit to come upon us and liberate us from our post-Christian pessimism. We need the Holy Spirit to enable us to proclaim the gospel to the nations; people that are no longer at the ends of the earth, but making their home in Canada. The chapters in this volume endeavour to do just that.

This volume derives from select papers presented at the conference "Pentecostal Preaching and Ministry in Multicultural and Post-Christian Canada" at McMaster Divinity College in January 2016.[14] This conference was also the inaugural event of the Centre for Post-Christendom Studies at McMaster Divinity College.[15] The conference goal was to consider and to propose ways that Pentecostal Christians and churches can respond to the challenges of the increasingly post-Christian, multicultural, secular, and religiously plural context of Canadian society. Given that cultural changes taking place in Canada mirror, in certain ways even portend, those occurring in the USA, our hope is that these essays will prove beneficial for our American neighbors as well.

In the first chapter, Michael Wilkinson and Bradley Truman Noel provide a helpful context for the remainder of the book and argue that,

---

14. This conference was the third conference focused on Pentecostalism at McMaster Divinity College. The first was "Defining Issues in Pentecostalism: Classical and Emergent" (October 2006) and the second "Globalization and Pentecostal Theology and Ministry" (October 2008). Papers from these conferences were published as Studebaker, ed., *Defining Issues in Pentecostalism* and Studebaker, ed., *Pentecostalism and Globalization*.

15. See https://pcs.mcmasterdivinity.ca/.

although Christian influence in Canada has been in decline since the Second World War, the collapse of Christendom may actually be positive for future Christian vitality in the West. Observing that Christendom was never God's ideal, the authors contend that post-*Christendom* does not necessarily mean post-*Christian*. In reality, this new context releases Christians from policing the culture and instead affords them the opportunity to more actively demonstrate the transformative principles of the kingdom of God. Without the power to coerce the state, churches today must seek alternative routes to change society, which, according to the authors, will be most effective if believers rely genuinely on the Holy Spirit's guidance.

In the first of two chapters in this volume written by Gary Tyra, he argues that the effectiveness of one's ministry in the current religious landscape is contingent upon having a spiritual, moral, and missional faithfulness. This "three-fold faithfulness," as he identifies it, begins with a genuine relationship with the risen Christ through the Holy Spirit (spiritual), which then influences how one makes ethical choices in the world (moral), and pairs ultimately with an impulse that both contends and contextualizes the gospel for one's setting (missional). Inherent in Tyra's proposal is the prioritization of a posture of pneumatological realism, which, as he diagnoses, is a doctrine that has declined in emphasis in many Pentecostal churches. Therefore, those who wish to effectively minister to a post-Christian world must recover an emphasis on experiencing the Holy Spirit.

If Tyra's first chapter diagnoses the problem of a declining emphasis on pneumatological expectancy in Pentecostal churches and how it negatively effects how one ministers in post-Christendom, his second chapter resumes the conversation and offers something of a solution in the form of what he identifies as "missional Pentecostalism." Building on his previous chapter, Tyra observes that the Holy Spirit works through believers to achieve God's purposes, which cannot be discerned unless the believer adopts a posture of pneumatological realism. Further, Tyra argues that missional Pentecostalism builds a "kingdom-representing" context in the manner by which it fosters community and encourages servanthood and proclamation. Finally, using the global growth of Pentecostalism as his model, he observes that genuine experiences with the Holy Spirit have the potential to break down the barriers of religious relativism in twenty-first century Canada.

Moving the reader across the Atlantic Ocean, David Courey argues that although Christianity in Europe has declined over the last century, the "vestiges of Christendom" (visible in elements such as holidays and architecture) suggest that Christianity's social influence remains a pertinent part of society and that it is not dead, but simply lying dormant. Although Courey focuses on Belgium in particular, his conclusions speak to the larger European context, and offer insight into Canada's climate of post-Christendom. He observes that while indigenous Christianity has waned, the vibrancy of migrant churches has resulted in recent areas of growth, which has ensured that this decline is not ubiquitous. He suggests further that Christian churches in Europe need to reorient their focus from preservation to activism, and stand as a reflection of the kingdom of God to a needy world. In light of Europe's religious setting, Courey suggests that Pentecostals should dialogue with Roman Catholics and migrant churches, thus building bridges within the Christian community, and should find common ground and perhaps even partner with secularists and Muslims, using the unique position of its heritage to form a new social identity that has a genuinely Christian influence on society as a whole.

Much in the same way that Courey probes the past for insight into the present (and future), Van Johnson looks at three early Pentecostal newsletters that predate the Pentecostal Assemblies of Canada (1919) and observes the ways in which Pentecostal preaching has changed in Canada over the past century, especially as it relates to the declining emphasis on eschatological themes. For Johnson, the three newsletters that clearly demonstrate this shift include *The Promise* (Toronto, 1907), *The Apostolic Messenger* (Winnipeg, 1908), and *The Good Report* (Ottawa, 1911). These early Pentecostals saw the events of Acts 2 unfolding in their own time and believed that this meant Christ's return was imminent, which developed in them an urgency to minister to the lost. The expectation reflected an "already-not yet" eschatology that brought the present and future into conversation. In the twenty-first century, where eschatological themes have been minimized in preaching to some extent, Pentecostals must negotiate a way to harmonize their tradition with their present reality. Johnson concludes that Pentecostals must return to their roots and adopt an eschatology that does not focus solely on the future (and thereby rarely is preached), but must present one that focuses both on the "already" and the "not yet."

Among the most pressing areas of attention for ministering in Canada today is the question of multiculturalism, which Josh Samuel argues should be approached by using the Day of Pentecost in Acts 2 as a paradigm, especially its inherent emphasis on hospitality. As he observes, churches need to be hospitable to a variety of cultural backgrounds without falling prey to a "melting pot" ministry on one extreme or an affirmative action ministry on the other. Instead, churches need to prayerfully listen for the Holy Spirit's guidance, and earnestly acknowledge cultural differences as a means through which to enter into community with one another. This, he contends, is a closer reflection of the presence of multiple tongues on the Day of Pentecost, and creates a much more welcoming environment for minorities.

In the penultimate chapter, Peter Neumann suggests that highlighting the communal aspects of Pentecost may provide a way forward for Pentecostalism and satiate the hesitations of emerging adults in Canada. Of particular interest to Neumann is the next generation's criticism of traditional Pentecostal beliefs (especially tongues as initial evidence of the Spirit) as exclusive and therefore unappealing. In an effort to solve this tension, he looks for overlapping similarities between traditional Pentecostalism and today's emerging adults, and suggests re-reading Acts 2 through a communal lens in order to combat the overemphasis on personal experience and autonomy. He focuses on Pentecost as a formative event that drew together a diverse community defined by love, commitment, and unity. Employing this communal interpretation, he shows, paves a much more inclusive way forward for Pentecostals of all ages.

In the concluding chapter, Lyman Kulathungam argues that the spirituality inherent in Pentecostalism offers opportunities to engage contemporary Canadian society in a meaningful way. He observes that while organized religion in Canada is in decline, spirituality, which is dictated by one's desire to discover the unknown, is thriving. This spirituality is not necessarily "religious" in the traditional sense, and has taken root in religious and secular communities alike. In order to meet the apparent longing for meaning in this socio-religious context, Kulathungam maintains that Pentecostal spirituality must reflect the description of Pentecost found in Acts 2. Namely, he argues that if Pentecostalism focuses on being personal rather than individualistic, which includes communal worship of the triune God and fellowship with other believers, it will provide a healthy alternative to the North American consumer culture and will remain relevant in a society seeking answers on a spiritual level.

In 2019, the Pentecostal Assemblies of Canada celebrate their centennial. Amid the relatively uncharted waters of Canada's changing religious and social context, Pentecostals in Canada now face their second century. The task of ministering in post-Christendom will remain a challenge, to be sure; however, with the Holy Spirit as a compass and a pilot, it is not an insurmountable one.

BIBLIOGRAPHY

Bays, Daniel H. *A New History of Christianity in China*. Blackwell Guides to Global Christianity. Malden, MA: Wiley-Blackwell, 2012.

Bibby, Reginald W. *Beyond the Gods and Back: Religion's Demise and Rise and Why it Matters*. Lethbridge, AB: Project Canada, 2011.

———. "Continuing the Conversation on Canada: Changing Patterns of Religious Service Attendance." *Journal for the Scientific Study of Religion* 50 (2011) 831–37.

———. *The Emerging Millennials: How Canada's Newest Generation is Responding to Change and Choice*. Lethbridge, AB: Project Canada, 2009.

Bowen, John P. *Christians in a Secular World: The Canadian Experience*. Montreal: McGill-Queen's University Press, 2004.

Bramadat, Paul, and Seljak, David. "Charting the New Terrain: Christianity and Ethnicity in Canada." In *Christianity and Ethnicity in Canada*, edited by Paul Bramadat and David Seljak, 3–48. Toronto: University of Toronto Press, 2008.

Center for the Study of Global Christianity. "Christianity in Its Global Context, 1970–2020: Society, Religion, and Mission," Gordon-Conwell Theological Seminary, June 2013. Online: https://www.gordonconwell.edu/ockenga/research/documents/ChristianityinitsGlobalContext.pdf

Eagle, David E. "Changing Patterns of Attendance at Religious Services in Canada, 1986–2008." *Journal for the Scientific Study of Religion* 50 (2011) 187–200.

———. "The Loosening Bond of Religion in Canada: Reply to Bibby." *Journal for the Scientific Study of Religion* 50 (2011) 838–39.

Haskell, David Millard, et al. "Theology Matters: Comparing the Traits of Growing and Declining Mainline Protestant Church Attendees and Clergy." *Review of Religious Research* 58 (2016) 515–41.

Jenkins, Philip. *The Next Christendom: The Coming of Global Christianity*. New York: Oxford University Press, 2002.

Pew Research Center. "America's Changing Religious Landscape." 12 May 2015. http://www.pewforum.org/2015/05/12/americas-changing-religious-landscape/

———. "Global Christianity—A Report of the Size and Distribution of the World's Christian Population." 19 December 2011. Appendix C. http://www.pewforum.org/2011/12/19/global-christianity-exec/

Phillips, Tom, and Zhejiang Liushi. "China on Course to Become 'World's Most Christian Nation' Within 15 Years." *The Telegraph*, 19 April 2014.

Reimer, Sam, and Michael Wilkinson. *A Culture of Faith: Evangelical Congregations in Canada*. Montreal: McGill-Queen's University Press, 2015.

Reimer, Will. "Canadians split on summer jobs program funding controversy." *Global News*, 16 May 2018.

Studebaker, Steven M., ed. *Defining Issues in Pentecostalism: Classical and Emergent.* McMaster Theological Studies Series 1. Eugene, OR: Pickwick, 2008.

———. *Pentecostalism and Globalization: The Impact of Global Pentecostalism on Pentecostal Theology and Ministry.* McMaster Theological Studies Series 2. Eugene, OR: Pickwick, 2010.

Thiessen, Joel. *The Meaning of Sunday: The Practice of Belief in a Secular Age.* Montreal: McGill-Queen's University Press, 2015.

Thiessen, Joel, and Dawson, Lorne L. "Is There a 'Renaissance' of Religion in Canada? A Critical Look at Bibby and Beyond." *Studies in Religion* 37 (2008) 389–415.

Wood, Linda Solomon. "Science v. Religion and the new Governor General under Fire." *Canada's National Observer*, 6 November 2017.

2

The Decline of Religion and the Future of Christianity in Canada

Michael Wilkinson and Bradley Truman Noel

INTRODUCTION

MANY THEOLOGIANS, PASTORS, AND church leaders claim Canada is no longer a Christian country. While this assumes that Canada once was a Christian country, there was never a single vision of Canada as a Christian country. Rather, competing views were shaped by the "two solitudes" of English- and French-speaking Canadians, reflecting the regionalism of the country. Protestant churches, like the United Church of Canada and the Anglican Church of Canada, and evangelical churches, including the Pentecostal Assemblies of Canada (PAOC), were products of the time. These reflected a particular view of Canada as a Christian country, albeit a Protestant country that did not recognize the competing view of Roman Catholics. The churches were also bolstered by a growing sense of nationalism and a post-World War II economic and demographic boom that shaped an emerging Canadian identity and coincided with a growing satisfaction with family, jobs, and public life. But signs of decline were already emerging in this prosperous period that were exacerbated with the social upheaval of the 1960s. Since the 1970s, Canadian society has experienced growing levels of secularization, a social process that leads to the decline of religious participation, authority, privatization of faith, and the growth of "no religion" as a religious identity. Immigration is one of the most important factors for explaining religious change in Canada, with shifting numbers among Roman Catholics and Protestants from Europe to other regions of the world. Immigration also has an impact on the growth of religions like Islam, Buddhism, Sikhism, and Hinduism. The future of religion will continue to be shaped by ongoing waves of immigration and secularization. In this chapter, we review the changing religious landscape of Canada and raise questions about the implications for Christianity.

RELIGIOUS CHANGE IN CANADA

Religious change in Canada can be organized around four key storylines. The first is the general decline of Christianity—in Roman Catholicism, but especially among the historical or mainline Protestants like the United Church of Canada and the Anglican Church of Canada. Mainline Protestantism has faced massive decline over the past several decades with no signs of recovery. Roman Catholicism has maintained its numbers largely through immigration. Although the numbers of Roman Catholics remain about the same (approximately 12 million),[1] the overall population in Canada has grown and so while the numbers are not declining, the growth is slowing relative to the population.

The second storyline revolves around the general vitality among evangelical Protestants.[2] Evangelicals have roughly grown from about 8 per cent to 10 per cent of the Canadian population. However, the vast majority of growth is due to immigration.[3] Evangelicalism in Canada is undergoing a de-Europeanization process as it increasingly becomes more ethnically and culturally diverse. The growth, however, is tempered with a series of challenges for evangelical Protestants including some general dissatisfaction among clergy, especially youth pastors and assistant pastors. Evangelical pastors are also aging, with the vast majority of pastors in the PAOC, for example, now over the age of 55.[4] This ag-

---

1. Statistics Canada, *2011 National Household Survey*.
2. Reimer and Wilkinson, *A Culture of Faith*.
3. See Reimer and Wilkinson, *A Culture of Faith*, 68–89; Guenther, "Ethnicity and Evangelical Protestants in Canada," 365–414.
4. Unpublished figures compiled by the PAOC for Wilkinson. Also see Reimer

ing of the clergy also corresponds with a decline in enrolment figures at evangelical colleges and seminaries, where traditionally, clergy have been educated and prepared for congregational ministry.

The third storyline concerns the impact of immigration. We have noted that immigration is a major contributor to the changes within Christianity; however, it also accounts for the growth among non-Christian religions in Canada and the increase in religious diversity.[5] Immigration figures for Judaism, Islam, Hinduism, Buddhism, and Sikhism, for example, for about 100 years, accounted for about 4–6 per cent of Canadians. In the past two decades, the figures have grown to roughly 6–8 per cent of Canadians identifying with a non-Christian religion. This reflects the growing numbers of immigrants from Africa, Asia, and Latin America.

The fourth storyline is perhaps one of the most intriguing, for it describes the rapid growth in Canada of those who do not identify with any religion. The percentage of Canadians stating they do not identify with any religion was 4 per cent in 1971, 12 per cent in 1991, 16 per cent in 2001, and 24 per cent in 2011. Religious "nones" are not necessarily atheists or irreligious; some attend church and have religious beliefs. They are mostly young males, politically liberal, and recent immigrants. Sociologists also point out that it is increasingly more acceptable socially to identify as a religious none, and they note that numbers of those identifying as a religious none may continue to increase as individuals react negatively to the growing religious right and Christian fundamentalism.[6]

Often, the decline of Christianity in Canada is contrasted with the meteoric rise of Pentecostalism in the twentieth century. But what do we know about the Pentecostals when compared to other trends? What impact does immigration or secularization have on Pentecostalism? What is the future of Pentecostalism in Canada? What is the Pentecostal story in relation to the general decline of Christianity in Canada? When Ellen Hebden, leader of the East End Mission, announced that she received the gift of tongues in 1906, the Pentecostal movement in Canada found a home in Toronto.[7] Very quickly the news began to spread that the Spirit was baptizing Methodists looking for renewal, Holiness

and Wilkinson, *A Culture of Faith*, 134–36.

5. Beaman and Beyer, *Religion and Diversity in Canada*; Beyer and Ramji, *Growing up Canadian*.

6. Thiessen, *The Meaning of Sunday*, 96–99.

7. Stewart, "A Canadian Azusa?" 17–37.

missionaries looking for power to evangelize the world, and many other radical evangelical Christians looking for signs of the coming kingdom of God. Hebden's Mission saw people from all around the world coming to discover what God was doing and in turn the Mission sent missionaries throughout the world, including the most prominent Canadian missionary, Charles Chawner, whose family made a lasting impact on the PAOC.[8]

By 1909 the Pentecostals were asking questions about organizing at a camp meeting in Markham, Ontario. The English Anglican minister, Alexander Boddy, found some interest among those in attendance, but Ellen Hebden made it very clear that she was not interested in any organization and believed it would be the end of the movement.[9] However, the irony of all new religious movements is that without some organization they will come to an end; organization, however, does temper the charisms that surround the emergence of these types of movements. Still, it would take another decade before the first Canadian Pentecostal denomination would officially receive a charter from the government to organize congregations, establish theological schools, and send missionaries.[10] In the meantime, the Hebden Mission would face a number of crises and eventually come to an end followed by Ellen Hebden's death in 1923.[11]

In 1914 the Assemblies of God, USA (AG) organized and Pentecostals in Western Canada were officially linked as a district. This relationship would continue until the Pentecostals in Eastern Canada received their charter in 1919 when East and West joined. However, it was not until 1925 that the official relationship with the AG ended and the Canadian Pentecostals came to exist under one constitution as the Pentecostal Assemblies of Canada.[12]

The year 1925 was also important in Canadian religious history, for it was the year in which the Methodists, Congregationalists, and about one third of the Presbyterians formed the United Church of Canada.[13]

---

8. Wilkinson, "Charles W. Chawner," 39–54. The son of Charles Chawner, C. Austin Chawner was a key missionary for the PAOC in Africa and gave leadership to the PAOC mission work.

9. Wakefield, *Alexander Boddy*.

10. Di Giacomo, "Pentecostal and Charismatic Christianity in Canada," 22–23.

11. Sloos, "The Story of James and Ellen Hebden," 181–202.

12. Di Giacomo, "Pentecostal and Charismatic Christianity in Canada," 23.

13. Schweitzer, *The United Church of Canada*; Flatt, *After Evangelicalism*; Airhart, *A Church with the Soul of a Nation*. Airhart and Flatt offer two very different

These two denominations are case studies in contrast that reveal two different paths Christians with Methodist roots would follow. One would be the path of evangelical Pentecostalism and the other a national vision for a Canadian church. Both, however, are products of the time when early-twentieth-century Canada was still a colony of Britain, allegiance to the Crown was taken for granted in English-speaking Canada, and anti-Catholic and anti-French sentiments were high, as the country was trying to find its identity. Canada was broadly a Christian country in belief and practice. Most Canadians attended church. Sabbath laws meant no shopping on Sunday. Prayer was public. Still, there was no unified vision of a Christian Canada.

With their view of Quebec and the Church shaped by Catholic renewal and the ultramontane movement of the nineteenth century, French Roman Catholics envisioned the country and its Christian identity much differently than the Protestants.[14] Catholic conservatism and its reaction to modernity was a stronghold in Quebec until the 1960s, when about 90 per cent of Québécois identified as being Roman Catholic and about the same percentage attended church on a weekly basis. While the Second Vatican Council contributed to a new openness in the Roman Catholic Church, it was most likely the Quiet Revolution with accelerated modernization and secularization that impacted the Catholics in Quebec.[15] There was also no single Protestant vision of Canada as a Christian country. The Methodists saw Canada as "God's Dominion" where God would reign from sea to sea.[16] The Anglicans, on the other hand, saw themselves as *the* Church in the colony where the Church of England in Great Britain was the official state church that received certain benefits. The divide among

interpretations of the United Church. Flatt explains the decline of the United Church in relation to its adoption of liberal theology in the 1960s. Airhart, on the other hand, offers a social and cultural analysis that explores how the United Church's vision of Canada and the role of the Church changed with modernization, which had the effect of making the Church irrelevant in relation to the State. Airhart's social and cultural analysis is more nuanced and convincing. For another argument about the role of conservative theology and liberal theology and its impact on the United Church, see Haskell et al., "Theology Matters," 515–41. The argument by Haskell, Flatt, and Burgoyne adopts a rational choice or market model theory that focuses on the problem of supply. Basically, the argument is that the demand for conservative religion is higher than that for liberal theology but the suppliers (i.e., the churches) are not able to meet the demand.

14. Choquette, *Canada's Religions*, 173–77, 322–27.
15. Beyer, "Roman Catholicism in Contemporary Quebec," 140–44.
16. Clifford, "His Dominion: A Vision in Crisis," 23–42.

Protestants was notable in certain ways but especially among Protestants with differing views about Protestantism's relationship to the state.[17] In this sense, there was no single vision of Canada as a Christian country, but at least three distinct visions among Roman Catholics, Methodists (now the United Church of Canada), and Anglicans. Pentecostals did not share in this vision either except for some sense of being English and citizens of Great Britain. The allegiance between Church and State, while not formalized in the colony, was debated, and two world wars solidified a Canadian identity that was more nationalistic than religious.

The post-World War II era of Canada was characterized by a series of "booms" including economic and demographic change. These two variables together inflated church attendance after the war. Canadians experienced peace and a sense of comfort with good jobs and salaries that allowed for mothers to stay at home and raise children. This era provided a family and work context never experienced before, and yet it was so highly influential that many assumed the nuclear family living in the growing suburbs of Toronto, Montreal, and Vancouver was the norm for centuries. This economic security is the key for understanding the growing comfort among Canadians with views of progressive growth and economic certainty. As Canadians experienced this growth, which was very much a social anomaly, church attendance was already showing signs of slowing, especially in the United Church of Canada prior to the so-called liberalization of Canadian social values in the 1960s.[18] While the 1960s may have called into question the comfort of the 1950s, it was in no way the single cause for the problems that would face the United Church. Even the Pentecostals were yet to experience their attendance boom that occurred in the 1970s. PAOC growth, however, may have had more to do with the Charismatic renewal that was occurring among Roman Catholics and mainline Protestants who began visiting Pentecostal churches on Sunday evenings to share ecumenically the experience of seeking God for divine healing and gifts of the Spirit.[19]

---

17. Westfall, *Two Worlds*.

18. Bibby, *Fragmented Gods*, 13. Bibby notes that the attendance figures among Mainline Protestants did not suddenly decline in the 1960s but were not growing at the same rate as the rest of the population for years previous. In other words, the decline or slowing of growth was already beginning prior to the significant losses of the 1960s.

19. Butler, "The Interface of Two Canadian Renewal Movements."

Canada in the 1970s does start to change socially and culturally as a result of the Royal Commission to investigate the bilingual and bicultural nature of Canada.[20] By the time the study was completed and the fourth volume was written, the Canadian government realized that it was not just the English and the French who built the country but many "other" Canadians with European cultural histories including the Germans, Italians, Ukrainians, Scandinavians, and the Dutch. In this social context, the Canadian government brought forward a new vision for Canada: the multicultural society. However, the multicultural society was really a pan-European one. Canada was still primarily English and French with significant numbers of "other" Europeans. In the 1970s Europe was not as challenging a place to live as it was in the 1930s and 1940s and many Europeans did not want to leave. International laws and immigration were changing, with more opportunities for people to come to Canada from Africa, Asia, and Latin America. It would take another twenty years for full recognition that multicultural Canada was not simply English and Anglican or United Church or French and Roman Catholic.[21] Any sense of Canada being a Christian country was contested among Christians and with growing numbers of Christians arriving from Africa, Asia, and Latin America, a new understanding of Christianity was emerging largely linked with the de-Europeanization of world Christianity.[22] If Christianity throughout the world was not European, why were Christians in Canada so surprised to discover that African, Asian, and Latin American Christians were not like them?

POLARIZATION OR SECULARIZATION?

How do we begin to explain and understand these changes? There are two important ideas that have occupied sociologists in Canada. The most prominent voice in Canada is Reginald Bibby, who has consistently argued that religion in Canada has changed: it is characterized by fragmentation, high levels of interest in spirituality along with low levels of participation in religious institutions, and more recently with religion

---

20. *Report of the Royal Commission on Bilingualism and Biculturalism*, 1970.

21. Bramadat and Seljak, *Religion and Ethnicity in Canada*.

22. Wilkinson, *The Spirit said Go*; Bramadat and Seljak, *Christianity and Ethnicity in Canada*.

polarized between believers and non-believers.[23] Bibby is shaped by the theoretical views of Rodney Stark and the religious market model most prevalent among American sociologists.[24] The argument is that the demand for religion remains high but the providers vary. Secularization, it is argued, is characterized by the decline of religious providers who are eventually replaced by those who do a better job at meeting religious needs. Bibby argues that in Canada, we have experienced fragmentation, which accounts for the decline of churches like the United Church and the Anglican Church, and revitalization that is not measured by church attendance but in higher levels of belief, spirituality, and overall faith. The polarization view also recognizes the growing divide between believers and unbelievers with a large so-called ambivalent middle that could go either way on the continuum.[25] Bibby's work has been critiqued on several levels, but particularly by those who advocate for an explanation that revolves around the long-standing view of secularization.[26] Advocates of secularization argue that while currently it appears that society is polarized between believers and unbelievers, the trend is moving towards "no religion" with no evidence suggesting that the ambivalent middle is seriously considering a return to church.

The main proponents of secularization in Canada include sociologists like Kurt Bowen who argued that Canada is increasingly a secular and modern society.[27] The implications, according to Bowen, are as follows: (a) secularization as differentiation whereby the public role of religion loses authority; (b) disengagement among Canadians from congregations and more specifically, the decline of Church-based religion; (c) decline in faith with growing numbers of people claiming to be spiritual but not religious; and (d) the privatization of faith whereby religious

---

23. Bibby, *Fragmented Gods*; *Unknown Gods*; *Restless Gods*; *Beyond the Gods and Back*. In *Fragmented Gods*, Bibby makes his best case for understanding secularizing trends but also his views about the need for churches to connect with Canadians through the offering of specialized services. In *Unknown Gods*, Bibby continues his analysis of the decline in religion but one-third of the book focuses on the churches and their problems of marketing and messaging among other issues. *Restless Gods* focuses on high levels of spirituality in the Canadian marketplace.

24. There are numerous journal articles and books, but see especially Stark and Finke, *Acts of Faith*, for details about the theory.

25. Bibby, *Beyond the Gods and Back*, 34–61.

26. Thiessen and Dawson, "Is there a Renaissance of Religion in Canada?" 389–415; Wilkins-Laflamme, "Toward Religious Polarization?" 284–308.

27. Bowen, *Christians in a Secular World*.

commitment is increasingly insignificant. Bowen evaluated numerous studies and trends and argued that the decline of Christianity in Canada would result in the weakening of civic life precisely because Christianity played an important role in many areas, including volunteering and charitable work, education, and social services.

Joel Thiessen has also considered the question about secularization and specifically whether or not Canadians had any interest in churches.[28] In his study Thiessen interviewed people from three groups to ascertain just how much interest or demand for religion existed. The groups included (a) active affiliates, or those who regularly participate in church; (b) marginal affiliates, those who attend only on special occasions like Christmas and Easter; and (c) religious nones, those who do not attend or identify with any particular religion. Thiessen discovered that active affiliates are generally content with their involvement and the congregations they attend. Marginal affiliates, while enjoying the special times of the year that they attend, are not interested in higher levels of participation.[29] Religious nones clearly indicated that they have no interest in participating. Overall, the high demand for religion argument, according to Thiessen is weak in Canada, which is a cultural issue and not necessarily a congregational problem. There was no indication that Canadians saw the problem being primarily churches, but clearly, they did not see much need or relevance for increased levels of participation.[30]

IMPLICATIONS FOR FAITH IN A POST CHRISTIAN CANADA

Having presented the background to the collapse of Christendom in Canada, in all of its various forms, we may now discuss the many issues arising out of changing societal values around faith and religion, focusing in particular on the tremendous challenge to Pentecostalism that secularization is proving to be in a post-Christendom age. We wish to offer a way forward that includes the possibilities and opportunities inherent within an increasingly secular and post-Christendom context.

28. Thiessen, *The Meaning of Sunday*.

29. Also see Thiessen, "Marginal Religious Affiliates in Canada," 69–90.

30. This conclusion challenges the view of Bibby (e.g., *Unknown Gods*), that one of the primary problems is with the churches, and not culture, and if they would attend to issues like marketing and managing (i.e., be more relevant) then Canadians would return.

CHRIST AND CULTURE: NIEBUHR'S FIVE TYPES

The classic book around which discussion on religion and culture revolves is *Christ and Culture*, published in 1951 by H. Richard Niebuhr.[31] Written more than 60 years ago, Niebuhr offered five perspectives on Christian responses to contemporary culture in the middle of the last century. Beginning with definitions of Christ (acknowledging that our descriptions will always be incomplete) and culture ("the total process of human activity")[32] Niebuhr sought to summarize the possible relationships between Christianity and modern Western culture.

The first, termed *Christ Against Culture*, emphasized the opposition between Christ and culture. "Whatever may be the customs of the society in which the Christian lives, and whatever the human achievement it conserves, Christ is seen as opposed to them, so that he confronts men with the challenge of an 'either-or' decision."[33] This view uncompromisingly affirmed the Lordship of Christ and his authority over the Christian, and rejected absolutely any claims of loyalty by contemporary culture. For one to be completely loyal to Christ, one draws a clear line of separation from the world. On the opposite end of the spectrum, with option two, *The Christ of Culture*, proponents sought to ". . . hail Jesus as the Messiah of their society, the fulfiller of its hopes and aspirations, the perfecter of its true faith, the source of its holiest spirit."[34] There is no inherent tension between the Church and contemporary culture, the social laws and the gospel, or the workings of divine grace and human effort. Culture is interpreted through an understanding of Christ, and his teachings and actions which were believed to mirror the broader civilization.

Third, Niebuhr noted that the vast majority of Christianity refused to side with the "anti-cultural radicals" or the "accommodators," but sought a different approach, termed *Christ Above Culture*. In this view, the tension is not between Christ and culture, but between God and humanity. As God stands above culture, it is neither inherently good nor evil, but as a human sphere may exhibit both extremes. As humanity functioned in the social realm it also did so in the cultural realm, and thus culture

---

31. Niebuhr, *Christ and Culture*. For a helpful summary, see Kumar, "'Christ and Culture' by Richard Niebuhr: Book Summary." Also, Carson, *Christ and Culture Revisited*, 9–65.

32. Niebuhr, *Christ and Culture*, 32.

33. Niebuhr, *Christ and Culture*, 40.

34. Niebuhr, *Christ and Culture*, 83.

was a tool in the hand of God. D. A. Carson noted, "Synthesists seek a 'both-and' solution. They maintain the gap between Christ and culture that the cultural Christian never takes seriously and that the radical does not even try to breech—yet they insist that Christ is as sovereign over the culture as over the church."[35]

Similar to this is the *Christ and Culture in Paradox* type, which sought to clarify that viewing Christ as above culture may be desirable, but is ultimately very challenging due to the sin within culture. Like the "Christ Against Culture" position, these dualists see a clear distinction between Christ and sinful humanity, but in contrast place themselves fully in the sinful category with the rest of humanity who do not follow Christ. Finally, Niebuhr posited the *Christ as the Transformer of Culture* position. Those who hold this position "hold fast to the radical distinction between God's work in Christ and man's work on culture" but reject the road of isolationism from culture that has plagued exclusivist Christianity. While not seeking to modify Christ's judgment of sin as found in culture, they also believed that "culture is under God's sovereign rule, and that the Christian must carry on cultural work in obedience to the Lord." We may distinguish the approach of the "conversionists" from their "dualist" compatriots by their more "positive and helpful attitude toward culture."[36] Although Niebuhr did not embrace either of his five types explicitly, only the last option of the five received no negative criticism whatsoever; many scholars have interpreted this as his tacit approval.[37]

Classical Pentecostalism's emphasis on "separation" from the world as evidence of commitment to Christ, clearly places it in Niebuhr's first category, *Christ Against Culture*. Culture and its institutions were inherently evil, as a part of a fallen, sinful world. The Christian task was to introduce humanity to Christ, so others might also enjoy similar separation from the culture and its negative influence. This understanding, of course, does not fit well with Christ's description of believers as "*in*, but not *of*, the world" (a phrase adapted from John 17:14–15). Further, this separation from culture, at least on the surface, was far easier in a society structured by Christendom. Pentecostals could assume a posture of antagonism vis-à-vis culture, and feel secure in their "withdrawal" from the world, because Christendom supported all of the major societal

---

35. Carson, *Christ and Culture Revisited*, 21.
36. Niebuhr, *Christ and Culture*, 191.
37. Carson, *Christ and Culture Revisited*, 29.

structures around them. Pentecostalism could afford the luxury of posturing against "worldly endeavours" because many of these were, in the broad strokes at least, supported by the Canadian Christendom narrative.

Further, and less pejoratively, Pentecostals were loath to embrace any task that detracted them from their core focus of winning souls before the soon return of Christ. Kent Duncan notes that J. Roswell Flower, first General Secretary of the Assemblies of God (USA), declared in 1920 that institutional ventures (such as orphanages and schools) were "clearly out of bounds for Pentecostal missionaries serving in 'the last days.'" Pentecostal missionaries, he wrote, "cannot follow the methods laid down by those who have gone before them, neither can they bend their energies in building up charitable institutions, hospitals and schools as do the denominational societies. The Pentecostal commission is to witness, *witness, WITNESS*. . . . It is so easy to be turned aside to do work which is very good in itself, but which is short of the Pentecostal standard. Our missionaries are in danger of this."[38] Though this view did not prevail over the course of the decades that followed, it still appeared from time to time as Pentecostals grappled with the balance between the proclamation of the gospel and the desire to meet the real needs of hunger, housing, and medicine.

With the support of Christendom, early Pentecostals were therefore able to more easily maintain a cultural stance of separation. But as we have observed, culture and society have changed, raising an important question about the relationship between Pentecostalism and culture in Canada. Niebuhr's work is instructive even with its limitations. We recognize that Niebuhr's ideas reflect a Christendom assumption, and its perspective of transformation. Niebuhr did not imagine the end of Christendom as we now understand it. As Craig Carter notes, ". . . once one rejects the Christendom assumptions behind Niebuhr's book, the whole typology becomes suspect. . . . It is taken for granted by Niebuhr that, since Western culture is Christian, Christians therefore have a responsibility for culture . . . Christendom is presupposed, and the problem is how to relate Christ to it."[39] If this understanding is accurate, what is the value in Niebuhr's typology for a Canadian post-Christendom context?

---

38. Flower, "Pentecostal Commission," 12. Quoted in Duncan, "Emerging Engagement."

39. Carter, *Rethinking Christ and Culture*, 15, 17. Carter endeavours to engage Niebuhr's work via a post-Christendom perspective, and offers a new typology of understanding Christ and culture.

Without entangling ourselves in substantial debate relative to the details of Niebuhr's work, such as his particular understanding of "culture" or the placing of certain historical figures into specific categories of his five types, we may nonetheless observe value in his observations. Though the concerns raised by Carter and others have merit, the five types suggested by Niebuhr serve our purposes well as they raise important questions for how Pentecostals may consider engaging culture, even if culture is defined differently than Niebuhr suggested. We recognize that Christ did not come to establish a Canadian Christendom, but rather the kingdom of God. In this sense, we do not speak of "culture" as in any way suggesting "Christian culture." Rather, when speaking of culture we wish to consider simply how Christians can engage Canadians with the Good News of Christ through the everyday interactions of social life. The goal of the Incarnation was never to establish Christian governments or an official Christian society, but to establish God's kingdom in the lives of individuals called into community with one another. With that perspective, we may applaud the end of Christendom in the sense that it was never God's intention. Further we may recognize that the fight to preserve it has in many senses distracted Christians from the task originally given—announcing the good news of the kingdom of God—and not preserving the vestiges of a "Christian era" now past. As Stuart Murray observes, "The end of Christendom means, in the long run, *imposing Christianity does not work*; only if we celebrate this and move beyond dismissing Christendom to a more repentant response will we be truly free to develop a different strategy."[40]

THE CHALLENGE OF CHRIST AND CANADIAN CULTURE

Once the Church is able to embrace the demise of the Christendom narrative and structure, sober thought will be required to discern how it might shift its view of mission. Further, the Church must recognize the changes in the Canadian cultural milieu occurring as the demise of Christendom and its modern assumptions. As noted elsewhere,[41] a post-Christendom Canadian culture also exhibits signs of postmodernity. Shane Simms notes:

---

40. Murray, *Post-Christendom*, 208.

41. Noel, *Pentecostalism, Secularism, and Post-Christendom*, 68–82. Italics in the original.

> Penetrating a pagan or saturated culture that thinks in terms of post-modernity is one of the biggest challenges the church has ever faced in its history. Even though the postmodern milieu is potentially open to the narrative of God's Kingdom, it does not largely accept the role of the church in that narrative. The church needs to discover ways to be about the work of the Kingdom of God, not to proclaim itself as superintending the work of the Kingdom of God. *This change in ecclesiastical mindset may post a more significant challenge than actually reaching a postmodern generation with the message of Christ.*[42]

Lesslie Newbigin argues that a Christian response to secularization must involve more than simply affirming the way of salvation for the individual. Rather, the central call and life of the Church must be to call all people into discipleship. Acknowledging Christ's sovereignty over the personal and domestic issues of life, and the life of the Church, also implies acknowledging the Lordship of Christ over the public life of society. Believers cannot simply seek to follow Christ in their personal lives without also challenging the assumptions that govern the worlds of economics, politics, education, government, and culture. He observes:

> The Church can never settle down to being a voluntary society concerned merely with private and domestic affairs. It is bound to challenge in the name of the one Lord all the powers, ideologies, myths, assumptions, and worldviews which do not acknowledge him as Lord. If that involves conflict, trouble, and rejection, then we have the example of Jesus before us and his reminder that a servant is not greater than his master.[43]

REMAIN ORTHODOX: RESIST ASSIMILATION AND ISOLATIONISM

In the nineteenth and early-twentieth centuries, neither the conservative nor the liberal responses to the Enlightenment helped the cause of Christianity. "Conservatives, rejecting scientific explanations and trying to maintain a stranglehold on debate, weakened its appeal by associating Christianity with obscurantism and blinkered traditionalism. Liberals, attempting to reconfigure Christianity to fit comfortably into the culture

---

42. Simms, "Moving Forward in Mission," 54–55. Emphasis added.
43. Newbigin, *The Gospel in a Pluralist Society*, 220–21.

Pentecostal Preaching and Ministry

of scientific rationalism, produced an anemic religion that attracted little commitment and decreasing numbers."[44] Some groups in the twentieth century sought to fortify their position in Christendom by withdrawing into the church walls, avoiding contact with culture. In a culture that has moved beyond bounded set thinking, and desires to *belong* before it will *believe*, this approach simply will not work.

Other Christian groups sought to navigate the changes in culture by seeking to eradicate any position or doctrine offensive to Enlightenment thinking and its modern assumptions. Belief in the Scriptures as authoritative, the divinity of Christ, and any talk of Christ's atoning blood shed for "sinners," were among the first casualties. While these attempts to placate the supposed demands of a secular culture and bridge the gap between the message of Christ and the notions acceptable to the modern, educated person, seemed prudent, in reality the strategy had the opposite effect.

The correct approach is to take the middle of these two extremes: neither *Christ Against Culture* nor the *Christ of Culture* approaches will serve the church well in a post-Christendom society. Rather, churches would do well to hold to orthodoxy while engaging culture. Maintaining congregational vitality in a sea of secularizing trends is a challenge. Roger Finke and Rodney Stark note, "People tend to value religion according to how much it costs . . . because 'reasonable' and 'sociable' religion costs little, it is not valued greatly."[45] Bibby agrees, stating "In short, the more mainline a denomination becomes, the lower the value of belonging to it, resulting eventually in widespread defection."[46]

Newbigin observes,

> The facts are well known. The strongly conservative and evangelical elements in the Protestant church have undergone a remarkable renaissance, while the churches which have tried to adjust their beliefs and practices to the temper of modernity are in decline . . . It would seem to be proved beyond doubt that human beings cannot live in the rarefied atmosphere of pure rationality as the post-Enlightenment world has understood rationality. There are needs of the human spirit which simply must be met. It seems that those religious bodies which have tried to accommodate as much as possible of the rationalism of

---

44. Murray, *Post-Christendom*, 181.
45. Stark and Finke, *Acts of Faith*, 238–50.
46. Bibby, *Beyond the Gods and Back*, 39.

the Enlightenment are those which are in decline, and that those which have maintained a strong emphasis on the supernatural dimensions of religions have flourished.[47]

The reality is, those who value Christianity in Canada are surrounded by those who do not. Post-Christendom churches must focus on practicing and living the culture of the kingdom of God rather than defining and patrolling the boundaries of Canadian culture. Congregations must be places where those exploring faith and searching for authentic relationships are welcomed; cultures of faith that refrain from quick judgment, where doubts, questions, criticism, and fears are embraced. "They will also need to embody core values that are attractive, clear, demanding, and deeply owned. The term 'centred set' (rather than 'bounded set') is now popular to describe communities that welcome people to 'belong before they believe' but it is not always clear that the 'centred set' has a centre!"[48] We can hold strong to Christ as the centre while still ensuring that the margins are flexible and open.

Stuart Murray makes the excellent point that it is the surviving interest in the person of Jesus, exhibited in contemporary culture by individuals who have long given up on the church—and even in the Jesus portrayed by Christendom—that offers the greatest asset to the post-Christendom church. "In a society that is heartily and understandably sick of institutional Christianity, Jesus still commands interest and respect. However garbled his teaching may have become, and however little his story is known, many people suspect Jesus is good news, despite the shortcomings they see in our churches and the distaste for which they regard our evangelistic activities."[49] We must rediscover how to tell the story of Jesus, recognizing that many previous attempts by a Canadian church immersed in Christendom have fallen short. We cannot reduce Jesus to simple statements of dogmatism, a feel-good message to assuage guilt, or a safe "establishment Jesus" who came to make believers feel comfortable and secure. Rather, "we must present Jesus as (among much else) friend of sinners, good news to the poor, defender of the powerless, reconciler of communities, pioneer of a new age, freedom fighter, breaker

---

47. Newbigin, *The Gospel in a Pluralist Society*, 212–13. This is the key point of Reeves, *The Empty Church*.

48. Murray, *Post-Christendom*, 310. Paul Hiebert first used these terms in "Conversion, Culture and Cognitive Categories," 24–29. Also see Hiebert, "Sets and Structure," 217–27.

49. Murray, *Post-Christendom*, 316.

of chains, liberator and peacemaker, the one who unmasks systems of oppression, identifies with the vulnerable and brings hope."[50]

CONCLUSION: POST CHRISTENDOM NEED NOT MEAN POST CHRISTIAN

Some may fear that celebrating or even accepting the demise of Christendom automatically entails a tacit acknowledgment that we must *de facto* enter a post-Christian era also. In fact, the opposite may well be the case. The end of Christendom will in reality place the church in a context where the gospel—without the trappings of institutional Christianity—may once again be clearly heard. John Webster Grant, in *The Church in the Canadian Era*, wrote, "The end of Christendom does not imply the end of Christianity or necessarily even any diminution of the influence of the church on its members or on society . . . A period of exile to the periphery of power might well release Christian energies that have been smothered for centuries."[51]

We might argue that while the Church relied on the position and influence afforded by the overarching narrative of Christendom, she was less creative than might otherwise have been the case. Why seek earnestly for the creative empowerment of the Holy Spirit to engage culture, when one could count on Government to enact the laws needed to preserve the semblance of a Christian nation? With the structure of Christendom collapsing, the Church will be forced to once again rely upon the Spirit's guidance and power.

Stuart Murray declares:

> But post-Christendom need not mean post-Christian. The near future will be difficult for Christians in a society that has rejected institutional Christianity and is familiar enough with the Christian story not to want to hear it again. Inherited assumptions and Christendom models will not help us respond creatively to the challenges ahead. But perhaps—if we have the courage to face into this future rather than hankering after a fading past, if we resist short-term strategies and pre-packaged answers, if we learn to be cross-cultural missionaries in our own society, and if we can negotiate the next forty years—whatever culture emerges from the ruins of Christendom might offer

---

50. Murray, *Post-Christendom*, 316–17.
51. Grant, *The Church in the Canadian Era*, 216–17.

tremendous opportunities for telling and living out the Christian story in a society where this is largely unknown. Whether post-Christendom is post-Christian will depend on whether we can re-imagine Christianity in a world we no longer control. Christendom is dying, but a new and dynamic Christianity could rise from its ashes.[52]

BIBLIOGRAPHY

Airhart, Phyllis D. *A Church with the Soul of a Nation: Making and Remaking the United Church of Canada*. Montreal: McGill-Queen's University Press, 2014.
Beaman, Lori, and Peter Beyer, eds. *Religion and Diversity in Canada*. Leiden: Brill, 2008.
Beyer, Peter. "Roman Catholicism in Contemporary Quebec: The Ghosts of Religion Past?" In *The Sociology of Religion: A Canadian Focus*, edited by W. E. Hewitt, 133–56. Toronto: Butterworths, 1993.
Beyer, Peter, and Rubina Ramji, eds. *Growing up Canadian: Muslims, Hindus, Buddhists*. McGill-Queen's Studies in Ethnic History Series 2.32. Montreal: McGill-Queen's University Press, 2013.
Bibby, Reginald W. *Beyond the Gods and Back: Religion's Demise and Rise and Why It Matters*. Lethbridge, AB: Project Canada, 2011.
———. *Fragmented Gods: The Poverty and Potential of Religion in Canada*. Toronto: Irwin, 1987.
———. *Unknown Gods: The Ongoing Story of Religion in Canada*. Toronto: Stoddart, 1993.
———. *Restless Gods: The Renaissance of Religion*. Toronto: Stoddart, 2002.
Bowen, Kurt. *Christians in a Secular World: The Canadian Experience*. McGill-Queen's Studies in the History of Religion Series 2.27. Montreal: McGill-Queen's University Press, 2004.
Bramadat, Paul, and David Seljak, eds. *Religion and Ethnicity in Canada*. Toronto: Pearson, 2005.
———. *Christianity and Ethnicity in Canada*. Toronto: University of Toronto Press, 2008.
Butler, Ewen H. "The Interface of Two Canadian Renewal Movements: Classical Pentecostalism in the Pentecostal Assemblies of Canada and the Charismatic Movement, 1960–1985." PhD diss., Regent University, 2015.
Carson, D. A. *Christ and Culture Revisited*. Grand Rapids: Eerdmans, 2008.
Choquette, Robert. *Canada's Religions*. Ottawa: University of Ottawa Press, 2004.
Clifford, N. Keith. "His Dominion: A Vision in Crisis." In *Religion and Culture in Canada*, edited by Peter Slater, 23–42. Waterloo: CCSR, 1977.
Di Giacomo, Michael. "Pentecostal and Charismatic Christianity in Canada: Its Origins, Development, and Distinct Culture." In *Canadian Pentecostalism: Transition and Transformation*, edited by Michael Wilkinson, 15–38. McGill-Queen's Studies in

---

52. Murray, *Post-Christendom*, 8.

the History of Religion Series 2.49. Montreal: McGill-Queen's University Press, 2009.

Duncan, Kent. "Emerging Engagement: The Growing Social Conscience of Pentecostalism." *Enrichment Journal* [n.d.], http://enrichmentjournal.ag.org/201201/201201_EJO_Emerg_Engag.cfm.

Flatt, Kevin. *After Evangelicalism: The Sixties and the United Church of Canada*. McGill-Queen's Studies in the History of Religion Series 2.64. Montreal: McGill-Queen's University Press, 2013.

Grant, John Webster. *The Church in the Canadian Era*. 3rd ed. Vancouver: Regent College Publishing, 1998.

Guenther, Bruce L. "Ethnicity and Evangelical Protestants in Canada." In *Christianity and Ethnicity in Canada*, edited by Paul Bramadat and David Seljak, 365–414. Toronto: University of Toronto Press, 2008.

Haskell, D. M., et al. "Theology Matters: Comparing the Traits of Growing and Declining Mainline Protestant Church Attendees and Clergy." *Review of Religious Research* 58 (2016) 515–41.

Hiebert, Paul. "Conversion, Culture and Cognitive Categories." *Gospel in Context* 1.4 (1978) 24–29.

———. "Sets and Structures: A Study in Church Patterns." In *New Horizons in World Missions: Evangelicals and the Christian Mission in the 1980s*, edited by David Hesselgrave, 217–27. Grand Rapids: Baker, 1979.

Kumar, Nigel Ajay. "'Christ and Culture' by Richard Niebuhr: Book Summary." *Regeneration: A Tryst with (Indian) Theology*, January 17, 2008, https://regenerationayk.wordpress.com/2008/01/17/christ-and-culture-by-richard-niebuhr-book-summary/.

Leng, Felicity. *Consecrated Spirits*. Mahwah, NJ: Paulist, 2011.

Murray, Stuart. *Post-Christendom: Church and Mission in a Strange New World*. Milton Keyes, UK: Paternoster, 2004.

Newbigin, Lesslie. *The Gospel in a Pluralist Society*. Grand Rapids: Eerdmans, 1989.

Niebuhr, H. Richard. *Christ and Culture*. New York: Harper, 1951.

Noel, Bradley Truman. *Pentecostalism, Secularism, and Post-Christendom*. Eugene, OR: Wipf & Stock, 2015.

Reeves, Thomas C. *The Empty Church: The Suicide of Liberal Christianity*. New York: The Free Press, 1996.

Reimer, Sam, and Michael Wilkinson. *A Culture of Faith: Evangelical Congregations in Canada*. Montreal: McGill-Queen's University Press, 2015.

Report of the Royal Commission on Bilingualism and Biculturalism. Book IV: The Cultural Contribution of the Other Ethnic Groups. Ottawa: Minister of Supplies and Services, 1970.

Schweitzer, Don, ed. *The United Church of Canada: A History*. Waterloo, ON: Wilfrid Laurier University Press, 2011.

Simms, Shane A. "Moving Forward in Mission: Introducing Missional Life to a Rural Newfoundland and Labrador Pentecostal Church through Shared Narratives and Missional Experiments." DMin diss., Tyndale Seminary, 2011.

Sloos, William. "The Story of James and Ellen Hebden: The First Family of Pentecost in Canada." *Pneuma: The Journal of the Society for Pentecostal Studies* 32 (2010) 181–202.

Stark, Rodney, and Roger Finke. *Acts of Faith: Explaining the Human Side of Religion.* Berkeley, CA: University of California Press, 2000.

Statistics Canada. *2011 National Household Survey.* Catalogue 99-004-XWE. Ottawa: Statistics Canada, 2011.

Stewart, Adam. "A Canadian Azusa? The Implications of the Hebden Mission for Pentecostal Historiography." In *Winds from the North: Canadian Contributions to the Pentecostal Movement*, edited by Michael Wilkinson and Peter Althouse, 17–37. Leiden: Brill, 2010.

Thiessen, Joel. "Marginal Religious Affiliates in Canada: Little Reason to Expect Increased Church Involvement." *Canadian Review of Sociology* 49 (2012) 69–90.

———. *The Meaning of Sunday: The Practice of Belief in a Secular Age.* Montreal: McGill-Queen's University Press, 2015.

Thiessen, Joel, and Lorne L. Dawson. "Is there a Renaissance of Religion in Canada? A Critical Look at Bibby and Beyond." *Studies in Religion* 37 (2008) 389–415.

Wakefield, Gavin. *Alexander Body: Pentecostal Anglican Pioneer.* Milton Keynes, UK: Paternoster, 2007.

Westfall, William. *Two Worlds: The Protestant Culture of Nineteenth Century Ontario.* McGill-Queen's Studies in the History of Religion Series 1.02. Montreal: McGill-Queen's University Press, 1988.

Wilkins-Laflamme, Sarah. "Toward Religious Polarization? Time Effects on Religious Commitment in US, UK, and Canadian Religions." *Sociology of Religion* 75 (2014) 284–308.

Wilkinson, Michael. *The Spirit said Go: Pentecostal Immigrants in Canada.* New York: Peter Lang, 2006.

———. "Charles W. Chawner and the Missionary Impulse of the Hebden Mission." In *Winds from the North: Canadian Contributions to the Pentecostal Movement*, edited by Michael Wilkinson and Peter Althouse, 39–54. Leiden: Brill, 2010.

Wilkinson, Michael, ed. *Canadian Pentecostalism: Transition and Transformation.* McGill-Queen's Studies in the History of Religion Series 2.49. Montreal: McGill-Queen's University Press, 2009.

3

Even Pentecostals Need More of the Spirit
The Spirit and the Three-Fold Faithfulness Required to Reach this Generation for Christ

Gary Tyra

I will begin this essay by announcing some good news: my scholarly research and experience working with university students have led me to the conclusion that while the post-Christian dynamic is real, it is not insurmountable. *There is hope: our post-Christian family members, friends, neighbors, and co-workers can be reached for Christ!*

Just to be clear, in general, the post-Christians I refer to in this chapter are any of our cultural peers who consider themselves "over Christianity" and "done with the church." In particular, however, I will also make reference to the surprisingly significant number of university students I interact with each semester who have either adopted a post-Christian orientation, or are on the way to doing so.

You might be surprised at just how many of my students fall into this category even though I teach at a private, Christian liberal-arts university. Each semester I teach a theology course entitled "Developing a Christian Worldview." Since this course is part of the university's core curriculum, it is required of all students, regardless of their major. Just this past semester (at the time of this writing) I had a student approach me at the conclusion of the first class session to indicate a concern. In a manner that was both courteous and bold at the same time, she alerted me to the fact that, not only did she not consider herself a Christian, she did not even believe in the existence of God! It was in a subsequent conversation that I learned that the reason for her rather strident unbelief was that she had been bitterly disappointed by life and the Christians she had known growing up, both inside and outside her family. However, fifteen weeks later, at the conclusion of the semester, I received an email from this same student indicating that she had not only changed her mind about the existence of God, but had prayerfully surrendered her life to the lordship of Christ! *What had happened?*

During the semester we had met several times in my office to discuss her progress in the course and what was going on in her life. Mostly, I just listened as she told me her story and elaborated upon all the reasons why she did not feel that she could take the Christian message seriously. Rather than try to fix or correct her, I simply did my best to engage in some empathic *hearing* and promised to keep praying for her regardless of whether she considered this a waste of my time or not.[1] After the last conversation in my office, she had, at my encouragement, been reading the Gospel of Matthew while pondering the question: *So what is it about Jesus that causes so many people to be enamored with him?* I had also encouraged her, as an "experiment" based on Ps 34:8, to offer the prayer: "Jesus, if you are real, reveal yourself to me."

She had not gotten very far in this "taste and see" exercise before something dramatic occurred. The Spirit of Christ came upon this troubled university student in a remarkable way as she read the story in Matt 8 of Jesus calming a "*troubled* sea," and then exhorting his disciples to "overcome their . . . *unbelief.*" This young woman, so very disenchanted with the Christian faith, is one of many I have seen be led by the Holy Spirit to take another look at Christ and his church. Indeed, during the course of writing this chapter I have interacted with this student on several occasions. I am happy to report that in each conversation she has spoken of the progress she is making in her new life as a Christian disciple. So, yes, I know for a fact that post-Christians can be reached for Christ!

---

1. I tell my ministry-bound students that, though the words "listen" and "hear" can be used interchangeably (see Prov 1:5; 20:12), some qualifications need to be made. It is possible to hear without really "listening." It is also possible to listen without really "hearing." The goal should be to engage in a process of active, intentional "listening" that leads to genuine "hearing." Whatever the relationship, this empathic attending to the other is crucial to it.

Now with this good news ringing in our ears, there are three big ideas I would like to put forward in this chapter for consideration:

1. Ironically, a missional *fruitfulness* vis-à-vis our post-Christian peers requires a three-fold *faithfulness* vis-à-vis God.
2. Crucial to the cultivation of this three-fold faithfulness is an ecclesial environment earmarked by a *pneumatological realism*.
3. Even Pentecostal pastors need to go to work on this!

THE THREE-FOLD FAITHFULNESS A MISSIONAL FRUITFULNESS REQUIRES

Faithfulness is an important theme in Scripture. In passage after passage we read that the God of the Bible is faithful (e.g., Deut 7:9), and that faithfulness is one of his chief attributes (e.g., Ps 89:8). As well, the Bible tells us time and again that faithfulness is a very basic response God is looking for from his people (e.g., Josh 24:14; Hos 4:1; Rev 13:10). Thus, I have come to believe that there are three forms of faithfulness, in particular, which pastors should seek to cultivate in the lives of their parishioners: a *spiritual* faithfulness, a *moral* faithfulness, and a *missional* faithfulness. Put differently, I am convinced that if we want to reach our post-Christian peers for Christ (i.e., if we want to experience a *missional fruitfulness*), what is ultimately required is a *missional faithfulness* that is supported by a *moral faithfulness* that flows out of a *spiritual faithfulness*.

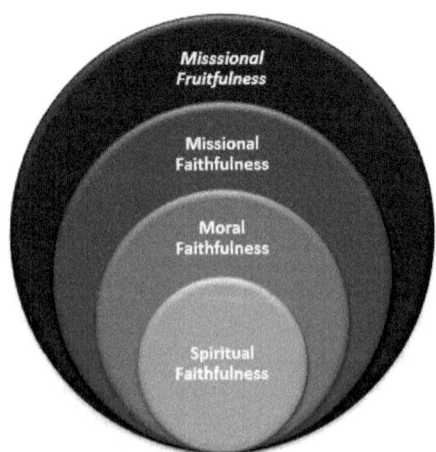

Figure 1

Now let us take a quick look at each of these crucial forms of faithfulness before God, taking special note of: its essence, why an intentional cooperation with the Holy Spirit is crucial to it, and how it contributes to a missional fruitfulness.

Spiritual Faithfulness

I am going to suggest here that the most fundamental type of faithfulness God expects from his people is spiritual in nature. It is impossible to exhibit a moral or missional faithfulness before God if a spiritual faithfulness is not also present.

The Essence of Spiritual Faithfulness

In the Old Testament, a primary manner in which one manifested faithfulness to Yahweh was remaining loyal to the covenant he had graciously entered into with Israel (see Pss 25:8–10; 78:32–37). Moreover, the New Testament also speaks of a covenant—a *new* covenant, which centers in the sacrifice of Christ (see Luke 22:20; 1 Cor 11:25; Heb 8:6–13; 9:15–28). Like the old covenant, the new covenant anticipates/expects a faithful response. At the very least, the New Testament makes it clear that fidelity to the new covenant requires that disciples *remain steadfast in their devotion to Jesus*, God's much beloved son (see Col 1:21–23; 2:6; Heb 3:1–6, 12–14; 4:14; 10:19–39). The question is: *What does this steadfast, ongoing devotion to Jesus involve?*

Many New Testament passages refer to the need to stay connected to Christ. I want to focus attention here on a very familiar passage from the Gospel of John:

> I am the true vine, and my Father is the gardener. He cuts off every branch in me that bears no fruit, while every branch that does bear fruit he prunes so that it will be even more fruitful. You are already clean because of the word I have spoken to you. Remain in me, and I will remain in you. No branch can bear fruit by itself; it must remain in the vine. Neither can you bear fruit unless you remain in me.
>
> I am the vine; you are the branches. If a man remains in me and I in him, he will bear much fruit; apart from me you can do nothing. If anyone does not remain in me, he is like a branch that is thrown away and withers; such branches are picked up,

thrown into the fire and burned. If you remain in me and my words remain in you, ask whatever you wish, and it will be given you. This is to my Father's glory, that you bear much fruit, showing yourselves to be my disciples (John 15:1–8).

This passage is famous for its call for Christ's followers to "continue," "remain," or "abide" (Greek: *meno*) in him. Some Christians tend to interpret the call to "remain" as an exhortation to maintain a *volitional-intellectual commitment* to Christ. In other words, to continue in Christ is to be careful to maintain an orthodox understanding/profession of who Jesus is and what he is about. Other Christians tend to interpret the call to "abide" as an exhortation to maintain a *mystical-experiential communion* with the risen Jesus—to interact with him daily in some sort of spiritual manner. So, which is it? Does a steadfast devotion to Christ involve a *volitional-intellectual commitment* or a *mystical-experiential communion*? As I have indicated elsewhere, I am convinced that the authors of the New Testament, especially the apostles John and Paul, were convinced that a spiritual faithfulness to Jesus involves *both* a volitional-intellectual commitment *and* mystical-experiential communion.[2] *In other words, a spiritual faithfulness that is Christian in orientation requires a personal, Spirit-enabled interaction with the risen Christ, as well as a careful maintenance of an orthodox opinion with respect to him.* Moreover, it is my contention that the writings of the New Testament authors, especially John and Paul, present us with the possibility of an *ongoing mentoring relationship* with Jesus—an intimate, interactive relationship that is designed to have a *transformational, fruit-bearing* effect upon our lives.[3] *Thus, to embody a spiritual faithfulness that is Christian in orientation is to do our part to maintain this ongoing mentoring relationship with the risen Christ.* Presented below is a graphic designed to portray the gist of my proposed understanding of what is at the heart of a spiritual faithfulness.

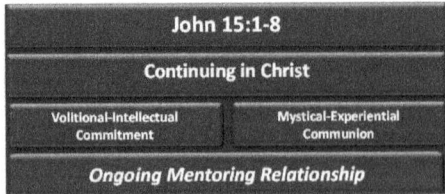

Figure 2

---

2. For more on this, see Tyra, *Christ's Empowering Presence*, 101–3.
3. For more on this, see Tyra, *Christ's Empowering Presence*, 99, 108–9, 184.

Even Pentecostals Need More of the Spirit

The Critical Role the Holy Spirit Plays in a Spiritual Faithfulness

Though the prospect of an ongoing mentoring relationship with the resurrected Jesus finds support in the New Testament as a whole, for the sake of expediency my focus here will be on the pneumatology presented in John 14 and 16, the two chapters which frame or *bookend* the "call to continue" sounded in John 15. To summarize, in John 14 and 16 we discover that the Holy Spirit is "another" *advocate, counselor, or mentor* (Greek: *paraklētos*) (John 14:15–18), whose role is to bring to the minds of Jesus' disciples everything that he has taught them (John 14:26), *and wishes (in an ongoing way) to teach them* (John 16:13). What I am suggesting here is that a careful consideration of the pneumatology presented in John 14–16 provides support for the notion that *one of the primary tasks of the Holy Spirit is to make it possible for Christian disciples to experience that ongoing mentoring relationship with Christ which John 15 exhorts us toward!*[4] Simply put, we are not experiencing the fullness of the Christ's Spirit in our lives if we are not allowing him to enable us to interact with Jesus in a moment-by-moment mentoring manner.

Spiritual Faithfulness and Missional Fruitfulness

My experience with post-Christians tells me that very few of them have actually rejected Christianity. What most post-Christians are struggling with is not Christianity per se, but "churchianity"—the sometimes egregiously imperfect manner in which many church members tend to represent the faith to one another and those outside the ecclesial community. To be more specific, my research into the post-Christian dynamic, along with my personal experience with thousands of students over the past two decades, tell me that one of the biggest reasons why so many of our contemporaries claim to be "over" Christianity and done with the church is because of the *Christian Pharisaism* they have experienced within conservative Christian congregations. While I include a brief discussion of what I refer to as "conservative Christianity's image problem" in my book *A Missional Orthodoxy: Theology and Ministry in a Post-Christian Context*,[5] I devote an entire chapter to this topic in an earlier work titled,

---

4. Moreover, some explicit support for this assertion can be discerned by comparing Matt 10:19–20 and Luke 21:14–15. For more on this, see Tyra, *Christ's Empowering Presence*, 99. See also, Tyra, "Proclaiming Christ's Victory," 72–78.

5. Tyra, *Missional Orthodoxy*, 38–42.

Defeating Pharisaism: Recovering Jesus' Disciple-Making Method.[6] In both books I cite the research reported on by David Kinnaman in his *Unchristian: What a New Generation Really Thinks about Christianity . . . and Why It Matters.*[7] Unfortunately, Kinnaman's findings indicate that conservative Christianity does indeed have an image problem, especially among the members of the emerging generations. Kinnaman summarizes his findings thusly:

> Our research shows that many of those outside of Christianity, especially younger adults, have little trust in the Christian faith, and esteem for the lifestyle of Christ followers is quickly fading among outsiders. They admit their emotional and intellectual barriers go up when they are around Christians, and they reject Jesus because they feel rejected by Christians.[8]

More precisely, I will offer that while Jesus exhorted his followers time and again to display grace and *mercy* toward others (e.g., Matt 5:7; 12:7; 18:21–35; 23:23), what many post-Christians report having experienced among conservative church members (Pentecostal and non-Pentecostal alike) are, instead, some of the same graceless attitudes and actions the New Testament ascribes to Jesus' ministry antagonists—the Pharisees. Some of these missionally problematic attitudes and actions include:

- *legalism* (e.g., Luke 18:9–14; John 5:39);
- *dogmatism* (e.g., Luke 7:29–35; John 9:24–34);
- *judgmentalism* (Luke 7:36–39; John 9:16);
- *separatism* (Matt 9:10–13); and especially
- *hypocrisy* (Matt 23:1–36; Luke 12:1).

Based on my experience with university students, this phenomenon of graceless Christianity is a very big deal! On the one hand, there seems to be an inverse relationship between Christian Pharisaism and missional fruitfulness, especially with respect to our post-Christian peers. On the other hand, I am also convinced that an ongoing mentoring relationship with Jesus cannot help but continually remind us of our need to *embrace* God's grace and mercy for ourselves, and *extend* this grace and mercy to others (e.g., Matt 5:7; Luke 6:36). So here is the bottom line with respect

---

6. Tyra, *Defeating Pharisaism*, 53–76.
7. Kinnaman, *Unchristian*.
8. Kinnaman, *Unchristian*, 11.

to the importance of a spiritual faithfulness to reaching post-Christians for Christ: *Since it is the lack of grace experienced by many that is at the heart of the post-Christian dynamic, it is precisely a grace-embracing and grace-extending approach to the Christian faith that needs to be lived out if we are to succeed at encouraging our cultural peers to give Christ and the church a second look!* Thus, the spiritual faithfulness I am promoting in this chapter (at the heart of which is an ongoing mentoring relationship with Christ made possible by the Holy Spirit) is indeed very important to reaching post-Christians for Christ!

Moral Faithfulness

Pressing on, the kind of spiritual faithfulness I am advocating for here cannot help but produce a second type of faithfulness: one which affects the moral dimension of the disciple's life.

The Essence of Moral Faithfulness

In a nutshell, at the heart of moral faithfulness is a commitment on the part of the moral agent to make ethical decisions by striving to *"hear" and honor the heart of God.*

Figure 3

Before elaborating upon what a moral faithfulness is, and why it is so important to reaching our post-Christian peers, I must first devote a brief discussion to what it is not. In a book titled *Lost in Transition: The Dark Side of Emerging Adulthood*, Christian sociologist Christian Smith and a team of co-authors include a chapter titled "Morality Adrift."[9] Based

---

9. Smith, *Lost in Transition*, 19–69. See also my treatment of this theme in Tyra,

on a nationwide, ongoing study of several thousand American youth into their young adult years—the National Study of Youth and Religion (NSYR)—Smith and his co-authors suggest that the moral lives of many of America's emerging adults can be said to be earmarked by: an embrace of *moral relativism*, a commitment to *moral autonomy*, and a capacity for *moral compromise*. To be more specific, according to the NSYR:

- 30 percent of America's emerging adults profess a belief in a strong moral relativism—the notion that "morals are relative, there are not definite rights and wrongs for everybody."[10]
- The other two-thirds of America's emerging adults should be thought of as "reluctant moral agnostics and skeptics" who cannot clearly explain why moral relativism is actually wrong.[11]
- 60 percent of emerging adults surveyed expressed a highly individualistic approach to morality; "morality is a personal choice, entirely a matter of individual decision. Moral rights and wrongs are essentially matters of individual opinion.[12]
- One in three (34 percent) of those interviewed said they might do certain things they considered morally wrong (e.g., lying, cheating, and stealing) if they knew they could get away with it.[13]

Obviously, what we are talking about here is just about the opposite of a moral faithfulness. And, while I would like to be able to say that this antithesis to a moral faithfulness only shows up in the lives of those outside the church, I cannot! The truth is that the moral lives of many of my students, even those who profess to be fervent Christ-followers, have been significantly influenced by the cultural soup in which we are all swimming!

It was this realization that prompted within me the haunting question: *Should not there be something distinctively Christian about the way Jesus' followers make ethical decisions and form moral opinions?* Based on my understanding of the moral manner and message of Jesus, I am of the opinion that a biblically informed answer to this crucial question has

Pursuing Moral Faithfulness, 141–58.
    10. Smith et al., *Lost in Transition*, 27.
    11. Smith et al., *Lost in Transition*, 27.
    12. Smith et al., *Lost in Transition*, 21.
    13. Smith et al., *Lost in Transition*, 47.

to be "yes!" Thus, I teach my students that we do not have to allow the cultural soup in which we are swimming to completely determine us. *A moral faithfulness is possible. We Christians can learn to, like Jesus, make important moral choices by hearing and then honoring the heart of God!*

The Critical Role the Holy Spirit Plays in a Moral Faithfulness

It is with the goal in mind of helping Christian disciples forge a moral faithfulness before God that I have put forward a moral model I refer to as the "ethic of responsible Christian discipleship."[14] I would like to think that what makes this approach to making ethical decisions and forming moral opinions somewhat unique is the manner in which it is not only biblically-informed and Christ-centered, but *genuinely Spirit-empowered* as well!

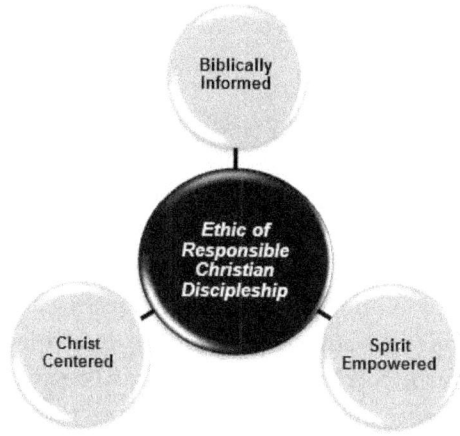

Figure 4

Based on what Prov 2 (and other biblical passages)[15] have to say about God's willingness to speak moral wisdom into the lives of people who are eager to hear it, and my own experience as a moral agent, I am suggesting that as we engage in certain spiritual discernment practices (Scripture study and prayer practiced in a theologically real manner)[16]

---

14. See Tyra, *Pursuing Moral Faithfulness*.

15. For more on this, see Tyra, *Pursuing Moral Faithfulness*, 183–88.

16. To engage in any spiritual discipline in a theologically real manner is to be careful to do so in a way that reckons with God's real presence. For example, to pray in a theologically real manner is to see ourselves conversing with God, himself, rather than simply talking toward the idea of God.

and engage in a deliberation process that strives to be both responsible and responsive, we put ourselves in a place where God's Spirit is able to help us *hear* or sense the heart of God with respect to this or that moral matter, virtually *speaking* wisdom, understanding, and insight to us through the Scriptures, the community of faith, and/or directly to the self by means of his still small voice.[17]

Thus, when I refer to this moral model as *Spirit-empowered* as well as biblically-informed and Christ-centered, I really mean it! Indeed, it is the manner and degree to which I emphasize the possibility of what I refer to as "prophetic moral guidance" that makes this approach to making moral choices somewhat unique and, for some evangelicals, provocative as well. It is my contention that the prospect of *prophetic moral guidance* is a biblically-supported game changer when it comes to Christian ethics!

Moral Faithfulness and Missional Fruitfulness

Given what we have discovered about the rather cavalier manner in which many emerging adults approach morality, we might be tempted to assume that more and more Christians endeavouring to hear and honour the heart of God would be off-putting rather than compelling to them. But I have discovered that just the opposite is true. If my students are any indication, many of our post-Christian peers are not studied moral relativists opposed in principle to the idea of hearing and honouring the heart of God. Indeed, many of the emerging adults I interact with each semester seem to be conflicted—intrinsically frustrated by the fact that the only two alternatives they see being presented to them are: their culture's embrace of an *abject moral relativism;* or a *strident ethical legalism* they associate with conservative Christianity.

The problem is that this false dichotomy suggests to our cultural peers that they only have two options when it comes to making ethical decisions and forming moral opinions: by focusing on how their decisions affect *people*, or doing their duty with respect to some biblical *principles*. It should come as no surprise that, when confronted with such a false antithesis, very few of our contemporaries are going to prioritize principles over people. Thus, they feel that moral relativism is their only option, and Christianity and the church take yet another hit!

---

17. For more on this, see Tyra, *Pursuing Moral Faithfulness*, 189.

However, here is the good news: the Gospels seem to portray Jesus resolving moral dilemmas in a way that strived to do justice to both principles and people.[18] My experience has been that when students flirting with a post-Christian orientation are offered a third alternative to moral relativism and legalism—a moral faithfulness that, like the one embodied by Jesus, is balanced in its emphasis upon both principles and people—they resonate with it.

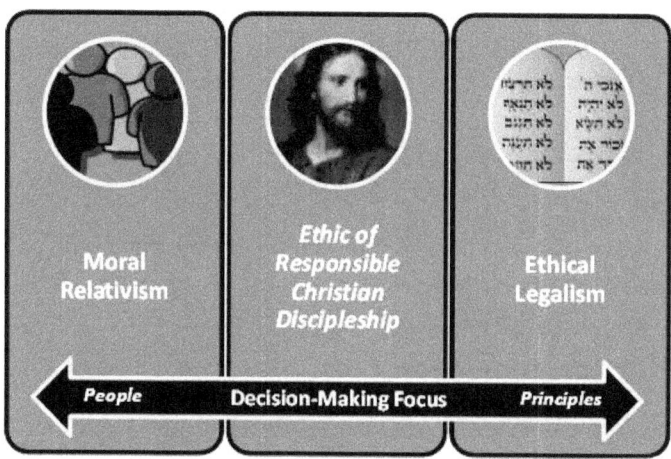

Figure 3

Indeed, I have actually had students indicate that their becoming aware of how Jesus embodied a moral faithfulness before God that is balanced and wholistic rather than unbalanced and restricted caused them to "want to study more about how Jesus lived" and to "fall in love with him all over again."[19] In sum, as counter-intuitive as it may seem, my experience has been that one way to encourage post-Christians to take another look at Christ and the church, is to talk turkey with them about the need for and possibility of *a moral faithfulness*!

Missional Faithfulness

As important as a spiritual faithfulness and moral faithfulness are to impacting our culture for Christ, they must be combined with yet another

---

18. For more on this, see chapters 7 and 8 of Tyra, *Pursuing Moral Faithfulness*, 205–53.

19. These are actual statements uttered by students during in-class discussions of the ethic of responsible Christian discipleship.

type of fidelity in order for God's ultimate purposes to be achieved. The "Cape Town Commitment"—created at Cape Town 2010: The Third Lausanne Congress on World Evangelization—refers to the Holy Spirit thusly: "He is the missionary Spirit sent by the missionary Father and the missionary Son, breathing life and power into God's missionary Church."[20] One of the implications of this extraordinary pneumatological statement would seem to be that: *in order to experience a missional fruitfulness at this critical time in the history of North American culture, we simply must allow the Holy Spirit to help us embody a faithfulness that is missional in nature!*

The Essence of Missional Faithfulness

Speaking broadly, a missional faithfulness requires that Christ's followers do justice to both the apostolic exhortation to *keep contending* for the historic Christian faith (Jude 3) and Paul's implicit encouragement to *keep contextualizing* the gospel in compelling ways within various cultural settings (1 Cor 9:20–22).[21] Unfortunately, church history tells us that Christians have not always done an adequate job of remaining faithful to both Jude 3 and 1 Cor 9:20–22. Traditional churches can so focus on the contending task that they fail to adequately contextualize the faith for new cultural groups. Progressive/Emerging churches can so focus on the contextualizing task that they fail to adequately contend for the faith that was "once for all entrusted to God's holy people." But according to the Bible: "It is good to grasp the one and not let go of the other. The man who fears God will avoid all extremes" (Eccl 7:18). In other words, a missional faithfulness occurs when we embrace the tension between the contending and contextualizing tasks and *faithfully* engage in *both at the same time!*

---

20. "The Cape Town Commitment," 1.5.

21. For more on this, see Tyra, *Missional Orthodoxy*, 11–12. See also Newbigin, *Gospel in a Pluralist Society*, 153–54.

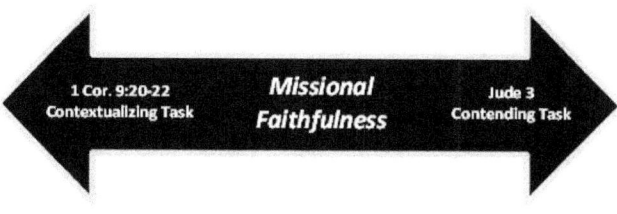

Figure 6

The Critical Role the Holy Spirit Plays in a Missional Faithfulness

The importance of the Holy Spirit to the missional endeavour has been underscored by some of the major voices in the missional conversation.[22] It is my contention that there are two primary ways the Spirit of mission contributes to missional ministry:

- first, by enabling the missional community to *discern* what God is up to in this or that ministry context (Prov 19:21); and

- second, by empowering the missional community to, through prophetic speech and action, adequately *represent* the kingdom of God to hurting people within the target community.

Since I elaborate upon these two principal contributions of the Spirit to missional ministry in another chapter included in this volume of essays, I will simply underscore here the assertion that *the recovery of a robust pneumatology is crucial to a fully faithful engagement in missional ministry*. Indeed, I am convinced that an enhanced partnership with the Holy Spirit can take our engagement in missional ministry to a whole new level![23]

Missional Faithfulness and Missional Fruitfulness

The type of missional faithfulness I am envisioning requires a presentation of the gospel that, precisely because it is faithful to the *biblical text* and sensitive to the *cultural context*, is one the Holy Spirit can use to

---

22. For example, see Newbigin, *Gospel in a Pluralist Society*, 118–19; Guder, *Missional Church*, 142, 145; Roxburgh and Boren, *Introducing Missional Church*, 122.

23. For more on this, see the companion essay included in this volume titled, "Missional Pentecostalism: What it is, why it is Needed, how to Unleash it in your Church."

entice post-Christians to take another look at Christ and the church. *In other words, the connection between a missional faithfulness and fruitfulness could not possibly be any stronger!* If the gospel presentation is not *sensitive to the cultural context*, it will not prove to be both *comprehensible* and *compelling* to the target audience. If the gospel that is being contextualized is not *faithful to the biblical text*, it will *lack saving, transforming power*. The bottom line is that there is indeed a connection between a missional faithfulness and missional fruitfulness—a connection of *immediate* importance!

This is the three-fold faithfulness that, I am suggesting, is critical to reaching our post-Christian peers for Christ: a *spiritual faithfulness*, *moral faithfulness*, and a *missional faithfulness*. I want to encourage the reader to imagine with me a multitude of evangelical church members empowered by the Spirit to exhibit the manifold faithfulness God desires and deserves, and that our post-Christian ministry context desperately needs. I am convinced we can do this but, that being said, allow me to press on to address two other vitally important matters.

ECCLESIAL ENVIRONMENTS EARMARKED BY A *PNEUMATOLOGICAL REALISM*

We have seen how important the work of the Holy Spirit is to the three-fold faithfulness that is crucial to reaching our post-Christian peers. However, it needs to be noted that throughout the first section of this essay I have simply presumed the presence of a particular type of ecclesial culture—one that encourages rather than discourages a certain understanding of, and experience with, the Holy Spirit.

In several of my books I have written of the need for a *theological realism*—the need for Christians to understand that God is not simply a philosophical idea or theoretical construct, but a *personal* being with whom it is possible to experience an *intimate, interactive relationship!*[24] Recently, I have begun to focus on the possibility and importance of a *pneumatological realism* as well—the idea that rank-and-file church members need to understand and experience the Spirit of Christ in a manner that is intimate, interactive, and existentially impactful rather

---

24. This theme runs throughout *Christ's Empowering Presence*; *The Holy Spirit in Mission*; *A Missional Orthodoxy*; and *Pursuing Moral Faithfulness*.

than merely theoretical and/or liturgical.[25] Moreover, a church environment impacted by a pneumatological realism will be one in which church members eagerly *expect* to interact with the Holy Spirit in ways that are *real* (personal, responsive, and existentially impactful) rather than merely *theoretical* or *ritualistic*. The issue here is the dynamic of *expectancy*—the *posture* that church members assume with respect to the working of the Spirit in their lives. A realist understanding of the Spirit tends to encourage a posture of *expectancy* toward the Holy Spirit, while a non-realist understanding of the Spirit tends to result in a posture of *presumption* (or even *indifference*) with respect to the Spirit.

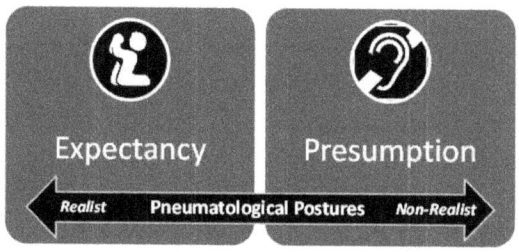

Figure 7

Given everything presented in this essay thus far about the importance of church members interacting with the Holy Spirit in ways that will nurture within them a spiritual, moral, and missional faithfulness, here is a pivotal question that all pastors concerned about reaching this generation for Christ should be asking themselves: *To what degree am I being careful to encourage the members of my congregation to adopt a "posture" of expectancy rather than presumption (or even indifference) with respect to the working of the Holy Spirit in their lives?*

I am absolutely convinced that this question should be taken very seriously. Breaking some new ground in this essay, I want to briefly indicate why I believe that very high on the ministry agenda of each and every evangelical church leader in North America should be the deliberate cultivation of ecclesial communities in which members are encouraged (and enabled) to interact with the Holy Spirit in real, transformational, ministry-engendering ways. My advocacy for the adoption and promotion of a pneumatological realism is based on four pivotal, possibly provocative, observations.

---

25. Merely implied in *The Holy Spirit in Mission*, I refer explicitly to a pneumatological realism in *A Missional Orthodoxy*; and *Pursuing Moral Faithfulness*.

Non-Realist Pneumatology and "Pneumatological Deficit"

The first observation I will boldly announce here is that in some post-Reformation Protestant theologies, the role of the Holy Spirit has been both truncated and overly conceptualized with the result that in too many evangelical churches the Spirit functions merely as an article in the creed or as a sanctifying force that is simply presumed to be operational in the lives of church members by virtue of their having engaged in this or that religious ritual. I will go on to suggest that an ecclesial environment, influenced by a non-realist pneumatology, is missing three important things: (1) a sufficient awareness of how important the Holy Spirit is to absolutely every aspect of the Christian life (including the disciple's engagement in mission);[26] (2) any sense that Christ's followers can and should *expect* to experience the Spirit in ways that are not only personal but sometimes phenomenal as well; and (3) the notion that through the Spirit the disciple can interact with the risen Christ in a genuinely *interactive* manner resulting in a profoundly impactful spiritual, moral, and ministry formation. In sum, the "pneumatological deficit"[27] observable in many evangelical churches is the direct result of an impoverished, non-realist doctrine of the Holy Spirit. The dramatic importance of this ecclesial development will be indicated below.

The Concurrent Emergence of a Functional Deism in Christian Churches

A second observation takes the form of a reminder concerning the National Study of Youth and Religion (NSYR) alluded to earlier in this chapter. One of the most significant results of the NSYR is the suggestion by Christian Smith and his team of researchers that a belief system they refer to as "Moralistic Therapeutic Deism" has become not only the "de facto dominant religion among contemporary U.S. teenagers,"[28] but a "widespread, popular faith" among American adults as well.[29] In other words, the suggestion is that huge numbers of Americans, even many Protestant church-goers, have embraced a belief system that more closely

---

26. For more on this, see Tennent, *Invitation to World Missions*, 94.
27. See Tennent, *Invitation to World Missions*, 94.
28. Smith and Denton, *Soul Searching*, 162–63.
29. Smith and Denton, *Soul Searching*, 166.

resembles *a functional deism with Christian trappings* than it does the historic Christian faith!

According to the findings of the NSYR, while many American church members profess a belief in the God of the Bible, the moralistic therapeutic deism (MTD) to which they are actually committed holds that:

- people earn their way to heaven by trying their best to be good, non-judgmental people (hence the term "moralistic");
- God's greatest desire is to help people become happy and successful in this life (hence the term "therapeutic"); and
- God only gets involved in our lives occasionally and on demand, when we need him to solve a problem we cannot handle on our own (hence the qualified use of the term "deistic").

Thus, Smith and his team suggest that the most basic problem with MTD is that in it the sovereignty of God has been replaced with the sovereignty of the self. As a result, *missing from MTD is any real understanding of the need for a spiritual, moral, and missional faithfulness before God.* Instead, God becomes a functional means toward our ends; what is really important is not our faithfulness toward him, but (only) his faithfulness toward us! Says Smith of the God of MTD:

> This God is not demanding. He actually can't be, because his job is to solve our problems and make people feel good. In short, God is something like a combination Divine Butler and Cosmic Therapist: he is always on call, takes care of any problems that arise, professionally helps his people to feel better about themselves, and does not become too personally involved in the process.[30]

It is not hard to see how this kind of belief system might promote an essentially narcissistic, consumerist, spectator-oriented church-goer who views the local church as a purveyor of therapeutic goods and services, and the worship gathering as a performance to be observed (and evaluated) rather than genuinely participated in.

Does this sound familiar? Indeed, the question must be asked: *To what degree is this non-biblical, faithfulness-frustrating understanding of God at work among evangelicals?*

---

30. Smith and Denton, *Soul Searching*, 166.

Unfortunately, my experience has been that when I make my students aware of the NSYR and its findings with respect to MTD, the majority of them readily acknowledge that they see this belief system operating not only among their family and friends, but in their own lives as well. Indeed, not a few of my students have actually expressed gratitude for my having made them aware of Smith's research, indicating that it provides them with the vocabulary they need to address the presence of MTD in their own religious experience, as well as that of their loved ones and peers. So, yes, it appears that MTD is at work in evangelical as well as Roman Catholic and mainline Protestant congregations. This is why I am so insistent that evangelical pastors of all stripes need to take seriously the possibility that significant numbers of our parishioners are *not* relating to God in the *realistic* manner we see occurring in the Bible.

Functional Deism and Pneumatological Presumption

My third observation has to do with the connection between the phenomenon of functional deism and the pneumatological presumption referred to above.

Figure 8

The relationship between pneumatological presumption and functional deism should be considered complicated (perhaps even dialectical) in the sense that it is difficult to discern which causes what. On the one hand, an ecclesial environment earmarked by a non-realist pneumatology provides the fertile soil in which a functional deism can take root and thrive. On the other hand, once it becomes established in the life of a disciple or congregation, a functional deism virtually prohibits the assumption of any pneumatological posture other than one of presumption/indifference. At the very least it must be acknowledged that a functional deism certainly does not engender an expectation of genuinely interactive encounters with the Spirit of God! Instead, it facilitates a narcissistic, consumeristic, spectator-oriented version of the Christian life which in no way resembles the spiritual, moral, and missional faithfulness God is looking for and that is vital to a fruitful contextualization of the gospel for our place and day.

So, what is the antidote for the functional deism currently plaguing too many Christian churches, even those that are evangelical (and Pent-evangelical) in brand? Is the cure for this faux version of the faith only a matter of our working harder at our current approach to the spiritual, moral, and ministry formation of church members? Or is there a more fundamental need to address the pneumatological presumption that might be at work in the lives of our members? The answers to these two key questions are provided below.

Pneumatological Expectancy, Experience, and Empowerment

Simply stated, the fourth and final observation I will present here is this: a lack of pneumatological *expectancy* regarding the empowerment of the Spirit cannot help but result in a diminished *experience* of the same. If we want to enable our church members to experience the Spirit in truly transformational, ministry-engendering ways, we have to encourage within them a sense of pneumatological expectancy rather than presumption or indifference.

Some support for this provocative notion is provided by evangelical theologian Gilbert Bilezikian, who, commenting on those churches in which the Holy Spirit is "reduced to an item of doctrine," makes a trenchant observation of his own:

> Being practically shut out of the lives of Christians and their churches, the Holy Spirit does not force his way into them. Every instance of the intervention of the Holy Spirit reported in the New Testament indicates that he cooperates actively in situations where he is expected and wanted.[31]

What Bilezikian seems to be suggesting here is that, when it comes to the intervention of the Spirit in the lives of believers, *a sense of expectancy (and welcome) tends to precede, perhaps even precipitate, experience.* If this assertion holds, it serves to explain why a functional deism really must be taken seriously: it is completely opposed to a Spirit-empowered engagement in the formational ministries of the local church! Moreover, it is my contention that, taken as a whole, the four observations presented above amply demonstrate that the cure for the functional deism so

31. Bilezikian, *Christianity 101*, 108–9.

injurious to a missional fruitfulness is not just practical, but is theological in nature. *In other words, the remedy for a functional deism requires nothing less than the recovery of a robust, fully Trinitarian doctrine of the Holy Spirit, leading to an eager embrace of a pneumatological realism that, in turn, encourages believers to expect to interact with Christ's Spirit in truly transformational, existentially impactful, and ministry-engendering ways.*

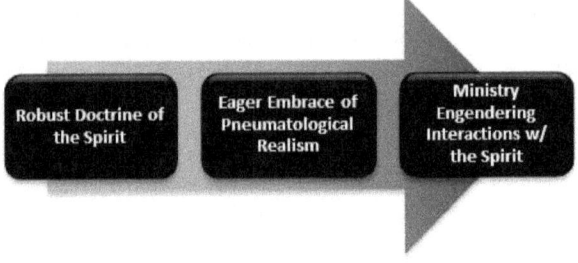

Figure 9

This is why rank-and-file church members must be encouraged toward a posture of pneumatological expectancy rather than presumption! *What I am advocating for is a functional-deism-defeating pneumatological realism that is crucial to the three-fold faithfulness the Scriptures enjoin upon the followers of Jesus.* To the degree the vital importance of a spiritual, moral, and missional faithfulness to a local church's ministry fruitfulness is granted, it is difficult to avoid the following conclusion: *the embrace and promotion of a pneumatological realism in evangelical churches really is critical to our reaching our post-Christian peers for Christ!*

WHY EVEN PENTECOSTAL PASTORS NEED TO GO TO WORK ON THIS!

To be honest, I struggled quite a bit with the title of this essay. Allow me, a Pent-evangelical pastor-scholar with over four decades of ministry experience, to conclude the chapter by briefly explaining what I mean when I suggest that even Pentecostals need more of the Spirit.[32]

---

32. My use of the term "Pent-evangelical" is an attempt to distinguish between Pentecostals/charismatics who are assiduously committed to the authority of Scripture and those whose embrace of a variety of highly sensational, extra-biblical ideas and practices can suggest to some non-Pentecostal evangelicals that they might not be. For more on this possibility, see Jones, "Kingdom Come in California," 30–37.

Essentially, my concern is that *many* (certainly not all) members of Pentecostal churches in the West are only Pentecostal in a nominal sense. Put differently, what I am suggesting is that it is possible to possess a Pentecostal heritage and/or profess a commitment to Pentecostal beliefs while actually living the Christian life day-to-day in a non-Pentecostal manner. Unfortunately, much could be said in support of this thesis. All I will do here, however, is offer a final personal anecdote.

I was having lunch one day with a former student who indicated that, having read my book, *The Holy Spirit in Mission: Prophetic Speech and Action in Christian Witness,* he had subsequently discussed its message with the youth pastor of his church—a congregation affiliated with a classical Pentecostal denomination. My former student indicated to me that he had become both confused and concerned when his youth pastor blithely remarked: "I do not see what the big deal is about prophetic speech. I spoke in tongues once a long time ago but have not done so since."

My concern is that this cavalier attitude toward not only glossolalia but prophetic speech and action in general is much more common among the leaders of Pentecostal churches than we might like to think. While I do not want to believe this, I have to admit that it does explain why many of my students who grew up in Pentecostal churches show up at the university with virtually no clue as to what it means to be Pentecostal, and why, the truth be known, there is precious little in terms of the three-fold faithfulness evident in their lives. What is more, some of my professorial colleagues have observed the phenomenon of students coming to the university without being aware of the fact that their home church is affiliated with a Pentecostal denomination. Apparently, there is nothing distinctively Pentecostal taking place in the churches in which these students have spent their formative years!

All of this leads me to say that I am fairly convinced that it is not just non-Pentecostal evangelical church leaders who need to work on encouraging a pneumatological realism among their parishioners. Many Pent-evangelical pastors need to do the same! Indeed, I believe the time has come for the adoption of a whole new pneumatological paradigm—something I refer to as a "Missional Pentecostalism."

What this new paradigm involves, why it is so important, and how it can be implemented in the local church are themes I address in the second chapter I have contributed to this collection of essays. Indeed, it is in that companion essay that I elaborate some on the specific things evangelical church leaders of all stripes can do to promote within their congregations a realist understanding and experience of God's Spirit.

While I certainly hope the reader will interact with that other chapter as well, I will conclude *this* one with a reiteration of my three-pronged thesis:

1. Ironically, a missional fruitfulness vis-à-vis our post-Christian peers requires a three-fold faithfulness vis-à-vis God.
2. Crucial to the cultivation of this three-fold faithfulness is an ecclesial environment earmarked by a pneumatological realism.
3. Even Pentecostal pastors need to go to work on this!

Once again, the good news is that the challenges created by the post-Christian dynamic are not insurmountable; the Spirit of mission can and will help us reach our post-Christian peers for Christ! But for this to occur, it is imperative that those of us who lead churches become intentional about promoting the pneumatological expectancy that really is crucial to the cultivation of a spiritual, moral, and missional faithfulness in the lives of our parishioners. My hope is that those reading these words will resolve to do this, inspired by the realization that, while the ministry needs currently confronting the church in an increasingly post-Christian North America are real, so is the Holy Spirit!

BIBLIOGRAPHY

Anonymous. "The Cape Town Commitment." http://www.lausanne.org/ctcommitment.
Bilezikian, Gilbert. *Christianity 101: Your Guide to Eight Basic Christian Beliefs*. Grand Rapids: Zondervan, 1993.
Dunn, James D. G. *Baptism in the Holy Spirit: A Re-examination of the New Testament on the Gift of the Spirit*. Philadelphia: Westminster John Knox, 1977.
Guder, Darrell, ed. *Missional Church: A Vision for the Sending of the Church in North America*. Grand Rapids: Eerdmans, 1998.
Jones, Martyn Wendell. "Kingdom Come in California." *Christianity Today* 60 (May 2016) 30–37. Online: http://www.christianitytoday.com/ct/2016/may/cover-story-inside-popular-controversial-bethel-church.html.
Kinnaman, David. *unChristian: What a New Generation Really Thinks about Christianity . . . and Why It Matters*. Grand Rapids: Baker, 2007.
Newbigin, Lesslie. *The Gospel in a Pluralist Society*. Grand Rapids: Eerdmans, 1989.
Roxburgh, Alan J., and M. Scott Boren. *Introducing the Missional Church: Why It Matters, How to Become One*. Grand Rapids: Baker, 2009.
Smith, Christian, et al. *Lost in Transition: The Dark Side of Emerging Adulthood*. New York: Oxford University Press, 2011.

Smith, Christian, and Melinda Lundquist Denton. *Soul Searching: The Religious and Spiritual Lives of American Teenagers*. New York: Oxford University Press, 2005.

Tennent, Timothy C. *Invitation to World Missions: A Trinitarian Missiology for the Twenty-first Century*. Grand Rapids: Kregel Academic, 2010.

Tyra, Gary. *A Missional Orthodoxy: Theology and Ministry in a Post-Christian Context*. Downers Grove, IL: IVP Academic, 2013.

———. *Christ's Empowering Presence: The Pursuit of God through the Ages*. Downers Grove, IL: IVP, 2011.

———. *Defeating Pharisaism: Recovering Jesus' Disciple-Making Method*. Downers Grove, IL: IVP, 2009.

———. *Pursuing Moral Faithfulness: Ethics and Christian Discipleship*. Downers Grove, IL: IVP Academic, 2015.

———. "Proclaiming Christ's Victory Over Sinful, Personal Desires," *Enrichment Journal* 18 (2013) 72–78. Online: http://enrichmentjournal.ag.org/201303/201303_072_personal_victory.cfm.

4

Missional Pentecostalism

What it is, why it is Needed, how to Unleash it in your Church

GARY TYRA

NEEDED TODAY IS AN entirely new pneumatological paradigm—a fresh, compelling way for Trinitarian Pentecostals to understand their experience of Christ's Spirit, and to commend this experience to others. As some of the essays included in this volume have indicated, the challenges currently confronting the Christian church in North America are great. In this chapter I will put forward a new/ancient version of Pentecostalism that, I am convinced, has the potential to unite all good-hearted, gospel-promoting evangelicals (Pentecostal and non-Pentecostal alike) toward a collegial, Spirit-empowered engagement in missional ministry.

The thesis prompting this essay is two-pronged. First, the time is ripe for the recovery of a robust, biblically-informed, fully Trinitarian doctrine of the Holy Spirit. Second, it is not only possible but crucial for Pentecostal and non-Pentecostal evangelicals to get past the old debates and down to the ministry business at hand: *fruitfully impacting an increasingly post-Christian and religiously relativistic North American culture with the gospel of Christ.*

While not wanting to suggest that I have coined the term, it is the manner in which a "missional Pentecostalism," as I understand it, is both biblically-supported and committed to Christ's mission that causes me to believe it has what it takes to garner the support of both Pentecostals and non-Pentecostals alike. Having treated the notion of a "missional pneumatology" in two of my previously published works,[1] this essay will break some new ground, responding to such crucial questions as: What is a "missional Pentecostalism"? Why is it needed? What is involved in its implementation in the local church?

WHAT I MEAN WHEN I REFER TO A *"MISSIONAL PENTECOSTALISM"*

The first thing required in an essay such as this is a quick survey of the current Pentecostal landscape. Since no firm consensus exists regarding the best way to categorize the various versions of Pentecostalism at work in the world,[2] I am going to, for the sake of simplicity, suggest that we think in terms of two primary types of Trinitarian Pentecostalism currently on offer in our North American context: *classical Pentecostalism* and *neo-Pentecostalism* (with neo-Pentecostalism functioning in this essay as a broad category encompassing the adherents of the "Charismatic" and "Third Wave" movements as well).[3]

Of course, were we to be completely honest, we would have to acknowledge that there is actually yet another version of Pentecostalism quietly at work in many North American churches: the *nominal Pentecostalism* practiced by more than a few congregants who, though they profess a commitment to traditional Pentecostal doctrine, actually live their lives on a day-to-day basis in a *de facto* non-Pentecostal manner. Because of the prevalence of this pallid version of Pentecostalism, I feel the need to treat it here as a lamentable but real possibility as far as possible Pentecostal expressions go.

So how does a missional Pentecostalism compare and contrast with the other three versions currently dotting the Pentecostal landscape? For reasons that will soon become clear, I am suggesting that a missional

---

1. See Tyra, *The Holy Spirit in Mission*; also, Tyra, *A Missional Orthodoxy*.

2. For a helpful yet concise survey of several typological proposals or "terminological suggestions," see Vondey, *Beyond Pentecostalism*, 9–13.

3. It is not uncommon for the charismatic movement to be associated with neo-Pentecostalism. For example, see RegionFacts.com, "Neo-Pentecostalism." For more on the relationship between neo-Pentecostals, charismatics, and "third wavers," see Yong, *Discerning the Spirit(s)*, 154–57; Friesen, *Norming the Abnormal*, 129–31.

Pentecostalism should be viewed on a continuum of Pentecostalisms progressing toward the goal of *missional fruitfulness*.

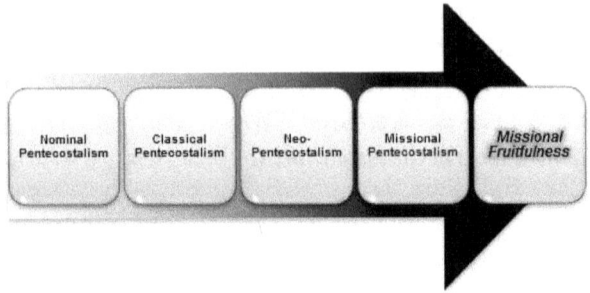

Figure 1

Presented below is a cursory indication of how I see these four versions of Pentecostalism differing from one another, and the degree to which each of them tends to produce the dynamic of missionality in the lives of Christ's followers and the churches to which they belong.

Nominal Pentecostalism

As I have indicated already, this is my way of referring to the reality that in some Pentecostal churches (those in which a *pneumatological realism* is not sufficiently emphasized)[4] many parishioners behave on a day-to-day basis just as many non-Pentecostals might: not really *expecting* to interact with the Holy Spirit in a personal, phenomenal,[5] transformational, ministry-engendering manner. To be sure, no one actually refers to himself or herself as a nominal Pentecostal. It is just that it happens! Depending on how strong the tie is between the local church and the denomination with which it is affiliated, the need for a more robust evidence of the congregation's Pentecostal heritage may occasionally be voiced. Still, it has likely been some time since anyone only nominally Pentecostal has actually engaged in any kind of "prophetic" (Spirit-prompted and enabled) activity, including *glossolalic* prayer. Why this reticence? I am of the opinion that, in addition to the absence of a genuine sense of pneumatological

---

4. For a thorough discussion of the importance of an ecclesial environment earmarked by the embrace of a "pneumatological realism," see the companion article included in this volume: "Even Pentecostals Need More of the Spirit."

5. I am using the term "phenomenal" in this essay to refer to the possibility of experiencing the Spirit of God in a way that is immediate and evident to the senses.

expectancy in these congregations, another reason for this failure to engage in Spirit-inspired speech and action is that the edificational and missional value of the member's prophetic capacity has not been sufficiently emphasized (I will have more to say about the nature and importance of a Spirit-filled Christian's prophetic capacity below).

Classical Pentecostalism

While the Pentecostalism birthed at Azusa Street was, in its early days, quite committed to the evangelization of the nations,[6] soon the focus of many *traditional* Pentecostals in the West turned toward the forging and defense of a boundary-marking doctrine—*glossolalia* as the initial physical evidence of Spirit baptism.[7] Certainly there are many classical Pentecostals who are passionate about personal evangelism and who support world missions. However, my interaction over the years with many of the ministers and members affiliated with the classical Pentecostal denomination of which I am a part indicates that not a few believe that the organization's reason for being is to get people to speak in tongues, rather than to win the world for Christ.[8]

Moreover, while references to *empowerment* for ministry abound in classical Pentecostal literature, it is not uncommon for congregants to possess an understanding of prophetic speech that essentially limits its occurrence to personal prayer times, corporate prayer meetings, and an occasional, especially anointed church service during which a "word of prophecy" or "message in tongues" followed by an interpretation might take place. Unfortunately, the biblically supported connection between prophetic activity (Spirit-enabled speech and action) and day-to-day ministry—especially missional ministry—seems not to be well understood by rank-and-file members of many classical Pentecostal churches.[9]

6. Newberg and Olena, *Children of the Calling*, 24–25.

7. Newberg and Olena, *Children of the Calling*, 25–26. For a critical survey of this development, see Friesen, *Norming the Abnormal*, 83–119.

8. Functioning at the time as a presbyter (mid-level leader) within my denomination, I once found myself actually having to debate this issue with a veteran pastor during a regional meeting of ministers!

9. The astute reader will intuit from this that I view *glossolalia* as a form of prophetic speech that possesses both evidential significance and edificational benefit toward an empowered engagement in missional ministry. Thus, the point needs to be

Neo-Pentecostalism

This form of Pentecostalism, despite the value it places on *glossolalia*, differs from classical Pentecostalism in three primary ways: (1) the more diverse sociological and ecclesial backgrounds of its adherents; (2) its openness to other gifts of the Spirit functioning as indications of Spirit-indwelling; and (3) its lack of a perceived need to affiliate with traditional Pentecostal denominations.[10] I am pleased to report that in some churches where a neo-Pentecostalism holds sway,[11] there is a strong commitment to a prophetic (Spirit-prompted and enabled) ministry which is not confined to the weekly worship gathering. However, in those neo-Pentecostal (or charismatic) ecclesial settings where, historically, personal evangelism has not been much emphasized (e.g., some Roman Catholic, Eastern Orthodox, and mainline Protestant churches), it is not uncommon for the exercise of the charismata to be limited to institutional, edification-oriented gatherings such as prayer meetings and worship services. Thus, I am not able to affirm an immediate, unqualified correlation between neo-Pentecostalism and the Spirit-empowered engagement in missional ministry our current ministry context urgently requires.

Missional Pentecostalism

This brings us to the type of Pentecostalism I am advocating for in this essay. As its name suggests, at the heart of a Missional Pentecostalism is the dynamic of *missionality*.

---

made that while a missional Pentecostalism in no way diminishes the value of *glossolalia*, it does emphasize its import to missional ministry in a way often neglected by the other versions of Pentecostalism.

10. See Yong, *Discerning the Spirit(s)*, 157.

11. I have in mind here some Vineyard congregations, some non-denominational Pent-evangelical congregations, and some congregations that, while they are formally affiliated with a classical Pentecostal denomination, have actually come to embrace a neo-Pentecostal understanding and experience of the Holy Spirit.

Figure 2

To be more precise, my understanding of missional Pentecostalism is influenced by the six theological, exegetical, and missiological observations presented below:

- The Holy Spirit is a missionary Spirit committed to fulfilling God's mission *(missio Dei)* in the world.[12]

- The Holy Spirit has a penchant for using God's people to accomplish God's purposes.[13]

- There is a connection in the Bible as a whole between the coming of the Spirit and the phenomenon of prophetic activity (Spirit-inspired speech and action).[14]

- There is a connection between prophetic activity and the missional faithfulness we observe in the Book of Acts.[15]

---

12. See Tyra, *The Holy Spirit in Mission*, 11–12.

13. See Tyra, *The Holy Spirit in Mission*, 12.

14. See Num 11:25–29; 1 Sam 10:6–11; 19:19–24; 1 Chr 12:18; 2 Chr 24:20; Joel 2:28–29; Luke 1:41–45, 67; 2:25–28; Acts 2:4; 4:8; 8:4–19; 9:17–18 (cf. 1 Cor 14:18); 10:44–46; 13:9; 19:6; Eph 5:18–20.

15. In no less than 21 of the 28 chapters that make up the book of Acts, I am able to identify an explicit reference to some form of prophetic activity taking place: Spirit-filled disciples praising God with prophetic speech, hearing personal words of encouragement, receiving special ministry assignments, speaking to others in God's name, etc. For more on this, see Tyra, *The Holy Spirit in Mission*, 64–68.

- The same Spirit-empowered missional faithfulness that is currently fueling the prolific growth of Pentecostal Christianity around the world[16] can also be engaged in here in the West.[17]
- What is needed here in the West is a *missional pneumatology* that can unite all evangelicals around the goal of forming Spirit-empowered, missionally faithful churches![18]

To be even more specific, my thesis is that both the Old and New Testaments teach that when the Spirit of mission comes upon God's people in an empowering manner, something missionally significant occurs: *the impartation of prophetic capacity*. This prophetic capacity involves a Spirit-enabled ability to—like Ananias of Damascus—hear God's voice, receive ministry assignments from him, speak and act into the lives of hurting people on his behalf, making disciples and building up Christ's church in the process (see Acts 9:10–22).[19]

In sum, aware of the radical commitment of the Holy Spirit to the missional endeavour, and mindful of the critical import of prophetic activity to a missional faithfulness vis-à-vis God and the world, *the aim of a missional Pentecostalism is to encourage and enable all mission-minded evangelicals to humbly open themselves to the phenomenon of prophetic speech and action for the purpose of kingdom ministry.*[20]

WHY I BELIEVE A MISSIONAL PENTECOSTALISM IS DESPERATELY NEEDED

In the companion essay titled "Even Pentecostals Need More of the Spirit" (also included in this volume), I alluded to the crucial importance of a missional faithfulness to a missional fruitfulness. In this chapter I am going to boldly suggest that there is also a dynamic connection between a missional Pentecostalism and the phenomenon of missional fruitfulness.

---

16. See Tyra, *The Holy Spirit in Mission*, 102–28.
17. See Tyra, *The Holy Spirit in Mission*, 129–58.
18. See Tyra, *The Holy Spirit in Mission*, 21–22, 129.
19. See Tyra, *The Holy Spirit in Mission*, 68, 98, 129.
20. See Tyra, *The Holy Spirit in Mission*, 33.

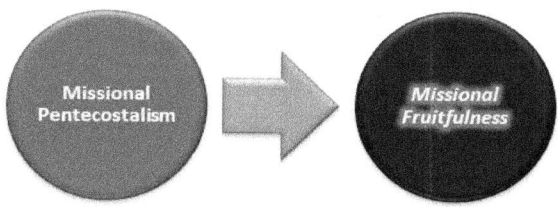

Figure 3

Obviously, I do not mean to suggest that non-Pentecostals cannot engage in fruitful missional ministry. However, the reader should take note of how in the companion essay to which I just alluded I took pains to point out how very important the work of the Holy Spirit is to a missional faithfulness, which, in turn, is critical to a missional fruitfulness. This is what makes the discussion of *pneumatological realism* presented in that companion essay so very important. *Pneumatological realism is the ground out of which a Spirit-empowered missional faithfulness grows!*

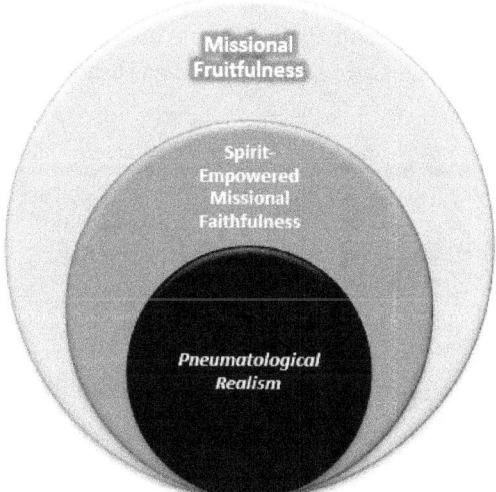

Figure 4

Refining our understanding of a missional Pentecostalism even further, since the pursuit of a Spirit-empowered missional faithfulness that leads to missional fruitfulness is what a missional Pentecostalism is all about, we might even say that *missional Pentecostalism is what happens when church members who have embraced a pneumatological realism begin to take the missional task seriously.* Thus, it is the vital importance of the Holy Spirit to fruitful missional ministry that leads me to offer the following ministry suggestion: *the embrace of a missional Pentecostalism can take an engagement in missional ministry to a whole new level!*

There are three main lines of support for this bold suggestion:

1. The crucial role a missional Pentecostalism can play in the *ministry discernment dynamic.*

2. The crucial role a missional Pentecostalism can play in the *kingdom-representing dynamic.*

3. The proven ability of a missional Pentecostalism to impact a ministry context earmarked by religious relativism.

Presented below is a brief elaboration of each of these lines of support.

Missional Pentecostalism and the Ministry Discernment Dynamic

Some missional experts have insisted that a contemporary engagement in the process of ministry contextualization, in order to qualify as missional, must involve an *imaginative dialogue* between the scriptural text and the cultural context.

Figure 5

These missional experts go on to stipulate that the purpose of this dialogue is to help the members of the missional community discern what God is already up to in this or that ministry location so they can cooperate with him in it (Prov 19:21).[21] Implicit in this assertion is the conviction that such a dialogue will enable the members of the missional community to *discern the ministry leading of the Holy Spirit for this or that ministry milieu.*[22] Such discernment is considered crucial to the ministry contextualization task.

Thus, one of the reasons why I believe a missional Pentecostalism can make a huge contribution to missional ministry is because at the

21. For example, see Roxburgh and Boren, *Introducing the Missional Church*, 99.
22. Tyra, *A Missional Orthodoxy*, 85.

heart of missional ministry is a contextualization question that is pneumatological in nature: *What is the Spirit of mission up to in this ministry context, and how might/ought we cooperate with him in the fulfilling of God's purposes within it?*[23]

With this in mind, please note that if a Spirit-sensitive approach to ministry discernment is to be engaged in authentically, it will require that the members of the missional community actually believe that it is possible to interact with Christ's Spirit in a personal, interactive, prophetic manner. After all, it makes no sense to pose this pneumatological question if we do not actually *expect* the Holy Spirit to in some way *respond*, providing some situation-specific ministry direction in the process! What this suggests, therefore, is that for an ecclesial community to adequately discern the leading of the Spirit with respect to missional ministry, something akin to what I am referring to as pneumatological realism is required. Moreover, as I have already indicated, another name for a missionally-oriented pneumatological realism is *missional Pentecostalism*.

Missional Pentecostalism and the Kingdom-Representing Dynamic

According to many missional thinkers, the ultimate goal of a properly contextualized missional ministry is a faithful representation of the *kingdom of God* to a particular ministry neighbourhood. For his part, missional theologian Lesslie Newbigin famously insisted that the New Testament seems to indicate that, in the first century, Christian proclamation was not so much a lecture forced on uninterested ears, but an enthusiastic response to a question continually being put to the church by those in the surrounding community: *"What is going on among you Christians?"* According to Newbigin, this crucial, ministry-generating question was prompted by a "new reality" at work in the church and perceptible to those outside it.[24]

But what is really important for my proposal is the fact that, ultimately, Newbigin went on to suggest that the "new reality" at work in the

---

23. Roxburgh and Boren, *Introducing the Missional Church*, 20, 52, 70, 86.

24. Lesslie Newbigin, *The Gospel in a Pluralist Society*, 116–17. See also Devadatta, "Strangers but Not Strange," 117–18.

church is the presence of the Holy Spirit—the *arrabōn* or foretaste of God's coming kingdom (Eph 1:13–14).[25]

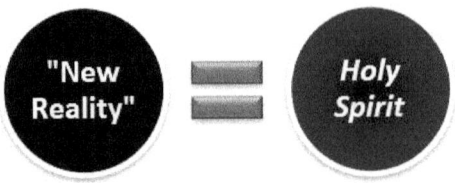

Figure 6

It is my contention that Newbigin's identification of the Holy Spirit as the "new reality" in the church supports the emphasis I am placing on the need for a realist rather than non-realist understanding and experience of the Spirit by rank-and-file church members.

Furthermore, as for how this "new reality" is to be manifested in the local church, the multiple authors of the widely read *Missional Church: A Vision for the Sending of the Church in North America* assert that by studying "Jesus' way of carrying out God's mission, we discover that the church is to represent God's reign as its *community*, its *servant*, and its *messenger*." Thus, this much respected work issues a call for churches in the post-Christian West to engage in missional ministry by means of three Christocentric kingdom-representing activities: *community*, *service*, and *proclamation*.[26]

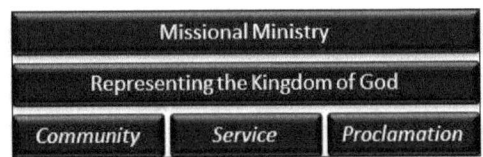

Figure 7

To the authors' credit, scattered throughout *Missional Church* are numerous references to the Holy Spirit.[27] However, I maintain that, while the allusions to the importance of the Spirit to missional ministry in *Missional Church* are a step in the right direction, they are nevertheless

---

25. Newbigin, *The Gospel in a Pluralist Society*, 120.

26. Guder, *Missional Church*, 102.

27. Over and over again, *Missional Church* speaks of the importance of the Holy Spirit to missional ministry. For example, see Guder, *Missional Church*, 4, 8, 12–13, 69, 82, 86–87, 96, 108, 114, 123, 134, 140–41, 142–82, 183–84, 199–200, 214, 223, 226, 231, 236, 238–39, 242, 247, 255–56, 259, 265, 267.

insufficient. There are three primary reasons for this bold critique. First, given the manner in which Newbigin was careful to describe the "new reality" in pneumatological as well as Christological terms, I will assert here the need for *a more explicit understanding of just how crucial a pneumatological realism is to an ecclesial environment productive of a missional faithfulness.* Second, I feel the need to remind my colleagues engaged in the missional conversation that, according to the Book of Acts, it was in an undeniably "prophetic" (i.e., Spirit-prompted and empowered) manner that the earliest Christians engaged in the three kingdom-representing activities prescribed in *Missional Church.* Third, an argument can be made for the idea that, in our own era, the prolific growth of Pentecostalism around the globe (especially in the majority world) is due at least in part to a similarly prophetic engagement in these three ministry activities.[28] The upshot is that an implicit commitment to a missional Pentecostalism seems to be observable in some of the most fruitful missional endeavors the Christian church has ever engaged in! Surely, these three lines of argument serve to support my suggestion that the importance of the Holy Spirit to the kingdom-representing dynamic merits an even closer look. If we really want to do an adequate job of representing the kingdom of God in our place and day, a missional Pentecostalism would seem to be key.

Missional Pentecostalism and a Religiously Relativistic Ministry Context

It is well known that a chief earmark of the North American post-Christian ministry context in which we evangelicals currently find ourselves is a rampant embrace of *religious relativism*—the notion that all religions are equally salvific. But are we also aware that this is not the first time in the history of the church that a group of sincere Christ-followers has had to minister in such a context? There is both historical and biblical support for the idea that religious relativism was rife in the world the earliest Christians inhabited.

Historian John Ferguson asserts that "the attitudes of many in the ancient Roman Empire in the first century concerning alien religious beliefs and practices were marked by tolerance, accommodation, and

---

28. Tyra, *The Holy Spirit in Mission*, 102–7.

openness to syncretism."²⁹ Also, Harold Netland, referring to the Roman Empire in the first century, alerts us to the fact that "[t]he idea that there are multiple ways in which to relate to the divine, with each culture having its own distinctive traditions for doing so was widespread."³⁰ Thus, the historical evidence strongly suggests that a commitment to religious relativism was commonplace in the first-century Roman world.

Moreover, biblical support for the idea that the early church's first-century ministry context was awash with religious relativism is not lacking either. For example, New Testament passages such as Acts 17:22–23 and 2 Cor 6:14–18 strongly suggest a multicultural milieu earmarked by religious relativism.

Thus, it certainly appears that the first-century world in which the earliest Christians were forced to function had much in common with our own. Indeed, it seems that our *post-Christian* ministry context is, ironically, eerily similar to the *pre-Christian* one inhabited by the earliest followers of Christ.

Herein lies the problem (as I see it): because the Christian faith purports to put people in touch with the truth about the way things are (e.g., 1 Tim 2:4; 2 Tim 2:25; Titus 1:1; Heb 10:26; 1 John 2:20–21; 2 John 1:1–4), the way humans beings should behave (e.g., Eph 5:1–17), and the true path to God and eternal blessedness (e.g., John 14:6; Acts 4:12; 1 Tim 2:5–6), a rampant religious relativism represents a ministry challenge that, as Paul's experience in Athens shows, can be quite formidable. What is a contemporary evangelical Christian (who sincerely believes that the way of Jesus is true in a manner that other religious paths are not) supposed to do?

I am convinced that we must emulate the prophetic—Spirit-prompted and enabled—missional ministry practices of the early church. Nearly every page of the Book of Acts presents us with a reference to some sort of prophetic, Spirit-enabled activity.³¹ As Canadian theologian Roger Stronstad is fond of saying, Luke viewed the church as a "community of Charismatic prophets" on a mission to re-present the risen Christ to the world through prophetic words and works.³² Moreover, the record

---

29. Ferguson, *The Religions of the Roman Empire*, 211–43, as cited in Netland, *Dissonant Voices*, 12. See also Netland, *Encountering Religious Pluralism*, 25.

30. Netland, *Encountering Religious Pluralism*, 25–26.

31. For more on this, see n. 15.

32. Stronstad, *The Charismatic Theology of St. Luke*, 34. See also, Stronstad, *The Prophethood of All Believers*, 15, 25, 65–66, 70, 71–84, 114, 115–21; Macchia, *Baptized*

Luke provides also indicates how successful these early Christians were at turning their religiously relativistic world "upside-down" (see Acts 17:6, KJV).[33]

Thus, I am firmly committed to the idea that, if we evangelicals are to succeed at countering the embrace of religious relativism by our cultural peers, the missional ministry practices required will need to be ones that are *prophetic*—Spirit-prompted and enabled—in nature.[34] The history of Christian mission has demonstrated that it is hard, if not impossible, for people, once they have witnessed the reality of the risen Christ through Spirit-inspired, mercy-saturated words and works, to relativize Jesus as just another religious option. So, when it is all said and done, *perhaps the biggest reason why a missional Pentecostalism is desperately needed in our place and day, is its proven ability to enable a missional fruitfulness in a cultural context that is rife with religious relativism!*

These, then, are the three main reasons why I am convinced that the embrace of a missional Pentecostalism can take an engagement in missional ministry to an entirely new level: (1) the crucial role a missional Pentecostalism can play in the *ministry discernment dynamic*; (2) the crucial role a missional Pentecostalism can play in the *kingdom-representing dynamic*; and (3) the proven ability of a missional Pentecostalism to bear fruit within a ministry context earmarked by religious relativism. Assuming that these arguments are at least somewhat persuasive, I want to shift the focus of this essay now to matters much more practical in nature.

---

in the Spirit, 76; and Yong, *The Spirit Poured Out*, 140.

33. Roland Allen emphasizes the fact that the earliest witnesses for Christ were motivated by a Spirit-instilled conviction that "the need of men [and women] could be satisfied only in Jesus Christ" (Allen, *The Compulsion of the Spirit*, 65). He goes on to insist that the experience that cemented this conviction in place was the earliest Christians' experience of the Holy Spirit. He writes "When the Holy Spirit reveals Christ to the soul, whatever the previous religion or morality of the man may have been, he is conscious that he could not do without Christ" (Allen, *The Compulsion of the Spirit*, 67).

34. In chapter 4 of *The Holy Spirit in Mission*, I elaborate upon the manner in which the phenomenon of prophetic activity can impact ministry in our current post-Christian context. See Tyra, *The Holy Spirit in Mission*, 129–58.

Pentecostal Preaching and Ministry

HOW TO UNLEASH A MISSIONAL PENTECOSTALISM IN YOUR CHURCH

Actually, what I intend to elaborate upon here is the process of cultivating a *missionally-oriented pneumatological realism* within a church's culture. As I have already indicated, a missional Pentecostalism requires an ecclesial environment that is earmarked by an eager embrace of a *pneumatological realism*.

Figure 8

Since I have written elsewhere on the topic of what local church leaders can do to encourage among congregation members an engagement in prophetic speech and action for missional purposes,[35] I want to bring this essay to a close with several practical suggestions regarding how the leaders of evangelical churches can accomplish an even more foundational task: the cultivation of an ecclesial environment that is earmarked by the *realist* understanding and experience of the Spirit which makes a missional Pentecostalism possible.

I will begin by simply making the assertion that *we can do this!* I sincerely believe that it is possible for leaders of evangelical churches to successfully encourage their parishioners to open themselves to the possibility that the Holy Spirit can and should be experienced in personal, interactive, ministry-engendering ways. Presented below are several suggestions as to how to achieve this very important outcome.

---

35. Tyra, *The Holy Spirit in Mission*, 162–76.

Prayerfully Partnering with the Spirit

The very first step in this process will involve some serious praying on the part of the church's leadership. It only makes sense that if the goal is to see the members of a church become more aware of the crucial need for a theologically real partnership with the Holy Spirit as it relates to their spirituality, morality, and missionality, those endeavouring to achieve this shift in church culture need to prayerfully enter into such a partnership with the Spirit themselves. Attempting to alter the culture of a church is a huge undertaking, and not for the faint of heart. To accomplish this significant endeavour, we are going to need wisdom and empowerment from above. Ongoing prayer offered in a theologically real (interactive, responsive) manner is the key to experiencing both.[36]

Raising Awareness Regarding Pneumatological Realism

Moving forward in the process, it should go without saying that, at an early stage within it, church leaders will need to help their congregants understand what a "pneumatological realism" is. While I would like to think that both of the chapters I have contributed to this volume will help with this important endeavour, I want to encourage the leaders of local churches to contextualize this dynamic for their parishioners. The central message is that the Holy Spirit is more than an idea, concept, or article of faith; he is the third person of the Trinity who can and should be interacted with in ways that are *personal, phenomenal,* and *genuinely impactful.* Perhaps the term "pneumatological realism" is not the best way to refer to this crucial dynamic in your ministry context. If not, how will you do so? How will you explain to the members of your congregation what it means for them to assume a pneumatological posture of expectation rather than presumption or indifference?

---

36. One version of prayer offered in a theologically real manner is the practice of "praying in the Spirit" (Rom 8:26; Eph 6:18; Jude 20). However one conceives of this practice—as merely extemporaneous prayer, literally groaning before God in prayer (Rom 8:26), or *glossolalic* prayer (cf. 1 Cor 14:13–15)—it would seem appropriate for church leaders wanting to forge and model a theologically real partnership with the Holy Spirit, to take seriously the multiple exhortations provided in the New Testament to engage in it.

Acknowledging Any Pneumatological Presumption

My experience as a pastor has been that, done in the right manner and with the right spirit in place, a congregation will not only tolerate, but will ultimately appreciate some prophetic challenge now and then. So, my suggestion here is that one of the ways in which both evangelical and Pent-evangelical leaders can succeed in encouraging their parishioners toward a more realist experience of the Spirit is to make them aware of the presence and impact of any Spirit-related non-realism that may currently be at work in their lives. Our congregants need to know how amazingly easy it is for any of us to adopt a posture of pneumatological presumption (or even indifference), with the result that we live our everyday lives not really expecting to interact with the Spirit of Christ in ways that will help us cultivate a spiritual, moral, and missional faithfulness before God. To the degree it is true that the New Testament seems to indicate that a sense of pneumatological expectancy is crucial to pneumatological experience,[37] and given what the New Testament has to say about the possibility of the Holy Spirit being *resisted* (Acts 7:51), *grieved* (Eph 4:30), *rejected* (1 Thess 4:8), *quenched* (1 Thess. 5:19), and even *insulted* (Heb 10:29), any pneumatological presumption/indifference present in the local church really does need to be recognized, repented of, and then carefully replaced.

Recovering a Robust Pneumatology

Building on the previous suggestion, I will go on to offer that, in order to create a genuine sense of pneumatological expectancy, church members need to be routinely reminded of how important the Holy Spirit is to just about every aspect of their walk with Christ. What I am arguing for here is a recovery within the local church of a robust, comprehensive doctrine of the Spirit. For an *ethos* of genuine pneumatological expectancy to be cultivated in a church, the members have to be made aware of the full scope of the Spirit's work in their lives, and what this portends for their cultivation of a spiritual, moral, and missional faithfulness before God. By means of sermons, seminars, retreats, Sunday School studies, worship

---

37. For more on the importance of the three-fold faithfulness referred to here, and the connection between pneumatological expectancy and experience, see the companion essay included in this volume titled "Even Pentecostals Need More of the Spirit."

themes, counseling sessions, hallway conversations, et cetera, church members can be encouraged to consider the spiritual, moral, and ministry implications of the fact that it is the Holy Spirit's job to:

- convict people of sin and their need for a saviour (John 16:7–11);
- enable believers to experience the *new birth* and *new life in Christ* (John 3:3–8; Eph 2:18, 22; 3:16–17; and Gal 5:25);
- assure Christ's disciples that they have become God's children (Rom 8:15–16; Gal 4:6);
- lead disciples into a deeper and ongoing interaction with Christ (John 16:12–15);
- serve as a guarantee of our heavenly inheritance (2 Cor 1:22; 5:5; Gal 4:6–7; Eph 1:13–14; 4:30);
- inspire us toward a vital, joyful, prophetic, theologically real worship experience (Eph 5:18–20);
- manifest his presence and power in our lives in various edifying, community-building, ministry engendering ways (1 Cor 12:4–8; 14:24–25);
- energize us to actually obey God's moral commands (Rom 8:1–4);
- help us overcome our habituated sinful tendencies (Gal 5:16–21);
- produce within us the very personality/character traits of Christ himself (Gal 5:22–25);[38]
- intercede for us and through us according to the will of the Father (Rom 8:26–27);
- empower us to boldly and effectively bear witness to the risen Christ (Acts 1:8);
- provide us with an amazingly precise degree of ministry guidance (Acts 16:6–10);
- motivate us to stand firm in the faith and to intercede for others in this regard (Eph 6:10–18); and
- endow us over and over again with a dynamic, despair-defeating sense of hope (Rom 15:13).[39]

---

38. See Tyra, *Pursuing Moral Faithfulness*, 273–74.
39. See Tyra, *The Holy Spirit in Mission*, 28–29.

All of the effects listed above indicate how very important the Holy Spirit is to the Christian life. Even some decidedly non-Pentecostal evangelicals have been willing to acknowledge this reality. The British churchman and biblical scholar John Stott once opined: "The Christian life is essentially life in the Spirit, that is to say, a life which is animated, sustained, directed and enriched by the Holy Spirit. Without the Holy Spirit true Christian discipleship would be inconceivable, indeed impossible."[40] Indeed! The bottom line is that, in order to create an *environment of expectancy* with respect to the Spirit, all evangelical church members must be continually reminded of how crucial the Spirit of Jesus[41] is to true Christian discipleship. We simply must take the Spirit seriously in order to live the Christian life. This is what a pneumatological realism is all about!

Advocating for a Spirit-Sensitive Spirituality

Yet another step in the process being discussed here calls for some rather consistent reminders of the need for Christ's followers to prayerfully, continually surrender themselves to the leadership of the Holy Spirit. Such an observation is validated by the fact that the writings of Jesus' apostles are replete with passages which not only underscore the prominent role the Holy Spirit is to play in the Christian life, but also *how important it is for Christ's followers to actively cooperate with him*. The Apostle Paul, in particular, was emphatic about the need for church members to: *live according to the Spirit* (Rom 8:5–13), *keep in step with the Spirit* (Gal 5:24–25),[42] and *continually be filled with the Spirit* (Eph 5:18).[43] Thus, crucial to a theologically-real experience of the Spirit is a spirituality that facilitates an *ongoing* surrender to the leadership of the Spirit. Because of the dialectical relationship that exists between a Spirit-sensitive spirituality

---

40. See Stott, *The Message of Romans*, 216.

41. See Acts 16:7; Rom 8:9; Gal 4:6; Phil 1:19; 1 Pet 1:11.

42. For more on how this passage indicates the need to cooperate with the Spirit's work in our lives, see Fung, *Epistle to the Galatians*, 272–73.

43. Commenting on the exhortation found in Eph 5:18 to be filled with the Spirit, Frances Foulkes writes: "the tense of the verb, present imperative in the Greek, should be noted, implying as it does that the experience of receiving the Holy Spirit so that every part of life is permeated and controlled by Him is not a 'once for all' experience. In the early chapters of the Acts of the Apostles it is repeated a number of times that the apostles were 'filled with the Holy Spirit.' The practical implication is that the Christian is to leave his life open to be filled constantly and repeatedly by the divine Spirit." Foulkes, *Ephesians*, 152.

and the phenomenon of a pneumatological realism (such a spirituality is, ironically, both the root and the fruit of a pneumatological realism), it is imperative that both evangelical and Pent-evangelical pastors encourage their congregation members to develop a daily devotional practice of *prayerfully, sincerely surrendering their lives to the leadership of Christ's Spirit.*[44] It is difficult to overstate how important this pastoral activity is toward the promotion of a pneumatological realism and the missional Pentecostalism it supports.

Promoting the Notion of Prophetic Capacity

Because it is at the heart of the "missional Pentecostalism" being discussed in this chapter, I will also stress here the importance of some serious study of what the Bible as a whole has to say about the relationship between the indwelling of the Spirit and the impartation of prophetic capacity. Once again, when I speak of "prophetic capacity," I am referring to a Spirit-enabled ability to: hear God's voice, receive ministry assignments from him, and then to speak and act into hurting people's lives in a way that achieves God's missional purposes in the world.[45]

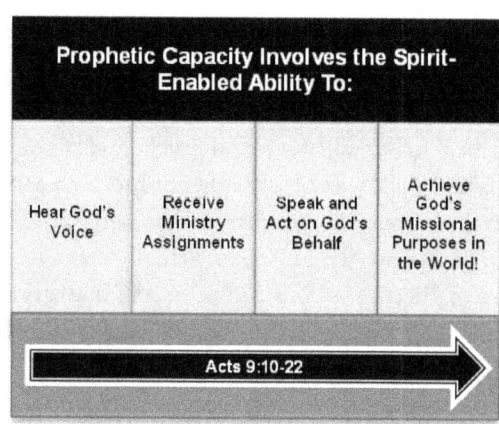

Figure 9

---

44. As well, I will suggest here that being careful to obey the several biblical exhortations to pray/intercede "in the Spirit" (see n. 36) should also be considered a vital part of a Spirit-sensitive spirituality. At the very least, such prayer has the effect of encouraging a sense of pneumatological expectancy (rather than presumption or indifference). Because of this, it is my custom to encourage students and congregants to incorporate this type of Spirit-enabled prayer into their everyday spirituality.

45. See Tyra, *The Holy Spirit in Mission*, 98.

Biblical passages supporting such a notion really are there (e.g., Acts 9:10–22), but church members need to be exposed to them.[46] Having expounded on this theme in various settings, even in some decidedly non-Pentecostal ones, I can attest to the fact that it is possible to, in a compelling manner, make the case for the notion that the Spirit of mission can and will use rank-and-file church members (like Ananias of Damascus) in missionally fruitful ways if we will simply take seriously those occasional promptings of the Spirit to speak and act into the lives of hurting people as he directs. Getting this message out is crucial. Encouraging our church members to embrace rather than ignore the phenomenon of Spirit-imparted prophetic capacity is not only at the heart of a missional Pentecostalism, it is the key to avoiding one that is merely nominal in nature!

Confronting the Demand for Certainty and Control

The problem is that the story of Ananias in Acts 9 also demonstrates how unpredictable the Christian life can become once a pneumatological realism is embraced. Who knows when the Spirit might speak, prompting us to engage in some unanticipated missional ministry? Therefore, it is also important for church leaders to keep reassuring anxious church members that, while the adoption of a pneumatological realism can make those of us who tend to obsess over *certainty* and *control* a bit uneasy, it is for this very reason critical to our spiritual (and psychological) development.

The fact is that all human beings inherently crave a sense of certainty and control in their lives. The problem is that some church members go beyond *desiring* these two dynamics, to virtually *demanding* them. For a variety of reasons, this is a serious problem. As I have argued elsewhere, it is my belief that an inordinate and unbridled *demand* for a sense of *certainty* and *control* is at the heart of the phenomenon of Christian Pharisaism.[47] Thus, *one of the most loving things a pastor can do is to encourage those church members who tend to obsess over certainty and control to*

---

46. For more on this, see Tyra, *The Holy Spirit in Mission*, 39–74 and 75–101.

47. In my book *Defeating Pharisaism* I argue that at the heart of a pharisaical reduction of the Christian faith to a myopic focus on the obedience of rules and observance of rituals is a deep-seated, obsessive need for certainty and control. See Tyra, *Defeating Pharisaism*, 68–74. Unfortunately, Christian Pharisaism is rife in many conservative churches, causing much pastoral burnout, the loss of members, and a great deal of missional dysfunction. See Tyra, *Defeating Pharisaism*, 53–67.

learn to live with some ambiguity in their lives. Inspiring church members to enter into a personal, interactive, existentially-impactful relationship with the often unpredictable Spirit of God (see John 3:8) is an important, divinely ordained way to do this.

Encouraging Pneumatological Nuance

Following up on the last two suggestions, I will also offer that church leaders committed to the type of culture change we are discussing here need to be prepared to deal with the messiness that can sometimes accompany the process. I have in mind, on the one hand, enthusiastic church members who tend to over-spiritualize just about everything going on in the church, and, on the other hand, those reluctant members who are deathly afraid that the church cannot take the Holy Spirit seriously without things getting weird. The fact is that sometimes the prophetic working of the Spirit *can* strike us as weird![48] Still, the instruction of the Apostle Paul is crystal clear: "Therefore, my brothers, be eager to prophesy, and do not forbid speaking in tongues. But everything should be done in a fitting and orderly way" (1 Cor 14:39–40). In other words, it is simply not okay to either *avoid* the prophetic working of the Spirit or *accept* every expression of it uncritically. Church leaders need to become adept at helping their congregants recognize the critical need for *nuance*, *discernment*, and *balance* with respect to just about everything that goes on in the church, especially its experience of the Spirit.

Embodying the Embrace

Finally, I will propose that perhaps the most important thing church leaders can do to encourage the embrace of a pneumatological realism (and the missional Pentecostalism made possible by it) is to exemplify such a commitment themselves. It does no good to talk to others about the need to be led by the Spirit if we ourselves are not attempting to take this apostolic exhortation seriously. We radiate a stunning and leadership-stunting lack of authenticity when we teach on the reality and propriety

---

48. This impression is exacerbated when church members insist on referring to themselves as prophets, and/or engaging in prophetic activity in a super-spiritual manner. I am of the opinion that both of these behaviors are unnecessary and should be lovingly discouraged.

of prophetic capacity while at the same time rarely, if ever, acting on the devotional, moral, and ministry promptings of the Spirit ourselves. At the end of the day, when it comes to a church's collective embrace of a pneumatological realism, *church leaders simply must lead the way!*

In this chapter's introduction I asserted the need in our place and day for a new pneumatological paradigm—one that, because of its biblical support, can unite Pentecostals and evangelicals toward a Spirit-empowered engagement in missional ministry. *Huge numbers of rank-and-file church members engaging in a Spirit-enabled proclamation and demonstration of the Christian gospel outside the four walls of the church*: this is my vision and the goal of the missional Pentecostalism for which I am advocating.

To reiterate, it is my sense that the time is ripe for the recovery of a robust, fully Trinitarian doctrine of the Holy Spirit *and the biblically supported, mission-focused form of Pentecostalism it engenders*. It is actually past the time for Pentecostals, Pent-evangelicals and non-Pentecostal evangelicals to move beyond the contentious debates that have historically occupied us, and to become mutually focused on the missional task at hand. Regardless of what kind of Pentecostalism we refer to it as, or whether we refer to it as a Pentecostalism at all, let us commit ourselves to a Spirit-empowered contextualization of the Christian gospel that has a proven track record of helping hurting people living in religiously relativistic cultural milieus experience the kingdom of God in a life-changing and eternity-altering manner. Given the ministry challenges currently confronting us, the future of both Pentecostalism and evangelicalism in North America may very well depend upon Pentecostals and evangelicals coming together at last, united by a common commitment to reach this generation for Christ. With the Spirit's help, we can do this. The question is: *Will we?*

> But you will receive power when the Holy Spirit comes on you; and you will be my witnesses in Jerusalem, and in all Judea and Samaria, and to the ends of the earth (Acts 1:8).

BIBLIOGRAPHY

Allen, Roland. *The Compulsion of the Spirit: A Roland Allen Reader*, edited by David Paton and Charles H. Long. Grand Rapids: Eerdmans, 1983.

Devadatta, Dan. "Strangers but Not Strange: A New Mission Situation for the Church (1 Peter 1:1–2 and 17–25)." In *Confident Witness—Changing World: Rediscovering the Gospel in North America*, edited by Craig Van Gelder, 110-25. Grand Rapids: Eerdmans, 1999.

Ferguson, John. *The Religions of the Roman Empire*. Ithaca: Cornell University Press, 1970.

Foulkes, Frances. *Ephesians*. Tyndale New Testament Commentaries. Grand Rapids: Eerdmans, 1983.

Friesen, Aaron T. *Norming the Abnormal: The Development and Function of the Doctrine of Initial Physical Evidence in Classical Pentecostalism*. Eugene, OR: Pickwick, 2013.

Fung, Ronald Y. K. *The Epistle to the Galatians*. New International Commentary on the New Testament. Grand Rapids: Eerdmans, 1988.

Guder, Darrell, ed. *Missional Church: A Vision for the Sending of the Church in North America*. Grand Rapids: Eerdmans, 1998.

Macchia, Frank. *Baptized in the Spirit: A Global Pentecostal Theology*. Grand Rapids: Zondervan, 2006.

Netland, Harold. *Dissonant Voices: Religious Pluralism and the Question of Truth*. Vancouver: Regent College Publishing, 1991.

———. *Encountering Religious Pluralism: The Challenge to Christian Faith & Mission*. Downers Grove, IL: IVP, 2001.

Newberg, Eric Nelson, and Lois E. Olena. *Children of the Calling: Essays in Honor of Stanley M. Burgess and Ruth V. Burgess*. Eugene, OR: Pickwick, 2014.

Newbigin, Lesslie. *The Gospel in a Pluralist Society*. Grand Rapids: Eerdmans, 1989.

ReligionFacts.com. "Neo-Pentecostalism." Online: http://www.religionfacts.com/neo-pentecostalism.

Roxburgh, Alan J., and M. Scott Boren. *Introducing the Missional Church: Why It Matters, How to Become One*. Grand Rapids: Baker, 2009.

Stott, John R. W. *The Message of Romans: God's Good News for the World*. Downers Grove, IL: IVP Academic, 2001.

Stronstad, Roger. *The Charismatic Theology of St. Luke*. Peabody, MA: Hendrickson, 1984.

———. *The Prophethood of All Believers: A Study in Luke's Charismatic Theology*. Cleveland, TN: CPT, 2010.

Tyra, Gary. *A Missional Orthodoxy: Theology and Ministry in a Post-Christian Context*. Downers Grove, IL: IVP Academic, 2013.

———. *Defeating Pharisaism: Recovering Jesus' Disciple-Making Method*. Downers Grove, IL: IVP, 2009.

———. *Pursuing Moral Faithfulness: Ethics and Christian Discipleship*. Downers Grove, IL: IVP Academic, 2015.

———. *The Holy Spirit in Mission: Prophetic Speech and Action in Christian Witness*. Downers Grove, IL: IVP Academic, 2011.

Vondey, Wolfgang. *Beyond Pentecostalism: The Crisis of Global Christianity and the Renewal of the Theological Agenda*. Grand Rapids: Eerdmans, 2010.

Yong, Amos. *Discerning the Spirit(s): A Pentecostal-Charismatic Contribution to Christian Theology of Religions*. Journal of Pentecostal Theology Supplement Series. New York: T. & T. Clark, 2000.

———. *The Spirit Poured Out on All Flesh: Pentecostalism and the Possibility of Global Theology*. Grand Rapids: Baker, 2005.

5

What does Brussels Have to do with Toronto?

Insights from the European Edge of the Post-Christian Frontier

DAVID COUREY

It was All Saints Day when I began to seriously consider this paper. It was a typical Belgian day, a little rain, a little sun. On my morning walk, I returned to a familiar theme of the last two years since we came to Brussels as missionaries: pondering what a different world Belgium is from Canada. One would not think so at first. This is not Katmandu, Samarkand, or Kerala. After all, once one accounts for the obvious old world/new world contrasts, we were both rocked in the cradle of Christendom, suckled at the breast of Western culture, and raised in the bosom of liberal democracy, and its companions: liberty, fraternity, and equality. Of course, one quickly learns the shorthand that culturally Canada sits somewhere in the center of the continuum between American and European extremes, particularly in matters of religion. America, we know, by a kind of cultural intuition retains a sizably Christian demographic, Europe is decidedly secular and, O, Canada—neither *icthys* nor foul!

But here it was, All Saints Day in secular Europe. Schools are closed, and so are the shops. Though it was once a holy day, it remains, nonetheless a holiday. I imagined explaining to my friends (believers and not) what All Saints Day is (after all, it lacks the brand awareness of Hallowe'en!), and why it is a statutory holiday here in much of post-Christian Europe. Truth be told, it would be difficult enough to explain to the average European. Yet, in spite of its touted secularity, most of the public holidays celebrated by the European Commission are Christian feast days surrounding Christmas and Easter, but also Ascension and Pentecost.[1] When it comes to Europe and religion, things are not as simple as it seems.

In what follows, I wish to examine the notions of secularity and Christendom in post-Christian Europe, and how they relate to the prospects of evangelical and Pentecostal Christianity in Belgium.[2] I contend that Christendom is not dead in Europe, but dormant and, considered from a cruciform perspective, that this condition offers obvious challenges but also great possibilities in three dimensions: what I call the globalization, colonization, and faithfulness factors. Finally, I will offer four possible options for fruitful ministry in this kind of a culture, whether here in Europe or in North America.

POST-CHRISTIANITY, SECULARIZATION, AND THE PERSISTENCE OF CHRISTENDOM

The key terms of this essay, secular, post-Christian, and post-Christendom, share complex interrelations. There was a time when Europe and Christianity were almost synonymous terms, when Western civilization was the bastion of Christianity. In the heyday of Christendom, the Euro-American world was the centre and chief exporter of Christian faith to the nations. Clearly, it succeeded in its mission, but in the process, seems to have expended itself. Philip Jenkins shows that while the two continents made up 82.4 per cent of the world's 558 million Christians in 1910, they represented only 31.2 per cent in 2010, and are predicted to total some 27.1 per cent of an estimated global population of 3.2 billion Christians by 2050.[3]

---

1. Thirteen of seventeen are related to Christian holy days. "Commission Public Holidays for 2015."

2. For a more theological consideration see the companion paper: Courey, "The Ozymandias Factor," 13–27.

3. Jenkins, "Changes and Trends in Global Christianity," 15–17.

Secularization in Theory and Reality

Typically, the decline of Christianity in Europe and North America has been reported as evidence of a process of secularization. The roots of classical secularization theory go back to Henri de Saint-Simon and Auguste Comte in the early nineteenth century. Essentially it argued that in the face of Enlightenment reason, and the technological advancement in its wake, the modern world would have little need for religion.[4] This was the conventional wisdom through much of the twentieth century. C. Wright Mills predicted the demise of religion in 1959: "[i]n due course, the sacred shall disappear altogether except, possibly, in the private realm."[5] Yet, Peter Berger, an earlier secularization theorist, could say in 1999 that "[t]he world today, with some exceptions . . . is as furiously religious as it ever was, and in some places more so than ever."[6] Indeed, Rodney Stark and Roger Finke wished "to carry the secularization doctrine to the graveyard of failed theories, and there to whisper 'requiescat in pace.'"[7] But in a 2010 survey of the field, Rob Warner demonstrated the continuing intensity of debate among secularization theorists concerning its viability as a model for understanding the influence of religion in modern and modernizing societies.[8] Secularization is clearly an "essentially contested concept" at the heart of the sociology of religion.[9] However, as Charles Taylor describes it, "the secular age" is hard to deny: "Belief in God is no longer axiomatic. There are alternatives."[10]

The religious situation in Europe is far from homogenous, and in many ways resists generalization. According to the European Social Survey (ESS), an EU-sponsored initiative, the five most secular countries in Europe, in each of which over half the population claim not to belong to a religion, are Estonia, the Czech Republic, Sweden, Belgium, and the Netherlands. On the other hand, in eight countries (Poland, Greece, Portugal, Ukraine, Turkey, Slovenia, Austria, and the Slovak Republic), over half the population belongs to some religious denomination, predominantly

---

4. Gorski, "Historicizing the Secularization Debate," 111.
5. Mills, *The Sociological Imagination*, 33.
6. Berger, "The Desecularization of the World," 2.
7. Finke and Stark, *Acts of Faith*, 78.
8. See Warner, *Secularization and Its Discontents*.
9. Gallie, "Essentially Contended Concepts," 167–98.
10. Taylor, *A Secular Age*, 3.

Roman Catholicism.[11] Clearly the European situation is wide-ranging, but tending toward an increasing erosion of institutionalized religion. In 2004 weekly attendance at religious services varied between 4 per cent in Protestant Estonia and 75 per cent in Catholic Malta. French and German figures were below 10 per cent, while Belgium, the Netherlands, Luxembourg, and the United Kingdom featured between 10 per cent and 15 per cent.[12] By comparison, some 37 per cent of Americans attended church weekly in 2013, and 70 per cent attended at least yearly, whereas in Canada similar numbers post at 28 per cent attending monthly, and 58 per cent at least yearly in 2008.[13]

In evaluating this situation, the ESS suggests an important distinction. There are two obvious groups, active believers (who *belong* to a religion and attend services at least on holy days), and non-believers, that is, those who claim not to belong to a religion. But the European wild-card is the third group: inactive believers who *belong* to a religion but never attend services.[14] This may be reflected in a remnant of deep and stubborn religiosity that underlies an outward secularity.

Post-Christian or Post-Christendom

Another way to consider the matter is as a demonstration, not so much of secularization, but the emergence of a post-Christian Europe. Four out of five European Union citizens maintain some kind of spiritual belief.[15] In even the most secular countries, the Czech Republic, or Estonia, for instance, where less than one in five affirm, "I believe in God," things change significantly when one adds the one in two who claim belief in some "sort of spirit or life force."[16] The move from a Christian system of belief appears more pronounced in Protestant and more secular countries, and less so in Catholic nations where the religious institutions have

---

11. Billiet and Meuleman, "Religious Diversity in Europe," 90. In this view secularisation is seen as a process that results in the decline of personal involvement in religious activities. These statistics reflect the situation in late 2004, and early 2005.

12. Manchin, "Religion in Europe: Trust Not Filling the Pews."

13. Lipka, "What Surveys Say about Worship Attendance"; Bibby, "Continuing the Conversation on Canada," 831–37; Eagle, "Changing Pattern of Attendance," 187–200.

14. European Social Survey, *Exploring Public Attitudes*, 11.

15. TNS Opinion & Social, *Social Values, Science and Technology*, 98.

16. TNS Opinion & Social, *Social Values, Science and Technology*, 10.

been historically strong, as well as in some Eastern European countries.[17] Rather than increasing secularization, such shifts suggest the declining vitality of formal Christianity in favour of a vaguer spirituality and privatization of faith.

Does the condition of post-Christianity suggest post-Christendom, though? These are two terms fraught with ambiguity. Lee Beach appears to equate the two notions in his book *The Church in Exile*. For Beach Christendom arose in an era when "Christianity held court" and was close to the levers of power. Beach (consciously following Walter Brueggemann) finds "exile" an appropriate metaphor for the church's position in a post-Christian, post-Christendom world.[18] With Anabaptist aplomb, Stuart Murray questions whether true Christianity ever shaped society in the way envisioned by the term *Christendom*. Murray decidedly declares that post-Christendom does not mean post-Christian. While post-Christendom is defined by the diminished societal influence of the church and Christianity, *post-Christian* implies the passing of Christian faith entirely. Murray is confident that Christianity will find fresh expressions in a post-Christendom world.[19] However, as Stanley Hauerwas has pointed out "Constantinianism is a hard habit to break."[20] He speaks of the church's addiction to a power position in determining society, but his insight serves as well to explain the stubborn cultural persistence of Christendom even after Christianity has left the building. "It is hard to break because all our categories have been set by the church's establishment as a necessary part of Western civilization."[21] This is not only true of the church's characteristic posture toward its declining influence, but in some sense like Pavlov's dogs, Western civilization retains an (albeit, diminishing) conditioned response to Christian values.

Thus, while active Christianity itself has a waning presence in Europe, the vestiges of Christendom remain, and continue to be felt. This legacy is sensed in the social infrastructure. In Belgium for instance, many hospitals and universities continue to have a distinctly Catholic feeling, and trade unions and social security insurance institutions have roots in Catholic social teaching and maintain some continuity with

---

17. TNS Opinion & Social, *Social Values, Science and Technology*, 98.
18. Beach, *The Church in Exile*.
19. Murray, *Post-Christendom*, 4–8.
20. Hauerwas, *After Christendom*, 18.
21. Hauerwas, *After Christendom*, 18.

Catholicism.[22] Statutory *holy days* have already been alluded to, but on a more permanent, if passive level, one can scarcely escape the architectural legacy of Christianity in Europe. One lives continually under the literal shadow of the church, and while the hollowness of cathedral life is proverbial, I have been personally surprised at its modest vibrancy, as I have stumbled across it occasionally. Latin American charismatics directed by a priest in vestments, and a guitar-playing worship leader in jeans fill Amsterdam's St. Nicholas Basilica with raised hands and hallelujahs on a Sunday afternoon. A crowded Catholic church in Budapest features video screens on pillars to guide the faithful through the liturgy on a Thursday evening.

Meanwhile in Belgium weekly attendance at mass dropped to 7 per cent in 2008 from 13.1 per cent in 1996 and 26.7 per cent in 1980. Nevertheless, given the choice between Catholic moral instruction and non-confessional ethics classes, 71.8 per cent of the children in Wallonia, and 82.6 per cent in Flanders choose Catholic religious instruction. This relates to the curious relationship between church and state in Belgium and across Europe where public funding of religious education and institutions remains a contested issue. In Belgium this has included Catholics, Protestants, and Jews since its inception in 1830, and has expanded to Islam since 1974, Orthodoxy since 1985, and non-confessional philosophical groups since 1993.[23]

The varied relationships between church and state across Europe remain yet another vestige of Christendom. A general axiom seems to hold that the apparent decline of Christendom in Western Europe is met with its resurgence in post-Communist states. For instance, Poland's constitution deliberately avoids any talk of separation of church and state, and while not formally establishing Catholicism, its laws certainly guarantee it a privileged position.[24] On the other hand, the Lutheran Church of Sweden was the state church until disestablishment in 2000, and until 1996, all children were automatically registered as members if one parent

---

22. "There definitely is a Catholic civil society consisting of a plethora of societies and institutions. Together they represent a majority of the Belgian population." Van de Poll, *Europe and the Gospel*, 260. See also Boeve, "'Katholieke' identiteit van organisaties," 109–20, cited therein.

23. Christians and Wattier, "Funding of Religious and Non-Confessional Organizations," 51–53. This entire volume discusses the thorny fiscal relations between church and state.

24. Stan and Turcescu, *Church, State, and Democracy*, 122–25.

was a member.[25] But the axiom is not absolute. Some nations still have state churches (e.g., Britain, where the Queen remains the head of the Church of England; or Greece, where Orthodoxy is the official state religion), some have formal relations with churches (Germany, where all citizens pay a church tax, unless they opt out and the fee is otherwise allocated; or Bulgaria, where Orthodoxy is officially called the recognized, traditional religion), and others like France are shaped by a constitutionally entrenched *laïcité* that ensures freedom, but circumscribes the role of religion in the public sphere.[26]

Thus, so-called "secular Europe" finds itself in a far more nuanced situation than it might at first appear. The depth of its secularity is neither at all clear, nor is the circumstance at all homogenous. This resilience of Christendom against the *corrosive acids of modernity* points to the possibility that Europe may have progressed beyond the threat of the secular. Indeed, it is argued by some that Europe may better be regarded as an example of post-secularized society. Jürgen Habermas considers the case of European exceptionalism (*Sonderweg*) against the background of global religious vibrancy. Having survived the rumors of its death, religion in Europe now appears to be remarkably resilient, even if more privatized among those from a *Christian* background. Habermas points to the resurgence of world fundamentalisms, and the emergence of large and active Islamic communities and the problems posed by their integration into European society. The effects of this on remnant Christianity in Europe should not be underestimated. In this context, the public voice of Christian faith becomes increasingly significant.[27] As Jewish constitutional scholar Joseph Weiler points out, "Christian thought offers us a range of instruments, conceptual challenges, ideas, which—handled with the right care—can be extremely useful in our attempts to define the specifically European modality of relations *ad gentes*, within and outside of the [European] Community."[28]

---

25. Alberts, *Integrative Religious Education in Europe*, 213–14.

26. Slomp, *Europe, A Political Profile*, 77, 629; Stan and Turcescu, *Church, State, and Democracy*, 24.

27. Habermas, "Notes on Post-Secular Society," 17–29. The post-secular model offers one way of reconceptualizing 'religion' within the framework of modern society. See Ziebertz and Riegel, "Europe: A Post-Secular Society?" 293–308.

28. Weiler, "A Christian Europe?" 146. Weiler refers here to insights from John Paul II's encyclical *Redemptoris Missio*.

Faced with such a complex situation, does one dare any generalizations? The situation in Belgium is unique, but can some remarks be made from this particular locus that may speak more broadly to both European and Canadian contexts?

THREE (CANADIAN) OBSERVATIONS OF POST-CHRISTIAN BELGIUM

I write as both a pastor and scholar. Thirty years of pastoral ministry in two churches of the Pentecostal Assemblies of Canada cannot help but inform my reflections on the place of Christianity in the mission field where I now find myself training young leaders for the church in Europe. As a former wannabe mega-church pastor, I write from three distances: first that of a teacher rather than a current practitioner; second from the distance of Europe, reconsidering North American pragmatism; third from an (admittedly artificial) lay perspective in Europe rather than a leadership perspective in Canada. My area of concern as a scholar has chiefly been the danger of triumphalism, particularly within Pentecostalism. Altogether, this standpoint creates a certain ambivalence in my perceptions. I see the quandary of the European church, but I am not sure that North American solutions are all that helpful. Not only are they contextually foreign, but does the European church need to be infected with our triumphalist disease? All the above, notwithstanding, I humbly offer three observations on trends I discern in the Belgian church. I imagine these to be, more or less, applicable to the European situation in general, probably instructive for Canadian leaders.

Globalized Christianity and European Christendom: Redefining 'Church'

Traditionally, Belgians have been firmly on the side of Catholicism. The Reformation was initially received with some enthusiasm, but by 1585 was sufficiently suppressed by the church and Catholic nobility that Protestantism has never gained a significant foothold in Belgian society.[29] Belgium became an independent state in 1830. When the first Protestant Synod for relating to the government was organized in 1838, it

---

29. Paul Arblaster sets the Belgian account within the history of the Reformation in the Low Countries in *A History of the Low Countries*, 112–30.

represented 16 churches. The arrival of free church evangelicals and Pentecostals, through the early and mid-twentieth century, along with the massive growth of diaspora Christianity since the 1990s, has brought that number to 720.[30] Colin Godwin estimates that the number of these churches has almost doubled since 1980.[31] Currently, Protestant churches articulate with the state through an umbrella organization, founded in 2003, that speaks for two separate Synods.[32]

While indigenous Protestantism, and particularly Pentecostalism, demonstrated vitality and growth in the twentieth century, that has generally subsided in recent years. Contemporary Protestant advancement has largely come from immigrant Christianity. Sarah Demart and her team estimate that there are some 200 Congolese Pentecostal churches in Belgium, of various sizes from less than a score to megachurch. Many of these, perhaps most, would not be represented by Administrative Raad van de Protestants-Evangelishe Eredienst (ARPEE). By far the largest church in Belgium is the Congolese Église de la Nouvelle Jérusalem. Established in 1986, and related to the Church of God (Cleveland, TN), this church claimed membership of over 3,000 in 2010. In addition, it features some 26 satellite churches in Belgium, and seven elsewhere in Europe and the USA.[33]

Lest the impression be given that the only Diaspora churches in Belgium are Congolese, it should be noted that there are several other churches with national and tribal identities, some originating in the other former Belgian colonies, (Burundi, Rwanda); others not, including both French-speaking (Cameroon, Togo) and English-speaking groups (Ghana, Nigeria).[34] Dibudi Way-Way notes the transience of such churches: "In the Brussels region . . . churches appear and disappear easily."[35] Thus, the more permanent, perhaps, reflect a more pan-African flavour.

---

30. Creemers, "Evangelical Free Churches," 180.

31. Godwin, "The Recent Growth of Pentecostalism in Belgium," 90.

32. Creemers, "Evangelical Free Churches," 192. The umbrella group is known as ARPEE/CACPE: Administratieve Raad van de Protestants-Evangelische Eredienst / Conseil Administratif du Culte Protestant et Évangélique (Administrative Council of the Protestant and Evangelical Religion).

33. Pfister, "The Development of Pentecostalism in Francophone Europe," 126.

34. In the year 2000, Dibudi Way-Way found ten Congolese, five Ghanaian and three Nigerian churches where English was the language of worship; Way-Way, "The African Christian Diaspora in Belgium," 452.

35. Way-Way, "The African Christian Diaspora in Belgium," 453.

But the globalization of the Belgian church extends beyond Africa. In 2012, ARPEE reported 29 Portuguese-speaking and 12 Spanish-speaking congregations in Belgium, along with Italian, Russian, Romanian, Korean, Turkish, and Arabic churches (in descending order of numbers from 13 to 3).[36] In Brussels two or three of these churches feature attendances of over 500. The presence of these Portuguese and Spanish churches is noteworthy due to their size and evangelistic passion.[37] In 2015, Belgium received 44,660 asylum applications, roughly double the average for previous years.[38] The Arabic congregations become significant in view of the recent influx of Islamic refugees, offering assistance, community meals, and gospel proclamation.

While the state of Christianity in Europe wanes, the revitalization afforded by immigrant churches cannot be underestimated. Muslims, coming from a world of "Islamdom," to use Marshall Hodgson's term, judge the relative weakness of Christianity by the condition of declining Christendom.[39] They may be inclined to view diaspora churches as outsiders, and socially and culturally irrelevant, as indeed, European churches may do. But this would be a grave mistake, for immigrant Christianity is essentially related to its European counterpart, both historically, and spiritually. I will later consider briefly what that bond may look like, and its value in contemporary Christian witness. For the moment it suffices to add that Americans may look at Europe and peer into their own future. Canadians, further down the road of globalization and secularization than America, and but less secularized than Europe, may find themselves looking into something of a mirror, finding novel insights. In Europe, however, the experience of a vibrant global Christianity in the ruins of a defunct Christendom will involve a more dramatic recognition of that curiously North American phenomenon of voluntary Christianity.

---

36. Godwin, "The Recent Growth of Pentecostalism in Belgium," 91.
37. This is anecdotal.
38. "Asylum and first time asylum applicants," [n.d.]
39. "The term 'Islamdom' will be immediately intelligible by analogy with 'Christendom'. 'Islamdom' is, then, the society in which the Muslims and their faith are recognized as prevalent and socially dominant, in one sense or another–a society in which, of course non-Muslims have always formed an integral, if subordinate, element, as have Jews in Christendom." Hodgson, *The Venture of Islam*, 58.

The Church as Colony or Outpost? Redefining Mission

As far back as 1989, Stanley Hauerwas and William Willimon had diagnosed the enculturated condition of the North American church after the demise of Christendom. They called for a reassessment of the Christian's role in culture, proposing the concept of "resident alien" as a metaphor for the believer's ambiguous position living *in the world* but not *of the world*. They describe the church, then, as a colony, "a beachhead, an outpost, an island of one culture in the middle of another, a place where the values of home are reiterated and passed on to the young, a place where the distinctive language and life-style of the resident aliens are lovingly nurtured and reinforced."[40]

At the risk of quibbling, I wish to make a distinction between two terms they use: *colony* and *outpost*. Hauerwas and Willimon's description of a colony agrees well with the Oxford English Dictionary, which offers one definition as "a settlement in a new country; a body of people who settle in a new locality, forming a community subject to or connected with their parent state." On the other hand, it shades outpost variously as "a detachment of an army . . . at a distance . . . esp. as a guard against surprise attack . . . an isolated or remote branch of something . . . the outermost limit . . . the furthest territory of an empire."[41] I find these definitions suggestive as descriptions of the church's mission. The outpost as far-flung, isolated, and primarily defensive; the colony as a bridge, settled in the far country but clearly subject to the occupying King.

The European church struggles in mission between these two models. At its most dejected, it seems like a lonely outpost. George Weigel popularized a term coined by Joseph Weiler: "christophobia." Weiler points out the almost vehement renunciation of Christian heritage by European politicians. It is, as Weigel claims, a "resistance to any acknowledgement of the Christian sources of Europe's democratic present."[42] Such attitudes, unchallenged in the public square, eventually enter the realm of conventional wisdom, even shaping the church's conception of itself. On this reading the church becomes *the Other* in its own cradle. It is the last outpost, holding on to its lonely narrative, and holding out, against the encroaching world. Without wishing to seem uncharitable, it

---

40. Hauerwas and Willimon, *Resident Aliens*, 12.

41. Both from the *Oxford English Dictionary Online*.

42. Weiler, "A Christian Europe?" 143–50 and George Weigel, *The Cube and the Cathedral*, 72.

sometimes seems that the chief goal of some Belgian churches is simply survival.

The image of the *colony* seems more hopeful. While still admitting its Otherhood, it sees its purpose differently. The colony embodies the Fatherland in miniature, it exists in foreign territory to express the character of its Kingdom. Hauerwas and Willimon take up John Howard Yoder's notion of the "confessing church." This is the church of the cross: not the church that quietly submits to the world system's cruel execution, but the church of "revolutionary participation" in Christ's triumph over those powers. "The cross is a sign of what happens when one takes God's account of reality more seriously than Caesar's."[43] That victory includes the resurrection side of the cross. For the church as colony, the goal ceases to be survival, but becomes challenging the status quo by proposing a vibrant alternative; offering a counter-cultural critique while expressing radical love within the system. At its best, the Belgian church demonstrates these qualities through ministries like the Breaking Chains Network that works with women caught up in human trafficking on the streets of Antwerp and Teen Challenge Belgique Francophone that operates a coffee house for street people in Charleroi, and a home for young women.

While the outpost, with its defensive stance, loudly claims its independence from the world, its very retreat causes it to melt into it. The colony remains vibrant by its living connection with the kingdom and its bold advances into the surrounding world. Both European and Canadian Pentecostalism face the challenge of maintaining their distinction from the world without retreating but by finding novel ways of infiltrating it.

Success, Failure, and Faithfulness: Redefining Ministry Effectiveness

North American paradigms of ministry are addicted to success. Back in 1986 Vernon Grounds decried the idolatry of American Evangelicalism to what William James called "the bitch goddess of success." "The right kind of thinking, plus the right kind of programming and motivation, plus the right battery of techniques will change any failure into shining success."[44] The critique still stings in the megachurchianity of today.

---

43. Hauerwas and Willimon, *Resident Aliens*, 47.

44. Grounds, "Faith for Failure," 4, as cited in Webster, *Selling Jesus*, 125. The well-known James image comes from a letter to H. G. Wells, 11 Sep 1906 in *The Letters of*

William Willimon laments that we fall too easily into worldly norms of achievement when we contemplate the meaning of ministerial success. "[W]e become the victims of whatever cultural images of success happen to be in ascendancy at the moment."[45] But what are the best means of evaluating pastoral effectiveness? How does one assess disciple-making, clear proclamation, missional deployment, or pastoral care? The elusiveness of gauging such activities makes it easy to default to numeric indicators like attendance, budget, and building size.[46]

Beside its pragmatic superficiality, this template for grading ministry leads to discouragement, burnout, and in the extreme, abandonment of vocation. Particularly in the European context, it fails to offer any kind of helpful assessment. In Belgium, one might count French or Flemish churches over 200 on one's fingers. While some clergy are state-funded, many smaller groups, and some with ideological aversion to state-subsidy are led by bi-vocational pastors who must support themselves, often with fulltime work. Anecdotally, it seems the story of starting with 50 parishioners and ending with 48 twenty years later is not uncommon. Measuring meaningful ministry by the standard metrics is useless in this milieu. A completely different scale is required in Europe than is typically used in Canadian Evangelicalism.

The incisive critique of European Christianity in the shadow of rising Nazism that Dietrich Bonhoeffer made in *The Cost of Discipleship* resonates with the contemporary North American situation. Bonhoeffer complained that "costly grace" had been replaced by a "cheap grace without discipleship" that was non-transformative.

> I can therefore cling to my bourgeois secular existence, and remain as I was before, but with the added assurance that the grace of God will cover me. It is under the influence of this kind of "grace" that the world has been made "Christian," but at the cost of secularizing the Christian religion as never before. The antithesis between the Christian life and the life of bourgeois respectability is at an end. The Christian life comes to mean nothing more than living in the world and as the world, in being no different from the world, in fact, in being prohibited from being different from the world for the sake of grace.[47]

William James, 259–60.

45. Willimon, *Pastor*, 302.
46. Lee and Fredrickson, *That Their Work Will Be a Joy*, 33.
47. Bonhoeffer, *The Cost of Discipleship*, 10.

In the present context Bonhoeffer's indictment carries particular irony. For it is the Christianity squeezed by secular Europe that may perhaps teach North American Christians how to escape their own endemic secularity. The success paradigm of North American ministry offers no "antithesis" between Christian effectiveness and "bourgeois" models of business success. Bonhoeffer amplifies Willimon's lament about worldly standards. The latter proposes a different, perhaps counterintuitive approach: "From what I have experienced as a pastor, the challenge is not to find some means of sure success, as the world measures these things, but rather to fail in the right way, for the right reasons."[48]

Faithfulness is the ultimate criterion of ministry (Matt 25:21; 1 Cor 4:2; 1 Tim 1:12). Indeed, Willimon and Hauerwas are tempted to claim faithfulness over effectiveness as the goal of the "confessing church," though finding it a false dichotomy.[49] The challenge in the postmodern, secular/post-secular context is to redefine faithfulness in terms of the obstacles such a world presents. Willimon implies that those who dare to fail properly are those who dare to risk greatly, that pastoral faithfulness is "a prodigal commitment" to calling people passionately to the life God envisions for them, a life larger than any or all of us are capable of sustaining.[50] Ministry in contemporary Europe as well as Canada requires a similar engagement with moving the church to colour outside the lines of secular expectation in radical ways, even at the risk of failure. A cruciform faith teaches us to live with failure as a necessary (read beneficial) corollary of existence. A cruciform faith, however, includes the surprise of resurrection and all its attendant possibilities. We will consider some ways this faith may be expressed in the next section.

PROPOSALS FOR ENGAGING (POST-) SECULAR EUROPE . . . AND CANADA?

The following ideas arise from pastoral reflection on the realities of life in contemporary Europe. Conversation with church leaders about the nature of ministry in Europe often turns to the challenges of confronting secular culture. Prospects for the future seem grim. Vision and faith are

---

48. Willimon, *Pastor*, 290.

49. Hauerwas and Willimon, *Resident Aliens*.

50. Willimon, *Pastor*, 289–90. See the quotation from Willimon's own teacher James L. Dittes.

in short supply, and where they are not, often realism is. Is it possible to take a more positive approach to Christian proclamation? Taking a theology of the cross as a starting place, one may find the current situation a suitably humble position from which to do Christ-like ministry.[51] Perhaps the most useful expression of the cross in this instance is the *diakonia* of hospitality.[52] Working from these assumptions, I make four optimistic proposals for future ministry in a post-Christendom culture.

Finding Common Cause with Roman Catholics

Mining Europe's dormant Christendom will mean going beyond the Thirty Years' War and the Reformation. The charismatic movement, and the International Roman Catholic-Classical Pentecostal Dialogue (IRC-CPD) offer an excellent model for the kind of fruitful discussion that can be had, highlighting areas of agreement, clarifying finer points of theology, and offering fresh perspectives for consideration from within one's own theological tradition.[53] Perhaps even more stunning was the Joint Declaration on the Doctrine of Justification signed in 1999 by the Roman Catholic Church and the Lutheran World Federation. Even in the wake of Vatican II, the unlikelihood of such an event was commonly accepted, yet careful discussion led to a document that describes a "common understanding" of justification without covering all that either teaches on the topic yet achieving a profound enough consensus that allows the historic condemnations both churches made to be set aside.[54]

Surveying historical paradigms of mission in *Transforming Ministry*, David Bosch suggests that the Eastern Orthodox approach starts with God's love rather than his justice, as Bosch imagines is true of Western notions. Bosch claims the Orthodox model of mission is kenosis: "inner voluntary self-denial which makes room to receive the other to whom

---

51. Space prohibits a proper development of the theology of the cross for ministry. One may consult Forde, *On Being a Theologian of the Cross*; Thomsen, *Christ Crucified*; Courey, *What Has Wittenberg to Do with Azusa?*; Moltmann, *The Crucified God*.

52. While the constraints of this paper do not afford the possibility of developing the notion of hospitality, the following shows what a fruitful concept it has become. See Pohl, *Making Room*; Richard, *Living the Hospitality of God*; Sutherland, *I Was A Stranger*; Byrne, *The Hospitality of God*; Yong, *Hospitality and the Other*.

53. Creemers, "Dance to the Beat of Your Own Drum," 58–68.

54. Lutheran World Federation and Roman Catholic Church, *Joint Declaration on the Doctrine of Justification*, para. 5, 10–11.

one turns." The self-emptying of Jesus led him to identify with those on the periphery. The corollary is that to be sent into the world as the Father sent the Son (John 20:21), Christians must practice such self-surrender.[55] In some ways this is the easiest, in other ways the most difficult context in which to make room for the *Other*. Perhaps this Evangelical/Pentecostal testing ground with Catholicism is the best place to discover whether or not the church is truly prepared for the kenotic ministry that Europe requires.

Such expressions go a long way to mutual reconciliation, but even more, offer the possibility of common witness to the Father's sending of His Son into the world (John 17:23). In the face of European secularity, the power of this witness is compelling, especially in the face of the divisions that Protestantism and Catholicism have foisted upon the continent. This step is essential to any effective recovery of Christian witness in Europe.

Beyond the symbolic value of such a rapprochement, there is the value of multiplying efforts toward the common cause of the gospel. In the postmodern context, which is more pronounced in Europe than North America, Catholics, Pentecostals, Evangelicals, and traditional Protestants increasingly will agree that personal engagement with Jesus Christ is the key to Christian experience and witness. While doctrinal differences will remain, they will become less significant against the alternative worldviews that surround them.

Common Cause with Migrant Churches

The mammoth growth of Christianity in the majority world, and the general decentering of Western Christianity asserted by Philip Jenkins' *Next Christendom*, augur for a strongly missional migrant church.[56] African immigration to Europe has been significant since the post-colonial era, and after the 1980s, particularly from sub-Saharan Africa.[57] It has been suggested that many of these migrants have come for missionary purposes. But as one British survey demonstrated, while religion is indeed a factor in migration, it is a small one. Only 7 per cent of Redeemed Christian

---

55. Bosch, *Transforming Mission*, 214, 525. The citation is from Voulgarakis "Mission and Unity," 301.

56. Jenkins, *The Next Christendom*.

57. Bade, *Migration in European History*, 220.

Church of God (RCCG) immigrants came for primarily missional purposes, and they are mainly pastors.[58] A chief reason for immigration has been financial. As B. A. Adedibu observes, "economic migrants traveled not only with their skills but also with their religious 'backpacks.'"[59]

The question of their missionary effectiveness is a thorny one. While African diaspora Christians have formed some of the largest churches in Europe, they remain primarily Black Majority Churches (BMCs). In 2000, Dibudi Way-Way estimated that European involvement in Afro-Belgian churches was no more than 10 per cent.[60] It was anticipated that such churches would exhibit *reverse mission*, the sending of missionaries from the formerly-evangelized back to the West. African churches have been moved by the image of Europe as the *dark continent* and prophecies spiritualizing their call to reach Europe. Their zeal to reach the world, and (at least, superficially) to eschew a distinctly African identity is demonstrated in their names, often including terms such as *worldwide*, *global outreach*, or *international*.[61] Thus, the notion of reverse mission is twofold: "reversing the direction of missionary-sending; and reversing the direction of colonization."[62] Richard Burgess, et al. note that these churches, particularly the RCCG, do make themselves known in the public sphere as agents of social action.[63] On the other hand, their success at reaching white European populations is negligible: in Adedibu's words they are more "'Migrant Sanctuaries,' reproducing African culture, than 'Reverse Missions.'"[64]

European Christianity can surely benefit from the vibrancy and commitment of diaspora churches. Indeed, it already does, from the number of diaspora believers who attend traditional Belgian churches. But is there a way to tap that vitality for effective proclamation? Both Adedibu and Paul Freston point to the barriers of race and culture between BMCs and the European public as major hindrances to their effectiveness.[65] Here, too the model of a ministry of hospitality commends itself. Both

---

58. Burgess et al., "Nigerian-Initiated Pentecostal Churches," 107–8.
59. Adedibu, "Reverse Mission or Migrant Sanctuaries?" 408.
60. Way-Way, "The African Christian Diaspora in Belgium," 453.
61. Godwin, "The Recent Growth of Pentecostalism in Belgium," 91.
62. Freston, "Reverse Mission," 155–56.
63. Burgess et al., "Nigerian-Initiated Pentecostal Churches," 97–121.
64. Adedibu, "Reverse Mission or Migrant Sanctuaries?" 428.
65. Freston, "Reverse Mission," 158–62; Adedibu, "Reverse Mission or Migrant Sanctuaries?" 418–22.

European and Canadian church leaders would do well to form strong ties to diaspora churches of African, Asian, and Latin American derivation, not only to help them bridge the gulf into the host society, but to learn from them lessons that transcend culture about spiritual vitality. This kind of reciprocity would be mutually beneficial, but beyond this, would cement common witness and unity before a watching world.

Common Cause with Secularists (?)

The recovery of social justice themes among evangelical and Pentecostal churches is to be celebrated. And recovery it is: social justice is not a theme foreign to evangelical or Wesleyan spirituality, but rather the unifying expression of faith in what was called the Benevolent Empire in nineteenth-century America, and the motivating impetus of that group of activists known as the Clapham Sect in Britain.[66] A contemporary observer of Evangelicalism might be forgiven for expressing surprise at the news that such churches are only now beginning to concern themselves with poverty, homelessness, and marginality.

The problem of inadequate response reaches the intellectual arena, as well. Andrew Hartropp observes that competing secular notions of justice lack any ontological basis or appeal to inherent truth, and that this provides an opening for Christian proposals, rooted as they are in the character and revelation of God. Sadly, Hartropp concludes that Christians have not adequately reflected on the nature of justice to articulate a theologically robust and culturally engaging response.[67] What is lacking is a resourceful appropriation of the theology of the cross that might offer both inspiration and imagination. Creative approaches to justice, as Jürgen Moltmann indicates, are not only beneficial, but essential to Christian mission. "Only where righteousness becomes creative and creates right both for the lawless and for those outside the law, only where creative love changes what is hateful and deserving of hate, only where the new man is born who is neither oppressed nor oppresses others, can

---

66. Handy, *A Christian America*; Tomkins, *The Clapham Sect*; For an assessment of this recovery, see Steensland and Goff, "Introduction: The New Evangelical Social Engagement."

67. Hartropp, *What Is Economic Justice?* 4–8.

one speak of the true revolution of righteousness and of the righteousness of God."[68] Theologizing must lead to action and cultural engagement.

If Hartropp is correct, both Christians and secularists find themselves facing gargantuan social challenges, and both are compelled to act, neither with an adequate ideological basis, but both with an activist compassion. I am not soft-pedalling differences, here. As Vic McCracken indicates, "The distinction between secular and Christian visions of justice matters." He advises that Christians practice the *politics of Jesus*, which will seem alien in a secular context.[69] But this is just the point. Common causes exist where the situation seems ideal for a team approach, and in that context an enlightening and fruitful dialogue can arise that will benefit both. This creates space for honing those *politics*, building needed bridges, and offering meaningful Christian witness, as well as making a practical difference.

Common Cause with Islam (?)

With the terseness of a statistical report, the Pew Research Center offers a clear summary as to its projections regarding European religious demographics.

> Europe's Christian population is expected to shrink by about 100 million people in the coming decades, dropping from 553 million to 454 million. While Christians will remain the largest religious group in Europe, they are projected to drop from three-quarters of the population to less than two-thirds. By 2050, nearly a quarter of Europeans (23%) are expected to have no religious affiliation, and Muslims will make up about 10% of the region's population, up from 5.9% in 2010.[70]

The drop in Christians is due to the aging Christian population and low fertility. Figures for Belgium reveal a similar trend. Muslims will double from 5.9 per cent to 11.8 per cent of the population, as with the rest of

---

68. Moltmann, *The Crucified God*, 178.

69. McCracken also considers the inconsistency of differing Christian views, such as pacifism and "just war." See McCracken, "Social Justice: An Introduction to a Vital Concept," 1–15 [12].

70. Pew Research Center, "The Future of World Religions: Population Growth Projections, 2010–2050," 27. Compare these numbers with those of the European Social Survey which claims that Muslims in Belgium grew from 11.2 per cent in 2010 to 15.8 per cent in 2014. I have given the more conservative numbers.

Europe, half biologically, half by immigration. The other startling statistic is the growth in the unaffiliated demographic from 18.8 per cent to 23.3 per cent.[71] Indeed Europe is the only continent on which the actual number of Christians will drop. These projections raise probing questions about the expression of a cruciform theology of hospitality toward Muslims between a declining Christianity and an ascending Islam.

But in fact, this is precisely what is required. In the increasingly politicized atmosphere of radical terrorism, can the church play a role in introducing a growing Muslim population to the West, while acknowledging their differences, respecting their faith, and still offering a sensitive Christian apologetic? This is the delicate balance the church must discover. In the current, and predicted climate of the future, kenosis appears as an appropriate model for ministry.

This must challenge Christian approaches to ministry to Muslims. If, as Bosch has shown about Orthodox mission, love is the motive force, this has significant implications. As long as Pentecostals and Evangelicals simply see Muslims as targets of evangelism, they can never succeed in properly loving them. Yale philosopher Gene Outka insists, "[s]elf-sacrifice must always be purposive in promoting the welfare of others and never simply expressive of something resident in the agent."[72] Thus the starting place for Islamic/Christian rapprochement must be conversation—but conversation of a distinct sort. Jane Linahan describes the nature of kenotic conversation in a creative 2003 paper: "The readiness to receive, the making of that empty space is just as crucial, just as much an act of love, as the act of giving itself. Openness to and reverence for the Other may be the most profound form of love, for without these we risk denying the unique truth and worth of the Other precisely as one who is other and different than ourselves."[73]

As Europe becomes more embroiled in the assimilation of Muslim refugees, as it continues to face jihadist pressures, it will be increasingly important for ministry to Muslims to uphold Islamic dignity. Such an approach need not ignore gospel proclamation, but rather creates the kind of environment that invites honest open-ended conversation in the place of aggressive evangelism. Canadians will immediately recognize that

---

71. European Social Survey, *Exploring Public Attitudes*, 82.
72. Outka, *Agape*, 278, cited in Linahan, "Kenosis," 305.
73. Linahan, "Kenosis," 307.

their new Muslim neighbors deserve this kind of introduction to their new nation and to the gospel.

CONCLUSION

Before coming to Belgium, I was quite aware of the "secular Europe" that has eclipsed Christendom, and its challenge of assimilating a vast Muslim diaspora. The picture was two-dimensional and easy to grasp. What I had not conceived was how deep were the currents of dormant Christendom and how easily both Europeans and outsiders dismiss its influence. I was alert to the presence of immigrant churches but was surprised to discover both how weak Christianity actually is, and yet how strong it was where I least expected it. I had read that Europeans perceived Islam as a kind of threat to European identity, but I had not contemplated the possibilities this presented for sensitive Christian participation.

I have endeavoured to provide a more optimistic view of Christian possibilities in Europe. I am persuaded that the facts do not substantiate the common view of European secularity. The statistical data suggest a more nuanced picture that indicates the possibility that Christianity has a significant contribution to make in bringing disparate populations together within the European context. With appropriate sensitivity, Roman Catholics and Protestants together could broker necessary relations with the diaspora church, Muslims, and secularists that might catalyze a needed revisioning of European identity in the twenty-first century.

A vibrant European Christianity revitalized by the global church, building on the shared identity of Europe's Christian heritage, a recalled, if not restored, Christendom possesses great promise for the future. Its hope lies not in triumphalist success paradigms, but in discovering cruciform ways of finding common cause with its neighbours, and as the church has always done in its best days, pouring out its life for others.

BIBLIOGRAPHY

Adedibu, Babatunde Aderemi. "Reverse Mission or Migrant Sanctuaries? Migration, Symbolic Mapping, and Missionary Challenges of Britain's Black Majority Churches." *Pneuma* 35 (2013) 405–23.

Alberts, Wanda. *Integrative Religious Education in Europe: A Study-of-Religions Approach*. Religion and Reason. Berlin: de Gruyter, 2007.

Arblaster, Paul. *A History of the Low Countries*. 2nd ed. New York: Palgrave Macmillan, 2012.

"Asylum and First Time Asylum Applicants—Annual Aggregated Data (Rounded)" [n.d.], http://ec.europa.eu/eurostat/tgm/table.do?tab=table&init=1&plugin=1&language=en&pcode=tps00191.

Bade, Klaus. *Migration in European History*. Translated by Allison Brown. Oxford: Blackwell, 2003.

Beach, Lee. *The Church in Exile: Living in Hope After Christendom*. Downers Grove, IL: IVP Academic, 2015.

Berger, Peter L. "The Desecularization of the World: A Global Overview." In *The Descularization of the World: Resurgent Religion and World Politics*, edited by Peter L. Berger, 1–18. Grand Rapids: Eerdmans, 1999.

Bibby, Reginald Wayne. "Continuing the Conversation on Canada: Changing Patterns of Religious Service Attendance." *Journal for the Scientific Study of Religion* 50 (December 2011) 831–37.

Billiet, Jaak, and Bart Meuleman. "Religious Diversity in Europe and its Relation to Social Attitudes and Value Orientations." In *European Social Survey, Citizenship and Cultural Identities in the EU: Old Questions, New Answers-Conference Proceedings*, 83–104. Ankara: Promeda Ofset Matbaacýlýk, 2008.

Boeve, Lieven. "'Katholieke' identiteit van organisaties en instellingen uit het cultureel-maatschappelijke middenveld." In *De 'K' van Kerk: De pluriformiteit van katholiciteit*, edited by Peter De Mey and Pieter de Witte, 109–20. Antwerp: Halewijn, 2009.

Bonhoeffer, Dietrich. *The Cost of Discipleship*. Translated by R. H. Fuller. London: SCM, 1948.

Bosch, David J. *Transforming Mission: Paradigm Shifts in Theology of Mission*. Maryknoll, NY: Orbis, 1991.

Burgess, Richard, et al. "Nigerian-Initiated Pentecostal Churches as a Social Force in Europe: The Case of the Redeemed Church of God." *PentecoStudies* 9 (2010) 97–121.

Byrne, Brendan. *The Hospitality of God: A Reading of Luke's Gospel*. 2nd ed. Collegeville, MN: Liturgical, 2015.

Christians, Louis-Léon, and Stéphanie Wattier. "Funding of Religious and Non-Confessional Organizations: The Case of Belgium." In *Public Funding of Religions in Europe*, edited by Francis Messner, 51–73. Farnham, UK: Ashgate, 2015.

"Commission Public Holidays for 2015." Accessed December 29, 2015. https://ec.europa.eu/europeaid/sites/devco/files/communication-commission-holidays-2015_en.pdf.

Courey, David J. "The Ozymandias Factor: Persistence, Memory, and European Secularism." *Journal of the European Pentecostal Association* 37 (2017) 13–27.

———. *What Has Wittenberg to Do with Azusa? Luther's Theology of the Cross and Pentecostal Triumphalism*. New York: Bloomsbury T. & T. Clark, 2015.

Creemers, Jelle. "Evangelical Free Churches and State Support in Belgium: Praxis and Discourse from 1987 to Today." *Trajecta* 24 (2015) 177-204.

———. "Dance to the Beat of Your Own Drum: Classical Pentecostals in Ecumenical Dialogue." *Journal of the European Theological Association* 35 (April 2015) 58–68.

Eagle, David Edwin. "Changing Pattern of Attendance at Religious Services in Canada, 1986–2008." *Journal for the Scientific Study of Religion* 50 (March 2011) 187–200.

Exploring Public Attitudes, Informing Public Policy: Selected Findings from the First Three Rounds. European Social Survey, n.d. http://www.europeansocialsurvey.org/

Finke, Roger, and Rodney Stark. *Acts of Faith: Explaining the Human Side of Religion*. Berkeley: University of California Press, 2000.

Forde, Gerhard O. *On Being a Theologian of the Cross: Reflections on Luther's Heidelberg Disputation, 1518*. Grand Rapids: Eerdmans, 1997.

Freston, Paul. "Reverse Mission: A Discourse in Search of Reality?" *PentecoStudies* 9 (2010) 153–74.

Gallie, B. "Essentially Contended Concepts." *Proceedings of the Aristotelian Society* 56 (1955–56) 167–98.

Godwin, Colin. "The Recent Growth of Pentecostalism in Belgium." *International Bulletin of Missionary Research* 37 (April 2013) 90–94.

Gorski, Philip S. "Historicizing the Secularization Debate: An Agenda for Research." In *Handbook of the Sociology of Religion*, edited by Michele Dillon, 110–22. New York: Cambridge University Press, 2003.

Grounds, Vernon. "Faith for Failure: A Meditation for Ministry." *Theological Students Fellowship Bulletin* 9 (March–April 1986) 3–5.

Habermas, Jürgen. "Notes on Post-Secular Society." *New Perspectives Review* 25.4 (2008) 17–29.

Handy, Robert T. *A Christian America: Protestant Hopes and Historical Realities*. 2nd ed. New York: Oxford University Press, 1984.

Hartropp, Andrew. *What Is Economic Justice? Biblical and Secular Perspectives Contrasted*. Eugene, OR: Wipf & Stock, 2008.

Hauerwas, Stanley. *After Christendom*. Nashville: Abingdon, 1991.

Hauerwas, Stanley, and William H. Willimon. *Resident Aliens: Life in the Christian Colony*. Nashville: Abingdon, 1989.

Hodgson, Marshall G. S. *The Venture of Islam, Volume 1: The Classical Age of Islam*. Chicago: University of Chicago Press, 1974.

James, William. *The Letters of William James, Volume II*, edited by Henry James. London: Longmans, Green, 1920.

Jenkins, Philip. "Changes and Trends in Global Christianity." In *The Globalization of Christianity: Implications for Christian Ministry and Theology*, edited by Gordon L. Heath and Steven M. Studebaker, 15–30. McMaster Theological Studies Series 6. Eugene, OR: Pickwick, 2015.

———. *The Next Christendom: The Coming of Global Christianity*. 3rd edition. Oxford: Oxford University Press, 2011.

Lee, Cameron, and Kurt Fredrickson. *That Their Work Will Be a Joy: Understanding and Coping with the Challenges of Pastoral Ministry*. Eugene, OR: Wipf & Stock, 2012.

Linahan, Jane E. "Kenosis: Metaphor of Relationship." In *Theology and Conversation: Towards a Relational Theology*, edited by Jacques Haers and Peter De Mey, 299–309. Leuven, Belgium: Leuven University Press, 2003.

Lipka, Michael. "What Surveys Say about Worship Attendance—and Why Some Stay Home." *Pew Research Center*, September 13, 2013, http://www.pewresearch.org/fact-tank/2013/09/13/what-surveys-say-about-worship-attendance-and-why-some-stay-home/.

Lutheran World Federation and Roman Catholic Church. *Joint Declaration on the Doctrine of Justification*. Grand Rapids: Eerdmans, 2000.

Manchin, Robert. "Religion in Europe: Trust Not Filling the Pews." *Gallup.com*, September 2004, http://www.gallup.com/poll/13117/Religion-Europe-Trust-Filling-Pews.aspx.

McCracken, Vic. "Social Justice: An Introduction to a Vital Concept." In *Christian Faith and Social Justice: Five Views*, edited by Vic McCracken, 1–15. London: Bloomsbury, 2014.

Mills, C. Wright. *The Sociological Imagination*. Oxford: Oxford University Press, 1959.

Moltmann, Jürgen. *The Crucified God: The Cross of Christ as the Foundation and Criticism of Christian Theology*. Minneapolis: Fortress, 1973.

Murray, Stuart. *Post-Christendom: Church and Mission in a Strange New World*. Milton Keynes, UK: Paternoster, 2004.

Outka, Gene. *Agape: An Ethical Analysis*. New Haven: Yale University Press, 1972.

Oxford English Dictionary Online [n.d.], http://www.oed.com/.

Pew Research Center. "The Future of World Religions: Population Growth Projections, 2010–2050," April 2015, http://www.pewforum.org/2015/04/02/religious-projections-2010-2050/.

Pfister, Raymond. "The Development of Pentecostalism in Francophone Europe." In *European Pentecostalism*, edited by William Kay and Anne Dyer, 113–64. Leiden: Brill, 2011.

Pohl, Christine D. *Making Room: Recovering Hospitality as a Christian Tradition*. Grand Rapids: Eerdmans, 1999.

Richard, Lucien. *Living the Hospitality of God*. Mahwah, NJ: Paulist, 2000.

Slomp, Hans. *Europe, a Political Profile: An American Companion to European Politics: An American Companion to European Politics*. 2 vols. Santa Barbra, CA: ABC-CLIO, 2011.

Stan, Lavinia, and Lucian Turcescu. *Church, State, and Democracy in Expanding Europe* Oxford: Oxford University Press, 2011.

Steensland, Brian, and Philip Goff. "Introduction: The New Evangelical Social Engagement." In *The New Evangelical Social Engagement*, edited by Brian Steensland and Philip Goff, 1–27. New York: Oxford University Press, 2014.

Sutherland, Arthur. *I Was A Stranger: A Christian Theology of Hospitality*. Nashville: Abingdon, 2006.

Taylor, Charles. *A Secular Age*. Cambridge, MA: The Belknap Press of Harvard University Press, 2007.

Thomsen, Mark W. *Christ Crucified: A 21st Century Missiology of the Cross*. Minneapolis: Lutheran University Press, 2004.

TNS Opinion & Social. *Social Values, Science and Technology*. Special Eurobarometer 225. European Commission, 2005.

Tomkins, Stephen. *The Clapham Sect: How Wilberforce's Circle Transformed Britain*. Oxford: Lion, 2012.

Warner, Rob. *Secularization and Its Discontents*. London: Continuum, 2010.

Webster, Douglas D. *Selling Jesus: What's Wrong with Marketing the Church*. Eugene, OR: Wipf & Stock, 2009.

Van de Poll, Evert. *Europe and the Gospel: Past Influences, Current Developments, Mission Challenges*. London: Versita, 2013.

Voulgarakis, Elias. "Mission and Unity from the Theological Point of View. *International Review of Mission* 54 (July 1965) 298–307.

Way-Way, Dibudi. "The African Christian Diaspora in Belgium with Special Reference to the International Church of Brussels." *International Review of Mission* 89 (July 2000) 451–56.

Weigel, George. *The Cube and the Cathedral: Europe, America, and Politics Without God*. New York: Basic, 2008.

Weiler, Joseph H. H. "A Christian Europe? Europe and Christianity: Rules of Commitment." *European View* 6 (2007) 143–50.

Willimon, William H. *Pastor: The Theology and Practice of Ordained Ministry*. Nashville: Abingdon, 2010.

Yong, Amos. *Hospitality and the Other: Pentecost, Christian Practices, and the Neighbor*. Maryknoll, NY: Orbis, 2008.

Ziebertz, Georg and Ulrich Riegel. "Europe: A Post-Secular Society?" *International Journal of Practical Theology* 13 (2009) 293–308.

6

The End of Pentecostal Preaching

VAN JOHNSON

THOSE FAMILIAR WITH PENTECOSTAL beginnings at the outset of the twentieth century know that an acute eschatological awareness played a formative role in the early years.[1] The belief in the imminent return of Jesus was explicit in their short catechism; the final affirmation of the Full Gospel is Christ as Coming King.[2] What is not sufficiently appreciated, though, was its primary role, not simply as one of the core beliefs and repeated emphases in early Pentecostal proclamation, but as *the* integrating factor for early Pentecostal belief and practice.[3] To put it another way, it shaped the plotline of their story. Even Spirit Baptism was understood eschatologically. Their experience of the restoration of tongues-speech signified God's selection of them as his people of the "last days"—the ones who had the power of the Holy Spirit to usher in one final great revival before the end. There was no Pentecostal message without an eschatological storyboard to give it shape and direction. I will

---

1. Regarding the centrality of eschatology for Pentecostalism, see Anderson, *Vision of the Disinherited*; Faupel, *This Gospel of the Kingdom*; and Land, *Pentecostal Spirituality*. Noteworthy is Jacobsen's observation about Charles Parham, who he credits as being the "founder of Pentecostal theology," that his "apocalyptic vision . . . set the context for Parham's theology as a whole" (*Thinking in the Spirit*, 20).

2. The original Pentecostal configuration was: Christ as Saviour, Sanctifier, Healer, Baptizer, and Coming King.

3. I develop this more fully in my article "Fulfillment of God's Promise," 181–201.

argue that if the return of Christ is no longer driving the plot behind contemporary Pentecostal proclamation of the gospel story, then Pentecostal preaching in its classical form has come to an end.

To illustrate the centrality of eschatology in the first phase of Canadian Pentecostal formation, this chapter analyzes three early newsletters representing the movement's beginnings in Toronto, Winnipeg, and Ottawa. They are primary sources for understanding pre-denominational Canadian Pentecostal proclamation because they reflect the oral nature of the movement. They are the printed record of what was being spoken among them. In the testimonies, pithy maxims, meeting announcements, and sermonic bits, we hear the echo of what they proclaimed when they gathered together. Much like the Gospels themselves, these newsletters represent an attempt to capture the spoken word and rebroadcast it in printed form. What we hear in them is an obsession with an eschatology focused on the return of Jesus. The constructs they used to proclaim the end times were variant expressions of Apocalyptic Eschatology, a system of thought that will need some explanation before we turn to the newsletters themselves. First, however, I will address the situation that prompts this essay.

My perception of the diminishing role for the return of Jesus in Pentecostal preaching is that of a participant in the Pentecostal Assemblies of Canada (PAOC), both as an ordained minister and as an educator. Although my concern derives from trends I have observed in my own fellowship, what I have heard in graduate classrooms and read in the literature on North American Pentecostalism suggests to me that the situation in the largest Pentecostal denomination in Canada is not unique. Admittedly, we cannot, with the data that exists, demonstrate an overall decline in eschatological urgency during 110 years of Pentecostalism in Canada, nor plot on a graph its intensity level in each decade.[4] The nature of the data on a century of attitudes toward the *parousia* (the return of Jesus) complicates any attempt at measurement.[5] Nevertheless, a few

---

4. What the reader of *The Pentecostal Testimony* will find in each decade are repeated exhortations to remember the soon coming of Jesus and to act accordingly.

5. The denominational periodical of the PAOC, *The Pentecostal Testimony* (1919–), would be the obvious starting point for such a search. One could track the frequency of articles devoted to eschatology, and the number of times the subject is raised in articles on other subjects, and then plot the numbers on a chart. But numbers alone would not tell the story. For example, an increase in mentions of the second coming in the denominational magazine in any period might reflect its currency as a topic in PAOC pulpits, or an editorial concern that the subject was in decline and

observations about changing attitudes may be made. First, as I will illustrate, the early Pentecostal movement in its pre-denominational phase (before 1919) was fixated on it. Against that standard, our current concern with the return of Jesus wanes in comparison. Second, we shared a blip of apocalyptic excitement with other evangelicals in the late 1960s and early 1970s. The soundtrack of the period was Larry Norman's *I Wish We'd All Been Ready*, the movie, *A Thief in the Night*, and the best-seller, Hal Lindsey's *The Late Great Planet Earth*—which reignited interest in Dispensational Theology.[6] If that era represents the high watermark of my lifetime, there has certainly been a decline in PAOC preaching about the return of Christ since then.

Third, we can speak more quantitatively about trends when we reach the 1980s. How the preaching of eschatology has fared within our movement between then and now is one of the areas studied by Adam Stewart and Andrew Gabriel. They compared the attitudes and behaviours of current PAOC pastors with those of their predecessors who were polled in the 1985/6 survey by Carl Verge.[7] While the 2014/15 study did show an overall decline in preaching about the return of Jesus since the mid-1980s, Stewart and Gabriel noted that educational level was a significant variable in the results. Those with some graduate education were actually a bit more likely than their 1980s counterparts to preach about the soon return of Christ (and Spirit Baptism, for that matter).[8] In contrast, those credential holders with a college degree or less, which made up the majority of respondents in both surveys, were slightly less likely to do so than similarly educated ministers in the PAOC thirty years previous, and even less likely to do so in comparison with current credential holders with some graduate education.[9] I am thankful that, on average, our pastors preach about the Second Coming about three times a year, yet this is still a radical departure from the seminal role its proclamation played in early Pentecostalism.

---

needed bolstering. The articles themselves would need to be interpreted.

6. Norman, "I Wish We'd All Been Ready"; Doughten and Grant, *A Thief in the Night*; Lindsey and Carlson, *The Late Great Planet Earth*.

7. Ready access to both surveys is available at https://paocbeliefs.weebly.com/findings.html. Surveys listed separately in bibliography for Verge, "Comparison of the Beliefs and Practices," and for Stewart et al., "Changes in Clergy Belief," 457–81.

8. In 1985, an average (or, mean) of 2 times a year; in 2014, 3.17 times a year.

9. Frequency decreased among college educated from 5 times a year to 2.82 times. Those with some graduate education are slightly higher at 3.17.

APOCALYPTIC ESCHATOLOGY

While I am pressing the point that early Pentecostal preaching was thoroughly eschatological in shape, the same could be argued for the *kerygma* (or, preaching) of the early church. Their proclamation was grounded in an eschatological perspective combining elements of fulfillment and expectation.[10] The Messiah had come, signaling the arrival of the promised age. He called for new wineskins to be gathered for new wine (Luke 5:38), and his death established a new covenant in his blood (Luke 22:20). Though he ascended to the Father with the work unfinished, his death and resurrection portended a different future for humankind that would culminate with his triumphant return to earth. The NT writings respond in various ways to this eschatological tension between what had been fulfilled and what remained unrealized (often referred to as "the already/not yet"). Yet, framing their negotiation of these two realities was the pervading notion that the period of expectation would be brief.

No generation of Christians has had a more acute sense of the soon return of Jesus than the first one. It was the worldview of Apocalyptic Eschatology—hinted at in the later sections of the OT, developed in Jewish writings in the period between the testaments and adopted and adapted by Jesus in his proclamation of the kingdom of God—that allowed the NT writers to make sense of what God had already done in Christ and what he was yet to do. When the first Pentecostals of the 1900s identified themselves with the apostolic era, they not only gained a biblical precedent for the charismatic phenomena occurring among them, but also an apocalyptic worldview by which to understand them. In particular, it was Peter's quotation from Joel 2 on the day of Pentecost, "in the last days I will pour out my Spirit" (Acts 2:17), that would impress on the collective Pentecostal psyche that they were people of the end.

There is a distinction to be made between Apocalyptic Eschatology and the type found in OT prophetic literature.[11] Whereas Prophetic

---

10. Adela Y. Collins advances the argument that apocalyptic is the framework for NT theology in "Apocalypticism and Christian Origins," 326–39.

11. See Hanson's differentiation of prophetic and apocalyptic expectation in *The Dawn of Apocalyptic*, 11. Despite the continuities between the two, and the emergence of an apocalyptic worldview in some prophetic texts (e.g., Zech 1–8), they still merit separate classification. As for the conceptual elements of apocalyptic material, J. J. Collins lists: "supernatural revelation, the heavenly world, angels and demons, and eschatological judgment" ("What is Apocalyptic Literature?" 7). See also Murphy, *Apocalypticism in the Bible and Its World*, especially chapters 1–3.

Eschatology foresaw the working out of God's promises to Israel within history—as a nation on a piece of sacred land—the apocalyptic perspective that emerged in Second Temple Judaism arose in a context of despair about the course of human history.[12] The apocalyptic solution to the seemingly endless oppression of Israel, first under the yoke of the Greeks and then the Romans, was to be discerned from *revelation*—what the word *apocalypse* means. Since the content of the revelations recorded in Jewish and Christian apocalyptic writings often describe a series of imminent cataclysmic events, marking the end of one world and the start of another, the term "apocalyptic" has become associated with the events themselves.

Although the word "apocalyptic" is commonly linked to a certain type of content, the term itself reminds us of the process through which the future is perceived. Divine revelation rather than human reasoning or deduction underlies this worldview. In other words, it reveals what the natural eye cannot see: a future radically different than all present appearances. Whereas the Hebrew prophets envisioned the glorious restoration of this world, the Jewish apocalyptic seers saw a whole other world. The future is revealed, not foreseen. Consequently, it will not be surprising for us when we turn to the newsletters to find that the sources of many of their expressions about the soon return of Jesus and the state of the world to come are visions and prophetic messages.

The early Christian adaptation of Jewish apocalyptic expectation introduced into the eschatological timetable an interim stage between Christ's arrival and his promised return, meaning, between the initial fulfillment of God's promises and their completion. The Messiah has come, therefore the age of Christ is inaugurated, yet the conditions of the age of Adam remain (Rom 5:12–21). Even though the present is a time of fulfillment, what Christians experience now is still essentially a preview. It is the completion of God's restoring work at the return of Jesus that spells the end of the age of Adam and so the *parousia* remains the great hope of the church.

Early Pentecostals located themselves in this temporal intersection: the "already" of the coming of the Son and the Spirit and the "not yet" of

---

12. Although the social function of apocalyptic literature certainly goes beyond consolation for the faithful who are in crisis and exhortation for the wicked, and the fact that scholarship is not of one mind on this (Collins, "What is Apocalyptic?" 5–6), I still find this a helpful starting point in understanding the emergence of apocalyptic literature and worldview within Second Temple Judaism.

Christ's return formed the ethos of early Pentecostalism. Perceiving that the Spirit had come upon them as he had at Pentecost, they saw themselves as restoring the conditions of the early church. Further, since it was the Spirit of power, the Spirit of witness (Acts 1:8), who had been poured out upon them, they became restorationists with a revivalistic bent. They were restoring to primacy the mission call of Jesus to preach to all the nations before the end. Spirit-empowered evangelism would prepare the world for the "not yet" but imminent return of Jesus.

Early Pentecostalism was a movement restoring a movement—or supplanting it. A close identification with the community of Acts 2 explains their self-proclaimed status as the community who inherited the promises spoken of by Peter on the Day of Pentecost. They justified their status with three nineteenth century constructs: Dispensationalism, Latter Rain, and The Promise. As we will argue below, each played a crucial role in early Pentecostal formation and proclamation.

By *revival* movement I mean something different than a *renewal* movement: in general, the former finds its success in salvation—both of the backslidden within the church and the lost outside of it; the latter, in a refreshing or stirring up of the faithful. With this distinction in mind, the early Pentecostal movement of the 1900s may be compared with the Charismatic Renewal of the 1960s. While there were certainly many shared experiences between them—speaking in tongues and healing, for example—this phenomenological overlap did not extend to a common proclamation that gave meaning and purpose to the phenomena. Whereas the renewalist might declare how the gifts of the Spirit were intended to bring vitality to congregational life, the early Pentecostals declared that the gifts of the Spirit were eschatological signs of the nearness of their Lord's return, which demanded of them expansion rather than consolidation, revival more than renewal. The presence of the Lord and all the phenomena of the Spirit's power were cherished by them, but they were told that Pentecostal power was not to be contained within the church walls. The Lord was coming soon, and they had to go out and do something about it. They were a revival-oriented restoration movement.

EARLY CANADIAN NEWSLETTERS

To illustrate the apocalyptic worldview of the first Canadian Pentecostals, we will look at the inaugural newsletters from three early centers of pre-denominational Pentecostalism, and we will do so in chronological order: *The Promise*, Toronto (1907), *The Apostolic Messenger*, Winnipeg (1908), and *The Good Report*, Ottawa (1911).

The Promise (Toronto)

The May 1907 issue of *The Promise* is the first edition of a series (most of which are not extant)[13] published at the East End Mission in Toronto by missionaries from Yorkshire, England—Ellen and James Hebden. The inaugural edition of *The Promise* is historically significant for the study of Canadian Pentecostal beginnings not just because it is the earliest of the newsletters. It shows that not all early influences on Canadian Pentecostalism came from south of the 49th parallel. First of all, it does not mention the revival on Azusa Street, Los Angeles, which began in April 1906, whereas the other two newsletters do. Secondly, Ellen's testimony makes clear she had no interest in speaking in tongues before her Spirit Baptism.[14] If she knew about Azusa and its reputation as the place where attendees were speaking in tongues, she did not want anything to do with it. As others have pointed out, the connection with this international hub of Pentecostalism would come later, suggesting an independent beginning for Canadian Pentecostalism—one connected to the UK Holiness movement.[15] And finally, an independent origin might go toward explaining why only the Toronto publication among the three employs the motif of "the promise" thematically.[16] Their use of "the promise" to express their restorationist *raison d'être* differentiates them from the

---

13. Only *The Promise* Nos. 1, 2, 14 (partial), and 15 have survived.

14. Ellen Hebden, "How Pentecost Came to Toronto," *The Promise*, May 1907, 2.

15. While the Hebden Mission began independently of the Azusa Street Mission—did the Hebdens even know about Azusa when the revival began in Toronto in Nov 1906?—it would become connected to it. As Sloos notes in his article "The Story of James and Ellen Hebden" (192 n. 61), five reports about the Hebden Mission appeared in *The Apostolic Faith* in four editions: Dec 1906; Jan 1907 (two reports); Feb–Mar 1907, Apr 1907. For more on the connection between the Hebden Mission and UK Holiness, see not only the article by Sloos, but also Stewart, "A Canadian Azusa?" 17–37.

16. Will Sloos, in several emails (July 12 and 14, 2018), provided some historical context: "promise" terminology was prominent in the newsletter *Tongues of Fire* that circulated in the UK in the 1890s. Ellen Hebden was part of the Pentecostal League of Prayer that published this periodical. The question remains: Is this formulation unique to UK holiness?

Azusa-influenced centers of Winnipeg and Ottawa, where the motif of former and latter rain is employed to link their communities with the one described in Acts 2.

Eschatology concerns the fulfillment of God's promises. In choosing *The Promise* for a title, the East End Mission identifies itself as the recipient of the eschatological blessing portion of Acts 2:39 taken from the conclusion to Peter's Pentecost sermon is cited below the title: "The promise is unto you, and to your children, and to all." By listing five NT verses that contain the word "promise" in the first column below the title, they clarify that they are the Gentile inheritors of the promise first given to the Jews by Jesus.[17]

The first three (Luke 24:49; Acts 1:4 and 1:8) anticipate Pentecost: the promise of the Father will be given to the disciples and power to witness to the ends of the earth will be the result. The other two, Pauline texts, emphasize that the promise, whether "the promise of the Spirit" (Gal 3:14) or "the promise in Christ" (Eph 3:6), is for Gentiles as well as Jews. This grouping of Lukan and Pauline texts as biblical commentary on the masthead text of Acts 2.39 ("The promise is unto you, and to your children, and to all") suggests that "the promise" has had a double fulfillment over two millennia: the "all" encompasses first-century Jews in Jerusalem and twentieth-century Gentiles in Toronto. The church is being restored as the promise is fulfilled again.

Almost half of the four pages that make up *The Promise* is given to the story of how it all began: Ellen's testimony of receiving Spirit Baptism and her report of what immediately transpired at the mission, which included one time when she spoke in twenty-two languages in a single service. She also notes that "hundreds of verses of poetry have been given by the Spirit, also the interpretation of many."[18] Only one of those poems is printed in the newsletter, which is transcribed in two verses as the spoken word of Jesus. The first stanza recalls the cross. The second reads: "I soon shall be returning / To fetch my precious bride / And then amid great glory / I'll place her by my side."[19] Two comments are ap-

---

17. Note also an article title from the Winnipeg newsletter: Ella Goff, "A Gentile's Pentecost in the 20th Century," *The Apostolic Messenger*, February–March 1908, 2. Nothing in the article itself, however, explains the title. The author describes a trip from the US to Ontario, Canada, without specifying the location of the meetings where she received "anointings." Her Spirit baptism would occur subsequently in Winnipeg.

18. Ellen Hebden, "How Pentecost Came to Toronto," *The Promise*, May 1907, 3.

19. Ellen Hebden, *The Promise*, May 1907, 4.

posite here: First, the point was made earlier (in the section Apocalyptic Eschatology) that apocalypse denotes a means of knowing, by revelation, what could not be known otherwise about the future of this world and the one to follow. Indeed, the fact that revelation was being given, that the heavens were now open, was thought to be an indication that the end was near. Consequently, both the reception by Ellen of a revelation as well as its contents about an imminent *parousia* suggest the restoration of an ancient Jewish and Christian tradition. Secondly, the location of the poem at the conclusion to the newsletter connects it with the opening section on promise-fulfillment, framing all the content in between as eschatological in nature. The promise is being fulfilled, and the Lord is returning.

In the body of the newsletter itself, we find numerous references that show early Pentecostalism in Toronto as a movement intent on restoring the NT emphasis on empowered evangelism. James Hebden, in the one article attributed to Ellen's husband, gives pastoral advice for the one seeking the power of the Holy Spirit to evangelize: "Above all things, seek Him. He shall baptize you with the Holy Ghost and Fire, and ye shall be witnesses."[20] Their emphasis on revival is seen in the summary statement on the same page: "The work is spreading rapidly; workers are going out."[21] Nowhere, however, is the association between the restoration of tongues and evangelism made more explicit, and for that matter, more compelling, than what we read at the end of Ellen's testimony:

> The gift of Tongues was God's gift to me, and as such I value it, for everything which God bestows is good; but I shall never cease to praise Him for the flood of love which filled my whole being and melted me into tenderness, and gave me such a yearning for souls as I had never had before.[22]

Her sentiments echo a long tradition, going back to John Wesley, which paired a second work of grace (what became known in Holiness circles as a Baptism of the Holy Ghost) with a transforming work of love. Here is the heartbeat of an emerging movement: the love of God now expressed as a passion for the lost.

---

20. James Hebden, *The Promise*, May 1907, 1. This article does not include a title.
21. James Hebden, *The Promise*, May 1907, 1.
22. Ellen Hebden, "How Pentecost Came to Toronto," *The Promise*, May 1907, 3.

The Apostolic Messenger (Winnipeg)

The first edition of *The Apostolic Messenger*, published by A. H. Argue in Winnipeg and dated February and March 1908,[23] dwarfs the other two newsletters in size and content. Whereas *The Promise* is four 8.5 x 11 inch pages, a tabloid with a reader-friendly font, *The Apostolic Messenger* is a four-page broadsheet of almost double the dimensions (16 x 20.5 inches) that was printed with a font type about half the size. *The Promise* has two columns per page; *The Apostolic Messenger* crammed news bits, testimonies and teaching segments into pages with seven columns. The size of *The Apostolic Messenger* accommodated a larger number and a greater diversity of contributors than *The Promise*, and thus a wider variety of eschatological expressions as well. *The Good Report* falls somewhere in the middle of the two in terms of overall content with its eight pages (9.125 x 11.25 inches) of three columns.

Like *The Promise*, the title of the Winnipeg newsletter conveys the restorationist and revivalistic worldview of the early Pentecostals in Winnipeg: "Apostolic"—the work of the NT church as seen in Acts is being restored; "Messenger"—the work itself is to evangelize. Of course, Argue's selection of "Apostolic" was intended to connect his ministry with what was occurring at the Apostolic Faith Mission on Azusa Street in Los Angeles, which Argue experienced for himself not in LA, but in Chicago under the ministry of one who had returned from there and was carrying on the work, the Baptist pastor William Durham.

The restorationist idea that primal conditions once lost will be restored before the end of time runs throughout the newsletter, and a primary example is in its second article on page one. "Extract From Bro. Lupton's Letter" is a shortened form of a report from a "Missionary Home" in Alliance, O[hio?], where intercessory prayer had been going on for nearly seventy days. They had been "weeping over the lost world, for a backslidden church, for laborers to be sent forth to the ends of the earth."[24] Levi Lupton expressed the conviction that the answer to their prayer for revival would coincide with the restoration of the gifts of the Spirit of 1 Cor 12, whose operation would convince the church and the world alike. What is noteworthy here is not only a restatement of a belief in the return of the charismata—an idea that may be tracked back to the

---

23. This is probably the only issue published under this title.

24. Levi R. Lupton, "Extract from Bro. Lupton's Letter," *The Apostolic Messenger*, February–March 1908, 1.

Holiness Movement of the 1800s and to A. B. Simpson in particular—but also the eschatological urgency underlying it. These are "the last, last days." The article concludes with an exhortation to pray, to search the Scriptures, and to observe the signs of the times, because "Everything indicates the near coming of Jesus."[25]

Likewise, the unnamed writer of the article "The Baptism of the Holy Ghost" interprets the reappearance of tongues as a sign of the imminent *parousia*. He also includes a short history of restorationism: tongues disappeared some time after the NT era during a period of spiritual darkness. Light began to appear when Martin Luther called for repentance and when John Wesley championed sanctification. And then, the Latter Rain prepared people for Baptism of the Spirit with the Bible evidence of speaking in tongues. Now that the gifts are being restored in greater measure, the author concludes, "Let us tarry, for James tells us: 'The coming of the Lord draweth nigh.'"[26] A similar view of church history appears in the subsequent article. Evangelists Birdsell, Mason, and Ralph (from Athens, Ontario) identify their era as the "closing age" and echo the hope expressed in the previous article for the gifts to be restored to the church. Once more, a sense of urgency propels their evangelism:

> With enlarged visions and great expectation of the near coming of the Lord, we feel more than ever like spreading this glorious light of Pentecostal power, and are praising God for open doors, hungry souls, and power attending the Word . . . [27]

A short statement of faith appears in the top left of the second page, with the newsletter title "The Apostolic Messenger" serving as its header.[28] The five emphases of the "Full Gospel"[29] are named: Justification by

---

25. Levi R. Lupton, "Extract from Bro. Lupton's Letter," *The Apostolic Messenger*, February–March 1908, 1.

26. "The Baptism of the Holy Ghost: 'The Latter Rain' or 'More of God,' Which Shall We Call It," *The Apostolic Messenger*, February–March 1908, 2. (These same themes are also emphasized by Thomas Smart in his article, "Jesus is Coming Soon," 3.) Somewhat unusual is the author's separation of the blessing of Latter Rain from the reception of Spirit Baptism: Latter Rain blessing is not enough. Baptism in the Spirit alone will satisfy the soul, convince the world, and give one the power. More typically, the two are equated.

27. "A Recent Letter from Evangelists Birdsell, Mason [and] Ralph, to be Read to the Saints at Winnipeg," *The Apostolic Messenger*, February–March 1908, 1.

28. This is similar to the layout of *The Apostolic Faith* (Vol. 1, No. 1).

29. The term "Full Gospel" does not appear here; we find it elsewhere in the newsletter. Note in particular where Thomas Smart equates the gospel that must be

faith, Sanctification, Baptism of the Holy Ghost, Divine Healing, and "The pre-Millennial, or the soon coming of Jesus." There is little doubt that the Rapture is the intended reading of "the soon coming of Jesus." This is seen in a lengthy article called: "Extracts From 'Jesus Is Coming: On the Rapture and the Revelation,'" which is presumably based on a pamphlet written by A. H. Argue. The Rapture is when Christ comes for his saints preceding the Tribulation, and the Revelation, when Christ returns to earth with them after the Tribulation.[30] Similarly, the article "The Thousand Years" (the final article in the newsletter) presumes the Rapture of the church in its detailed argument for pre-millennialism.[31] These two examples provide initial physical evidence in early Canadian Pentecostalism for the popularity of Dispensational teaching as a system that reinforced their sense of urgency. Whenever a Pentecostal preached the system, the return of Jesus would be featured and the audience would be told they were located right next to the end of God's timeline.

Dispensationalism is prominent in *The Apostolic Messenger*, but so is another expression of apocalyptic hope. The clearest articulation of Latter Rain in *The Apostolic Messenger* comes from a reprint of A. B. Simpson's "What is Meant by The Latter Rain." Simpson derives an eschatological template from the precipitation cycles of Palestine: the former rain coincided with planting, the latter rain, with reaping. This, Simpson writes, explains the "new thing" God is doing, namely, the latter rain has begun to fall, restoring to the Church the manifestations of the Spirit that accompanied the former rain. In a prophetic word that anticipates the emergence of Pentecostalism, Simpson pictures the near future—a return of the work of the Spirit, perhaps greater than before, that will include not only tongues, as described in 1 Cor 12, but also xenolalia, or in his words, "real missionary tongues like those of Pentecost through which the heathen world shall hear in their own languages 'the wonderful works of God.'"[32] The reappearance of "missionary tongues" was also a conviction of one of the founding fathers of American Pentecostalism. Charles

---

preached to all nations before Jesus returns as the Full Gospel ("Jesus is Coming Soon," *The Apostolic Messenger*, February–March 1908, 3).

30. "Extracts From 'Jesus Is Coming: On the Rapture and the Revelation,'" *The Apostolic Messenger*, February–March 1908, 4.

31. Dr. Seiss, "The Thousand Years," *The Apostolic Messenger*, February–March 1908, 4.

32. A. B. Simpson, "What is Meant by The Latter Rain," *The Apostolic Messenger*, February–March 1908, 3.

Parham would maintain, even when other Pentecostals became skeptical, that every legitimate experience of Spirit Baptism involved xenolalia. So influential was this idea in the earliest days of the movement that untrained, ill-prepared, but Spirit-baptized farmers and labourers boarded boats bound for the far regions of the world.

Although Dispensationalism and Latter Rain co-exist in this newsletter as they did in early North American Pentecostalism as a whole, they did so in contradictory fashion. The teaching of Dispensationalism that the church age is inaugurated with signs and wonders but does not end with them runs counter to the central assertion of Latter Rain expectation—the church age concludes as it began, with the same rain, meaning, the same pouring out of the Spirit. In passing, it may be noted that the Dispensational affirmation of cessationism (that the gifts ceased shortly after the time of the early church) contributed to the Pentecostal's self-understanding as restorationists. If, as they had been told, the gifts of the Spirit ceased early on, then, as they had experienced, God was bringing them back into existence.

How should we understand the circulation of logically inconsistent systems? Consistency is not to be found in the form, but in the function. Pentecostals benefited by employing these systems, both borrowed,[33] to tell their story about their place in salvation history. Dispensationalism reinforced the early Pentecostal conviction about the imminent return of Jesus by identifying signs in the heavens and on the earth as harbingers of the end. In subsequent generations, it would bolster the preacher's call for unflagging anticipation and appropriate action for an event that remained delayed. What Latter Rain provided, like The Promise did, was an organic rationale for their *raison d'être* that incorporated their experience. While Dispensationalism offered external indicators, both cosmic and geo-political, the Pentecostals found in the concept of a Latter Rain an experiential justification for their claim to be the inheritors of the apostolic faith. It was the life-transforming work of the Spirit among them, full of signs and wonders, that was the bedrock of their self-identification as the last days people of the Spirit. Eschatology was in their hearts, not just on the charts.

The effect of the dispensational preaching I heard back in the day was that it fixed the eye on what was to come and roused the mind to

---

33. Both ideas were circulating in nineteenth-century holiness circles. The book to read is Dayton's *Theological Roots of Pentecostalism*.

speculation (such as, who is Anti-Christ? And, when will he appear?).[34] But there was another aspect to our eschatological hope that was grounded in experience—and perhaps this has been lost. We once knew that the move of the Spirit was an eschatological indicator of the nearness of the end. Our experience of signs and wonders, tongues, and the gifts of the Spirit, which once enlivened our revivalistic tendencies, has been reframed as advantageous for personal renewal.

Two observations from the piece by Thomas Smart ("Jesus is Coming Soon") will conclude our survey of the integral role that eschatology played in *The Apostolic Messenger*. Smart files a report that prophetic utterances were being given about Jesus' soon return, which reinforces the point made earlier about the revelatory nature of the apocalyptic worldview. And, in light of the imminent appearance of Jesus, Smart exhorts his readers to holiness, because his return is "an incentive to holy living."[35] This is an early reference to a long-standing practice among Pentecostals, and a very Pauline practice at that, where sanctification is exhorted because of eschatological urgency. Once again we have an example of how the last element in the Full Gospel, Christ as Coming King, affected other facets of their lives.

The Good Report (Ottawa)

The title of the original newsletter from Pentecostalism in Ottawa, *The Good Report*, which is dated May 1911, takes its name from Prov 15:30, signaling to the reader that the content will be filled with testimony. As part of the masthead, there is an italicized motto directly under the title that incorporates the Full Gospel as it appeared in its earliest Pentecostal form (five aspects of the work of Christ are named rather than four).

> *Our Motto: A Whole Gospel, for a Whole Man, and to the Whole World. No Law but Love, no Creed but Christ. Jesus our Saviour, Sanctifier, Healer, Baptizer, Glorious Lord and Coming King. Everything in Jesus and Jesus Everything.*

---

34. Similarly, the idea of a horrific final chapter to human history, a Great Tribulation of seven years, has caused many Westerners to fear as they look ahead, whereas those in other parts of the globe, where persecution is the norm and martyrdom is common, see it as already present, or, at least, something an awful lot like it.

35. Thomas Smart, "Jesus is Coming," *The Apostolic Messenger*, February–March 1908, 3.

A restatement of the Full Gospel (here, "A Whole Gospel") comes at the bottom of the fourth page as the conclusion to a short summary of the Apostolic Faith movement.[36] It becomes readily apparent from the newsletter's first column that this is not an empty slogan, nor the reference to Jesus as Coming King at the end of it, a token expression. As we will see, the motto is an accurate description of the spirituality of early Pentecostals in Ottawa.

In column one, the editors of the newsletter—R. E. McAlister, H. E. Randall, and Harland Lawler—explain why they are still in Canada. With good intention they began a farewell tour in Portland, Oregon in August of the previous year, hoping to leave Ottawa for Egypt shortly after Christmas. But the breakout of a revival outside of Ottawa near Fitzroy, which spread to the capital city itself in March of 1911, delayed their trip. Although greater detail is given farther down in the newsletter as to the happenings in Fitzroy and Ottawa, the first column illustrates how they were living out the Whole Gospel.[37]

As missionaries bound for Egypt, they are acting as if the Whole Gospel *is* for the Whole World. The emphases in their testimony about what has been happening among them reflect the influence of the five elements of the Full Gospel: The first three elements—Jesus is Saviour, Sanctifier, and Baptizer—shape the report that "upwards of 70 souls have been saved, many sanctified, and some baptized with the Holy Ghost." They know Christ as Healer, as their reports of healing attest. And they are living in the narrative whose central character is Christ as Coming King.

> The Apostolic Faith work is surely commenced in Ottawa, the Capital of fair Canada, and is spreading to the surrounding country, and we believe that it will never stop till Jesus comes in the clouds of glory, and that there will then be a goodly company from this region to ascend to meet Him.[38]

There is one final great revival to precede the return of Jesus, and Ottawa is in the middle of it.

---

36. R. E. McAlister, "Apostolic Faith Movement," *The Good Report*, May 1911, 4. As in *The Apostolic Messenger*, the use of "Apostolic Faith" shows a conscious identification with the Azusa Street Mission.

37. "A Good Report," *The Good Report*, May 1911, 1.

38. "A Good Report," *The Good Report*, May 1911, 1.

The theme of the imminent return of Christ appears throughout the newsletter. For instance, in the second article, "Pentecost in the Ottawa Valley," a report is given about the conclusion of a convention held in Queen's Hall, Ottawa, in March 1911. "As we expressed our farewells it was with comforting assurance that if we met not again here, we would meet in the Rapture, caught up to be with Jesus and one another forever."[39] The theme is reiterated in many of the testimonies sent in to the editors. Florence Laws ends her report of healing with the adage: "Live as though Jesus died yesterday, Rose to-day, and is coming to-morrow."[40] J. A. Murphy concludes his testimony of salvation, sanctification, healing, and Spirit baptism with "Now I believe in the Deity and precious blood of Jesus, a real hell, and the soon coming of Jesus to reign."[41] Finally, Herbert Randall finishes his testimony of Spirit Baptism by stating his conviction that the Pentecostal movement "is God's last call and warning to this old sinful world before the coming again of His Son in judgment. Oh, let us be ready."[42]

It is highly significant that a reference to the Lord's soon return is the final statement in many of the pieces found in *The Good Report*. This reinforces the argument set out at the beginning of this essay that the soon return of Jesus was what made sense of their story and gave them hope for its ending. In an untitled paragraph on page 4, an admonition is given to remember the Lord's return. The reader is exhorted to be steadfast in this hope: since all of the promises and prophecies about the first coming have been fulfilled, then all the prophecies and promises about his second coming will be, too. "Jesus is coming soon. Hear it, ye cities and prepare to burn; hear it ye sinners and prepare to die; hear it ye righteous, and prepare to rise."[43]

Of the three editors of *The Good Report*, R. E. McAlister is the one most prominent in the publication. His influence on Canadian Pentecostalism is hard to over-estimate, both in the pre-denominational phase that concerns us here, and in the denominational phase when the PAOC absorbed much of the movement in Canada at its creation in 1919. Two

---

39. "Pentecost in the Ottawa Valley," *The Good Report*, May 1911, 1.

40. Florence Laws, "Salvation Army Soldier Receives Baptism," *The Good Report*, May 1911, 4.

41. J. A. Murphy, *The Good Report*, May 1911, 5.

42. H. E. Randall, "The Comforter Has Come to Herbert E. Randall," *The Good Report*, May 1911, 7.

43. *The Good Report*, May 1911, 4.

of his pieces stand out as worthy of comment, one reiterating what is by now a familiar theme and one that ventures to describe suffering as the lot of Pentecostals—a relatively unexplored subject in the other newsletters. In "Have Ye Received the Holy Ghost Since Ye Believed?" he explains that their shared conviction about the return of Jesus is confirmed by their experience of the Spirit's work among them. After quoting Rom 8:23 (where Paul connects the believer's groaning with receiving the firstfruits of the Spirit), he asks: "Is it any wonder that those who are baptized in the Holy Ghost look for Jesus to come?"[44] McAlister's question reflects their common experience. An intimate encounter with Jesus in Spirit Baptism is accompanied by a feeling that Jesus is near, not just spatially, but temporally as well. Intimacy and "imminency" are linked experientially. McAlister's reference to Rom 8 in regard to groaning—the sound of dissatisfaction with the present because of a yearning for the future—opens the door for a consideration of suffering.

Given that Pentecostals are known as a triumphalistic community with a bold message of deliverance, it is interesting that a piece devoted to the subject of suffering is featured in the inaugural newsletter from Ottawa. Early Pentecostals may not have had much to say to those who were still *not yet* healed (and perhaps their belief in Jesus' soon return mitigated the physical pain somewhat), but they gave voice to pain of another sort, that of rejection and persecution. In "Called to Suffer for Jesus," McAlister says that suffering for Jesus is to be expected. After all, the trial of one's faith is a means of preparation for future reward. In a moving and surprisingly frank manner, he describes the walk of faith like this:

> When we pray to be humbled the Lord begins in good earnest, and by one masterstroke all our living hopes are spoiled. Before a friendless, godless world we stand—misunderstood, the future veiled, the plan or thought of God for me unknown. Is this the answer to my prayer, O Lord? How strange thy dealings are![45]

The article concludes with a poem that offers resolution for his lament. He is cheered by the thought that he is witnessing a last great work of God.

> At last I see Thy work begun,
> And now I pray, 'Thy will be done.'

---

44. *The Good Report*, May 1911, 2.
45. R. E. McAlister, "Called to Suffer for Jesus," *The Good Report*, May 1911, 6.

Ultimately, though, it is his belief in the Lord's pleasure on his life that carries him forward. The last stanza reads:

> My calling is to live with Him alone,
> Unlike all others—lacking what they own,
> Content to be by all the world despised,
> Knowing that I by Him am loved and prized.[46]

CONCLUSION

The great critic of Canadian culture, Robert Fulford, describes in his 1999 Massey Lectures the human need for story-making to make sense of the world. By way of illustration, he recalls a scene from Peter Pan, where Peter tells Wendy that he is in charge of a group of lost boys—lost because no one told them any stories. As Fulford comments, growing up and finding one's way is impossible without stories.[47] The same is true for movements or fellowships, and even denominations.

The three earliest newsletters from the urban hubs of pre-denominational Canadian Pentecostalism all show the dominant role that the worldview of Apocalyptic Eschatology played in their stories. By reading themselves into the Acts narrative, the first Pentecostals not only gained an understanding of the phenomena occurring among them, but they cast themselves for the leading role of people of the last days. Their self-appointment as the lead actors in the final pages of God's script for human salvation fueled their evangelism and mission. Moreover, it reinforced their need for sanctification to be ready to meet Jesus, it caused them to see Spirit Baptism as an enablement to win the lost before it was too late, and it ameliorated the pain of persecution and rejection. The return of Jesus was their proclamation because it was their great hope—the climax of the divine story.

If we do not want to lose our story (and there is no plotline without a climax that features the Second Coming), how do we continue to preach the *soon* return of Jesus after a century of Pentecostalism and a couple millennia of Christianity? Obviously, there is no going back to an early stage of hyper-anticipation for an imminent appearance. We are too old for that now. Nor do we have much appetite for the charts of

---

46. R. E. McAlister, "Called to Suffer for Jesus," *The Good Report*, May 1911, 6.
47. Fulford, *The Triumph of Narrative*, 33–34.

Dispensationalism any longer, even though that system once gave us prepackaged material for sermons and Sunday School lessons.[48]

Maintaining hope among the faithful for the return of Jesus is not only a modern challenge. The belief in the soon return of Jesus was a reason that preaching, rather than writing, was the preoccupation of the eye-witnesses and servants of the word (Luke 1:2). Why write for a future that does not exist? But as the decades passed, the delay of the *parousia* called for adjustments, including the writing of narratives about Jesus to sustain the expanding church and extend the range of the apostolic message. Even in the Pauline letters, written over a short time span, we see adjustments in emphases with the delay of the *parousia*. For example, in 1 Cor 7, Paul is urging the unmarried to remain unmarried because time is short; in his later letters, he is giving marriage and family counseling (Col 3; Eph 5–6). Like the early church, then, we must adapt our proclamation without losing its essential eschatological dimension. We must continue to tell the old, old story proclaimed in the New Testament and witnessed to by the early Pentecostals that had its end in the return of Jesus. How do we adapt for the twenty-first century a proclamation rooted in an ancient apocalyptic perspective?

We could exchange our traditional worldview for one that appears to be more in step with the times. We could abandon our apocalyptically informed view that the world will be transformed suddenly at the return of Christ (a view embedded in our pre-millennial sensibilities) and adopt its rival: a post-millennial sensibility (whether framed with "millennial" terminology or not) that pictures the reality of heaven on earth emerging progressively through the faithfulness of the Church's witness, and culminating with the triumphant return of Christ. Part of the popularity of this approach is that it resonates with a current Western myth that the world will inevitably evolve for the better. This optimistic approach to life is appealing, inviting our wholehearted participation in the cultural call to make the world a better place.

I am not recommending the switch, however. Not only is it a departure from our tradition, but from the NT worldview itself. The great hope of the first century church and early Pentecostalism was the return of

---

48. This may partly explain the rate of decline in preaching about the return of Jesus in the PAOC between 1985/6 and 2014/5. Now that Dispensationalism has fallen out of favor in our ranks, and the charts have been folded up and stored, we may be preaching less about His return partly because we are at a loss to know how to preach about the end times.

Jesus. We are more like the New Testament writers in disposition: pessimistic optimists who are hopeful as we hear the groanings of an expiring world and echo them with our own—groans of longing for what is hoped for rather than groans of despair. If we see through an apocalyptic lens, then we will not believe our own eyes: the future is revealed from heaven, not foreseen by searching for signs of human progress on earth and then extrapolating forward. The desired future will appear suddenly in a dark period as a radical departure from current conditions. And this should be emphasized: an apocalyptic sensibility need not promote inaction. The early church in Acts was energized, not paralyzed. The Spirit has come, Jesus is returning, and we must do something about it.

So how will this preach? We have three systems that circulated in early Pentecostalism to choose from, and while they all served a purpose, I would suggest there is another approach that will serve us better because the popularity of systems ebb and flow. Let us preach the main events: the "already" of Christ's death, resurrection, ascension, and his sending of the Spirit; the "not yets" of his return, the judgment with its promise of justice for all, and the resurrection of the faithful to participate in the new heaven and the new earth. These events are ubiquitous in the NT, so if we preach the Word, we will find ourselves referring to them constantly. Eschatology is not an isolated subject in the NT best suited for presentation as a special series ("and now for something completely different"). An eschatological perspective, which accounts for the future *and* the present, underlies and informs all of the writings of the NT. May it underlie and inform all of our preaching of the text—as it once did.

Finally, let us not forget the insight behind Latter Rain and The Promise that fired the imagination of early Pentecostals: our experience of the Spirit is an eschatological event that (re)orients us towards the return of Christ. The Comforter has come because Jesus is coming. Each conversion is a sign of a coming salvation. Every healing is a sign that sickness is temporary. Every time the gathered saints experience the presence of God among them, it is just a taste—the firstfruits—of a glorious future.

Early Pentecostals found their identity in the story of Pentecost, when the Spirit was poured out as power to witness. To that end, they constrained themselves to be empowered participants. Let the one whose vision anticipated Pentecostalism now remind us of what the vision was. A. B. Simpson's beatific depiction of the end captures the historic, forward-looking proclamation of Pentecostals:

thousands of missionaries going forth in one last mighty crusade from a united body of believers at home to bear swift witness of the crucified and coming Lord to all nations and then join hands around the world and welcome back our coming King.[49]

The End

BIBLIOGRAPHY

Newspapers

The Apostolic Messenger (Winnipeg), 1908
The Good Report (Ottawa), 1911
The Promise (Toronto), 1907

Other

Anderson, Robert. *Vision of the Disinherited: The Making of American Pentecostalism.* New York: Oxford University Press, 1979.
Collins, Adela Y. "Apocalypticism and Christian Origins." In *The Oxford Handbook of Apocalyptic Literature*, edited by John J. Collins, 326–39. New York: Oxford University Press, 2014.
Collins, John J. "What is Apocalyptic Literature?" In *The Oxford Handbook of Apocalyptic Literature*, edited by John J. Collins, 1–18. New York: Oxford University Press, 2014.
Dayton, Donald. *Theological Roots of Pentecostalism.* Grand Rapids: Zondervan, 1987.
Doughten, Jr., Russell, and Jim Grant. *A Thief in the Night.* Directed by Donald W. Thompson. Spring, TX: Russ Doughten Films, 1972.
Faupel, D. William. *This Gospel of the Kingdom: The Significance of Eschatology in the Development of Pentecostal Thought.* Sheffield: Sheffield Academic Press, 1996.
Fulford, Robert. *The Triumph of Narrative: Storytelling in the Age of Mass Culture.* Toronto: Anansi, 1999.
Hanson, Paul. *The Dawn of Apocalyptic.* Philadelphia: Fortress, 1975.
Green, Joel. "The (Re-) Turn to Narrative." In *Narrative Reading, Narrative Preaching: Reuniting New Testament Interpretation and Proclamation*, edited by Joel Green and Michael Pasquarello, 1–36. Grand Rapids: Baker, 2003.
Jacobsen, Donald. *Thinking in the Spirit: Theologies of the Early Pentecostal Movement.* Indianapolis: Indiana University Press, 2003.
Johnson, Van. "Fulfillment of God's Promise in the Soon-to-Return King." In *Pentecostals in the 21st Century: Identity, Beliefs, Praxis*, edited by Corneliu Constantineanu and Chris Scobie, 181–201. Eugene, OR: Cascade, 2018.
Land, Steven. *Pentecostal Spirituality. A Passion for the Kingdom.* Sheffield: Sheffield Academic, 1993.

49. "What is Meant by the Latter Rain," *The Apostolic Messenger*, February–March 1908, 3.

Lindsey, Hal, and Carole C. Carlson. *The Late Great Planet Earth*. Grand Rapids: Zondervan, 1970.

Murphy, Frank. *Apocalypticism in the Bible and Its World*. Grand Rapids: Baker, 2012.

Norman, Larry. "I Wish We'd All Been Ready." *Upon This Rock*. Capitol, 1969.

Pentecostal Assemblies of Canada. *The Pentecostal Testimony*. Toronto: Pentecostal Assemblies of Canada, 1919–2018.

Sloos, William. "The Story of James and Ellen Hebden: The First Family of Pentecost in Canada." *Pneuma* 32 (2010) 181–202.

Stewart, Adam. "A Canadian Azusa? The Implications of the Hebden Mission for Pentecostal Historiography." In *Winds From the North: Canadian Contributions to the Pentecostal Movement*, edited by Michael Wilkinson and Peter Althouse, 17–37. Leiden: Brill, 2010.

Stewart, Adam, et al. "Changes in Clergy Belief and Practice in Canada's Largest Pentecostal Denomination." *Pneuma* 39 (2017) 457–81.

Verge, Carl. "A Comparison of the Beliefs and Practices of Two Groups of Pentecostal Assemblies of Canada Ministers: Those with a Master's Degree and Those with Only Three Years of Bible College Training." PhD Dissertation, New York University, 1987.

7

Samosas at the Pentecostal Potluck
Pentecostal Hospitality for Multicultural Ministry

Josh P. S. Samuel

INTRODUCTION

Some of the most popular events I have encountered in some Pentecostal churches in Canada are what are often referred to as "International Nights," where people may provide food, wear clothing, sing, wave flags of various countries, and possibly even dance in accordance with their ethnic background.[1] International Nights give churches an opportunity to highlight the various ethnic backgrounds of people within the church. These types of events are often coordinated with an emphasis on supporting ministries going on in various contexts locally and around the world. As a Canadian of Indian background myself, I have participated in these events by singing and bringing food native to India. Over the years, I have noticed that one of the most popular food items brought by those of Indian background are samosas.[2] These pastries are so popular, that now even those who are not of Indian background may

---

1. Special thanks to Joyce M. Samuel for her valuable feedback on this essay.

2. For those not familiar with samosas, they are pastries typically in the shape of a triangle, filled with vegetables and/or meat.

be the ones who bring samosas for some of these events. For some leaders, a successful International Night with various foods, dances, songs, and flags waving gives the impression of a successful multicultural ministry. Having multiple ethnic groups in attendance in church and even hosting something like an International Night, however, is not a clear sign that a church has embraced multicultural ministry. Churches that are seeking to embrace multicultural ministry can do so by incorporating a theology and practice derived from a distinctively Pentecostal theology.

When Pentecostals look for Scriptural precedent for their identity, they often look to Acts 2. Pentecostals like Charles Parham and William Seymour looked to this passage for impetus for the early Pentecostal movement, particularly as it related to Spirit baptism and the evidence of speaking in tongues.[3] Even contemporary Pentecostal scholars like Frank Macchia and Amos Yong turn to Acts 2 and the theme of Spirit baptism to discuss how the Pentecostal movement can experience renewal.[4] This essay shows how multicultural ministry can be effective by embracing a Pentecostal theology of multicultural ministry that demonstrates hospitality, which includes an intentional approach to welcoming other cultures, cultural competence, and a willingness to empower people of various cultures.[5] Toward that goal this essay examines biblical, historical, and theological issues arising from the Pentecostal emphasis on Acts 2. The discussion begins with a brief explanation of culture, followed by three important aspects of Pentecostal hospitality for multicultural ministry, concluding with a response to four misguided applications of Pentecostal hospitality.

CULTURE EXPLAINED: MULTICULTURAL MINISTRY IS NECESSARY FOR ALL LEADERS

Before examining some of the issues arising from a closer study of Acts 2, it is important to explain the word *culture*. Some leaders may feel that the topic of multicultural ministry is not relevant to them, since they do not

---

3. See Mittelstadt, *Reading Luke-Acts in the Pentecostal Tradition*, 20–26, 76–77. E.g., Parham, *A Voice Crying in the Wilderness*, 25–38; Seymour, "Bro. Seymour's Call," 1.

4. E.g., Macchia, *Baptized in the Spirit*; Yong, "The Spirit of Hospitality," 55–73.

5. Amos Yong has done work on connecting Pentecostal theology with hospitality to other religions. See Yong's "The Spirit of Hospitality," 55–73 and *Hospitality and the Other*.

think that there are various cultural groups in their church. Some may look at their ministry and note that most of the people look alike and talk alike. Thus, they may feel that a discussion on multicultural ministry is not relevant for their context. Multicultural ministry, however, is not relegated to those who minister in contexts with people of different ethnic and language groups.

Culture does not merely relate to ethnic groups, like people who are from India, Brazil, Ethiopia, or France. Culture can be defined as the way of life for a particular group, which they develop, communicate, and perpetuate.[6] Thus, when thinking about how to demonstrate multicultural ministry, leaders should not feel that this can only be possible when various ethnic groups are working together in ministry. Multicultural ministry can relate to working with various ethnic groups—but it can also relate to how leaders minister to people of different socioeconomic groups, age categories, or even among those who have special needs physically and/or mentally. Cultural differences exist due to a variety of factors. Therefore, it is clear that being purposeful about multicultural ministry as a leader is not optional, but crucial in order to disciple all types of people. For this reason, I illustrate key ideas with examples from various cultural groups throughout this paper. Delving into the Pentecostals' emphasis on Acts 2 will help bring clarity to how multicultural ministry can thrive.

PENTECOSTALS AND THE DAY OF PENTECOST

Pentecostals often highlight the moment that believers supernaturally spoke in various languages in order to communicate to a variety of cultural groups on the Day of Pentecost in Acts 2:1–11:

> When the day of Pentecost had come, they were all together in one place. And suddenly from heaven there came a sound like the rush of a violent wind, and it filled the entire house where they were sitting. Divided tongues, as of fire, appeared among them, and a tongue rested on each of them. All of them were filled with the Holy Spirit and began to speak in other languages, as the Spirit gave them ability.
>
> Now there were devout Jews from every nation under heaven living in Jerusalem. And at this sound the crowd gathered and was bewildered, because each one heard them speaking in

---

6. Hunsberger, *Bearing Witness of the Spirit*, 12–13.

the native language of each. Amazed and astonished, they asked, "Are not all these who are speaking Galileans? And how is it that we hear, each of us, in our own native language? Parthians, Medes, Elamites, and residents of Mesopotamia, Judea and Cappadocia, Pontus and Asia, Phrygia and Pamphylia, Egypt and the parts of Libya belonging to Cyrene, and visitors from Rome, both Jews and proselytes, Cretans and Arabs—in our own languages we hear them speaking about God's deeds of power" (NRSV).

The supernatural ability to speak in different languages was an important part of that event, and will be highlighted in this essay. However, an important question that may be minimized in getting to the divine ability to speak in other tongues, is how did so many different cultural groups come to that place in Jerusalem? Or similarly, how did believers get the opportunity to minister to so many different cultural groups through the speaking of tongues? These questions lead to an important part of the story: believers had come together in Jerusalem for the Feast of Pentecost. This story of Pentecost showcases the importance of hospitality for multicultural ministry. To begin, though, some background information on the Feast of Pentecost follows to better understand this event.

The Day of Pentecost was an important festival in the Jewish calendar, as it marked the end of the wheat harvest when the Israelites brought offerings to the Lord.[7] Israelites were "to bring a corporate firstfruits offering of new grain, in this case, from the wheat harvest. The wheat was to be baked in two loaves of *leavened* bread ([Lev] 23:16–17) and presented along with a group of animal sacrifices ([Lev] vv. 18–20; cf. Num. 28:27–31)."[8] Unlike other festivals, there was no fixed date (Lev 23:15–21). Thus, Israelites were expected to count "the day when the barley sheaf is elevated as day 1," so that the day of Pentecost "comes after seven complete Sabbaths" (Lev 23:15).[9] The day of Pentecost would be celebrated the day after the seventh Sabbath, which would be the fiftieth day from day one.[10] Thus, though this festival was referred to as "the feast of weeks" (Exod 34:22; Deut 16:10), "the feast of harvest" (Exod 23:16), and "the day of first ripe grain" (Num 28:26), it took on the name

---

7. Wenham, *Leviticus*, 304.
8. Gane, *Leviticus, Numbers*, 390 (emphasis original).
9. Gane, *Leviticus, Numbers*, 390.
10. Gane, *Leviticus, Numbers*, 390.

of Pentecost in the New Testament because it "comes from the Greek word meaning 'fiftieth' (*pentēkostos*)."[11]

PENTECOSTAL HOSPITALITY: INTENTIONALLY WELCOMING OTHER CULTURES

Embedded in the story of Pentecost (and also in Pentecostalism) is an emphasis on the importance of believers being willing to ensure that those who are culturally different—particularly the marginalized—are welcomed in practical ways. While the section above explains the timeframe used by the Israelites for bringing their offerings to the Lord for the Day of Pentecost, a relevant issue relates to *how* they were expected to reap their harvest. Immediately following God's instructions for presenting offerings before Him, God states "And when you reap the harvest of your land, you shall not reap your field right up to its edge, nor shall you gather the gleanings after your harvest. You shall leave them for the poor and for the sojourner: I am the Lord your God" (Lev 23:22, ESV). Even in the midst of bringing an offering to the Lord, being thankful for God's provisions in the harvest, God reminds the Israelites that they should not forget the poor and sojourner when they harvest. The Israelites were commanded not to gather everything from their harvest—they were to leave some of their harvest for the poor and the sojourner. Hospitality was to be extended to those who were marginalized in society.

One of the most important themes Pentecostals make use of is Pentecost. But what Pentecostals typically neglect regarding Pentecost is the importance of hospitality extended to the marginalized in society, which, however, is rooted in the story of Pentecost in the Old Testament. Those who do not have access to the same resources must be remembered, particularly the poor and sojourner. Extending hospitality to the marginalized may include sharing food, money, or even ministry resources.

The immediate context of the Day of Pentecost in Acts 2 also strengthens the case that hospitality must be included in any discussion on the Day of Pentecost. The reason people were able to communicate in tongues to people of different cultural groups is not only because God granted them supernatural ability on that day, but also because Jerusalem

---

11. Hartley, *Leviticus*, 385; Wenham, *Leviticus*, 304. While there are some indications that the Jews celebrated the giving of the Torah or even of covenant renewal with the time of Pentecost, this essay focuses primarily on the explicit teachings on Pentecost found in the Pentateuch. Keener, *Acts*, 785–86.

had become a hospitable context for this cross-cultural communication to occur in the first place. People from different cultural groups came to Jerusalem for the Day of Pentecost. "Pentecost was one of the three Jewish pilgrimage feasts to Jerusalem during the year, which explains why people from so many different nationalities are present" in Acts 2:9–11.[12] Yet it is not merely Jews from different regions who just happened to visit Jerusalem at this time, but it would include Diaspora Jews who had already returned to live in Jerusalem permanently.[13] The religious requirements for the Day of Pentecost ensured that Jerusalem became a place of hospitality, where people from all types of cultural backgrounds, though Jewish themselves, could come together. The Jews who came from a variety of different cultural groups found a home—even if temporarily for some—in Jerusalem for the Day of Pentecost.

Pentecostals often focus on the powerful act of speaking in tongues when describing the Acts 2 story, that the context for this moment of ministry can be forgotten. While speaking in tongues—and other gifts of the Spirit for that matter—are important for ministry, believers cannot neglect the people and the context in which they minister. Empowered ministers are crucial for effective ministry. But a ministry that is hospitable to those who may be different than the typical demographic already part of the ministry will determine the reach of that ministry. Will that ministry remain within its own traditional demographic, or will it extend its reach to those outside its traditional makeup of people? Are other cultural groups considered as important as the majority culture(s), even if other minority cultural groups cannot reciprocate the ministry with some form of support (e.g., financial support)? Hospitality that is extended without conditions ultimately finds its greatest expression in the love Christ has extended to humanity. Like Christ who, out of love, desires to bring all of humanity into full communion with God through his sacrificial life and death—without any conditions—believers likewise extend this type of love to others through unconditional love expressed through hospitality.[14] Engaging with how the early Pentecostal movement extended hospitality will help reveal how Pentecostals have and can further this approach to ministry beyond mere theory.

---

12. Bock, *Acts*, 95.
13. Bock, *Acts*, 99–100.
14. Cf. Boersma, *Violence, Hospitality, and the Cross*, 15–16.

Examining the early Pentecostal movement also helps Pentecostals wrestle with the importance of hospitality that is intentionally welcoming. The early Pentecostal movement forms the "heart and not simply the infancy of the movement" and its "spirituality," which is why it is quite important when dealing with the character of the Pentecostal movement today.[15] The Pentecostal movement, during the early 1900s under the leadership of Charles F. Parham and William J. Seymour, provides a case study in what to do and what not to do when it comes to hospitality. Though Seymour was the leader of the Azusa Street Revival, Parham taught Seymour some key teachings about Spirit baptism and the evidence of tongues. Parham was a white leader, and is considered one of the founders of the Pentecostal movement.[16] When Parham initially taught Seymour, Seymour was not permitted to sit in the classroom with the rest of the students. Seymour had to sit outside the class because he was black—typical of the Jim Crow laws in the States that legalized segregation between blacks and whites.[17] It must be stated, however, that Parham did allow Seymour to join him in the ministry of preaching to other blacks.[18] Nevertheless, while Parham's approach to teaching Seymour may seem more indicative of the racially segregated times of his day in the early 1900s, rather than his personal view of other cultural groups, Parham continued to be incapable of showing hospitality to a culture unlike his own. For instance, when Parham encountered the corporate worship at the Azusa Street Revival led by Seymour, one of his primary critiques of the revival was that it resembled the "old-fashioned Negro worship of the south."[19] Parham could not get over his disdain for a corporate worship expression that did not resemble his own cultural leanings, which revealed his inability to demonstrate effective hospitality to other cultural groups.

The Azusa Street Revival, however, provided an excellent model of hospitality in ministry extended through the leadership of Seymour during the early 1900s.[20] Seymour extended hospitality to various cultural

---

15. Faupel, *The Everlasting Gospel*, 309; Hollenweger, "Pentecostals and the Charismatic Movement," 551; Land, *Pentecostal Spirituality*, 1, 14–15; Anderson, *Introduction to Pentecostalism*, 45.

16. Cf. Goff, *Fields White Unto Harvest*, 164.

17. Goff, *Fields White Unto Harvest*, 107–9.

18. Goff, *Fields White Unto Harvest*, 107–9.

19. Parham, *The Everlasting Gospel*, 118.

20. Whether or not the Azusa Street Revival is where Pentecostalism originated,

groups within the context of his ministry at the Azusa Street Mission. During the early 1900s, discrimination and segregation was the norm in society. For instance, Seymour's own parents were former slaves in the American South.[21] But when it came to Azusa, one of the famous lines used to describe the revival comes from Frank Bartleman, who said: "The 'color line' was washed in the blood."[22] People of various cultural groups could feel welcome at the Azusa Street Mission. Seymour attempted to overcome the discrimination not just between ethnic groups, but also along gender, age, and socioeconomic distinctions—they were not only welcomed but they also served in ministry (a discussion taken up in the final section of this essay).

While the importance of remembering the "poor" in Lev 23:22 may have more obvious contemporary application for today, there is also a stress in this same passage on providing hospitality for the "sojourner," which readers occasionally neglect. Sojourners refer to those who may live among the Israelites, but are not Israelites themselves. The inclusion of the sojourner has immediate relevance for the church in North American in light of the current refugee crisis. God's heart for the sojourner reveals the type of heart needed for refugees. In 2014, the Canadian province of Ontario brought in 11,400 refugees from around the world.[23] The Syrian refugee crisis is one important issue that has been addressed in Canada recently, as over four million Syrian refugees have fled the civil war, and approximately fifty percent of them are children.[24] Moreover, as recent as 2015, the newly elected Liberal government in Canada committed to resettle 25,000 Syrian refugees.[25] Regardless of what one's political persuasion, extending hospitality to refugees is a commitment believers must be willing to take on. The Pentecostal Assemblies of Canada can be commended for their willingness to sponsor Syrian refugees as of 2015.[26] Emergency Relief and Development Overseas (ERDO), the

---

however, is not crucial for this discussion. Rather, Azusa can at least be deemed an influential centre of Pentecostalism, which popularized Pentecostalism worldwide. Robeck, *The Azusa Street Mission and Revival*, 8, 239; Cox, *Fire from Heaven*, 149; Anderson, *An Introduction to Pentecostalism*, 43.

21. Robeck, *The Azusa Street Mission and Revival*, 17–25.
22. Bartleman, *Azusa Street*, 51.
23. Government of Ontario, "Syrian Refugees."
24. Government of Ontario, "Syrian Refugees."
25. Zilio, "Not Enough Resources."
26. Douara, "Meet the Heroes."

humanitarian expression of the Pentecostal Assemblies of Canada, has provided over $250,000 for refugee aid over the past two years.[27] Some well-meaning Christians have resented the influx of refugees, citing fears of religious extremists among the refugees. But Pentecostals must be willing to continue to overlook the fears of religious extremism and political agendas, in order to extend genuine hospitality to all types of people regardless of their background.[28]

This inclusion of the poor and sojourners in a discussion on the day of Pentecost reminds believers that they must not be so involved in religious duties—whether bringing offerings to the Lord or singing songs of worship—that they forget the marginalized.[29] Like the Israelites, Pentecostals—and all Christians—must remember the marginalized. The marginalized are not just those who may be financially poor or sojourners, but they are anyone who is on the margins of society and in need. There are a number of people neglected in society to whom the church must seek to be hospitable. In the midst of the worshipping community, believers must be willing to welcome and care for those who are often forgotten, whether they are refugees, the physically and/or mentally challenged, young people, seniors, or ethnic minorities. Believers must discern who might be the marginalized and welcome them into their communities.

Young people are another important group of people to whom the church must be hospitable. The Fuller Youth Institute studied why some youth left the church while others remained. While they admit they did not find a "silver bullet" that found one solution for youth ministry, a key theme arose that relates to hospitality. The key theme that emerged was the important role of intergenerational relationships. Ministries that value intergenerational relationships ensure that youth are not merely an isolated ministry of the church, so that they are not segregated from the rest of the congregation. One important insight they arrived at was that "[i]nvolvement in all-church worship during high school is more consistently linked with mature faith in both high school and college than any other form of church participation."[30] They state that "[b]y far, the number-one way that churches made the teens in our survey feel

27. ERDO, "Syrian Refugee Crisis"; "Mission, Vision, Core Values & Milestones."
28. Cf. Jesus' story of the Good Samaritan in Luke 10:25–37.
29. Gane, *Leviticus, Numbers*, 391.
30. Powell et al., "The Church Sticking Together."

welcomed and valued was when adults in the congregation showed interest in them."[31] One student in their study stated: "We were welcomed not just in youth group; we were welcomed into other parts of the ministry of the church: the worship team on Sunday mornings, teaching Sunday school to kids and helping with cleaning and serving. All these other types of things really just brought the youth in and made them feel like they had a place and even feel like they were valued as individuals."[32]

Being hospitable to these young people not only strengthened their faith, but helped ensure longevity to the faith. This has serious implications for how youth ministry is accomplished. Some youth leaders may assume that they have to have the coolest, most hip ministry in order to be successful. What if youth leaders were told that it might even be better to get them connected to the rest of the church's ministries? What if youth leaders were told that youth might be better served by a mentoring elderly couple rather than investing in a smoke machine? A smoke machine may not need to be completely abandoned for some part of the ministry, but integrating a hospitable, mentoring elderly couple into the youth ministry would have more long-term benefits for the individual youth and the ministry as a whole.

Those on the margins of society and the church may not be able to make a difference in a church's budget, but they are worthy of investing in regardless of their socioeconomic situation—something God reminds believers in the theme of Pentecost. Those without sufficient resources must be remembered—both locally and abroad. For example, a church might house a local food bank or sponsor children overseas. Do local church leaders budget their programs in light of those who may give the most, or are they willing to remember the marginalized? Hospitality must be extended to all, and one of the key ways it begins is by becoming intentionally welcoming to people of different cultural backgrounds.[33]

PENTECOSTAL HOSPITALITY: CULTURAL COMPETENCE

In order to be more hospitable in a multicultural world, it is important to ensure that ministers are not only welcoming to other cultural groups,

---

31. Powell et al., "The Church Sticking Together."
32. Powell et al., "The Church Sticking Together."
33. See Rowlison's *Creative Hospitality* for practical suggestions on becoming more hospitable.

but are culturally competent to minister to others outside their own cultural identity. One of the primary ways Pentecostals have looked at Scripture as a source for cross-cultural ministry is the believers who spoke in tongues in Acts 2. Believers were sharing "the mighty works of God" in the various cultural groups' distinct languages in Jerusalem on the Day of Pentecost (Acts 2:11). But there is something that transpired in that cross-cultural communication that can sometimes be overlooked—the important issue of cultural competence when discussing hospitality and multicultural ministry.

When the Spirit moved on the Day of Pentecost in Acts 2, God did not supernaturally enable people to speak in one common language. Rather, believers spoke in the specific, unique languages of the various cultural groups assembled. God could have used a common language of that day like Aramaic or Greek for a diverse group of people in Jerusalem at that time. Rather, God in his wisdom intentionally chose to communicate to the audience in their own native languages, rather than a language that might be common to all.[34] This point about God communicating through specific languages, rather than one common language has important implications for multicultural ministry.

God's commitment to communicate to the various cultural groups in their native languages, rather than a common one on the Day of Pentecost, resists the approach to ministry in North America that insists on ministry that is solely—or even primarily—founded on a language and culture that is English and Western. God's approach on the Day of Pentecost reveals the need for cultural competence with other cultural groups when seeking to minister to others. This approach resists the desire to develop a ministry that reflects a *Wal-Mart* approach to ministry, whereby everyone is offered the same thing regardless of his or her cultural background. Even the early church had to work at being hospitable after Pentecost. Cultural tensions occurred in the early church between groups, such as the issue of circumcision among Gentiles (Acts 15). It may be easier for leaders to merely offer a ministry that is based on one's own cultural identity—a monocultural approach—but ministry on the Day of Pentecost shows that God respects and values the distinct features of each individual cultural group, which ministers must likewise do.

The early Pentecostal movement has a checkered past when it comes to the cultural competence it had with diverse cultural groups. First, they

---

34. Solivan, *The Spirit, Pathos and Liberation*, 114. Cf. Yong, *Hospitality and the Other*, chapter 2, locations 1646–53.

valued cultural competence for the diverse cultural groups that they encountered as demonstrated by their desire to gain new languages through Spirit baptism. They were "convinced that they had been given 'missionary tongues' through Spirit baptism and that when they reached their destinations they would be able to speak miraculously to the local people without having to undergo the arduous task of language learning."[35] One of the writers for *The Apostolic Faith*, the official publication out of Azusa, explained:

> The gift of languages is *given with the commission*, 'Go ye into all the world and preach the Gospel to every creature.' The Lord has given languages to the unlearned Greek, Latin, Hebrew, French, German, Italian, Chinese, Japanese, Zulu and languages of Africa, Hindu and Bengali and dialects of India, Chippewa and other languages of the Indians, Eskimaux, the deaf mute language and, in fact the Holy Spirit speaks all the languages of the world through His children.[36]

When these early Pentecostals felt someone had gained a new language through tongues, they tried to discern what language that person had gained and the country where that language might best be used. Subsequently, churches sent these believers to countries they deemed appropriate for the language the believer had gained. Although some claimed to have been successful with this approach to language learning and ministry, the majority were not able to speak in another language, and a few returned to the United States disillusioned.[37] Whether or not one agrees with their approach to Spirit baptism and language learning, it is clear they valued the role of gaining very unique languages, even "dialects of India," for instance, to communicate with other cultural groups.

Secondly, in light of a number of early Pentecostals inability to communicate in other languages through Spirit baptism, they shifted their approach, acknowledging multiple dynamics for cultural competence. For instance, the early Pentecostals acknowledged the importance of reaching the missionaries who were already in certain contexts with their message, particularly of Spirit baptism. Alfred and Lillian Garr, Pentecostal missionaries to India, admitted that the key to reaching Indians with the Pentecostal message was through the missionaries already there,

---

35. Anderson, *Spreading Fires*, 57–58.
36. "The Old-Time Pentecost," *The Apostolic Faith*, 1 (emphasis original).
37. Anderson, *Spreading Fires*, 57–58.

since they knew "all the customs of India and also the languages."[38] The Garr's approach—as early as 1907—show that some of the early Pentecostals began to acknowledge the importance of not only Spirit baptism with tongues for ministry, but ministers who knew the language and customs of the people well enough in order to communicate with cultural competence.

A helpful way of gaining cultural competency with other cultural groups is by acknowledging the various dynamics of cultural identities and activities. The image of an iceberg has often been used to show how what we see is not all there is to our world. While an iceberg may look fascinating to the eye, lying below the surface are aspects of that iceberg that are unseen. Similarly, culture includes at least three general components: the visible, the unspoken rules, and the unconscious rules. Too often when leaders seek to minister cross-culturally, attention is solely given to the visible: dress, food, music, language, and mannerisms. The visible is definitely important; leaders cannot neglect this dimension of culture. However, it is often the things that are not visible, such as unspoken rules and unconscious rules that can cause misunderstanding and conflict—even within the church. Unspoken rules refer to things like attitudes toward age, promptness, mannerisms, ways to express courtesy, and cleanliness standards. Unconscious rules refer to things like appropriate space, eye contact, touching, and nonverbal communication.[39] Cultural competence will require both the Spirit's empowerment and discernment, as well as godly wisdom. It may require leaders to ask questions, even uncomfortable questions in a most respectful manner. Leaders must seek resources in order to become more culturally competent for hospitality to occur.[40]

A number of years ago I was having lunch with another student who was studying theology with me. As he sat across from me, he had this very pointed question: "why do you brown people worship cows?" I was stunned. I realize that he may have been trying to be humorous, but he was not laughing, and neither was I at that moment. Why the phrase, *you* brown people? I was studying Christian theology at the same school as him! He may have been asking an honest question and trying to understand South Asian culture or even Hinduism, but the way he asked me

---

38. Garr and Garr, "The Work in India," 1; Anderson, *Spreading Fires*, 61.
39. Collins, *Christian Counseling*, 108–9.
40. E.g., Livermore, *Cultural Intelligence*.

had failed to be culturally sensitive. His cultural competence was lacking. I realize that I could have shown him some grace as well—maybe he was just ignorant and trying his best. I could not get over his approach and quickly switched the topic of conversation.

It is important, however, to ensure that cultural competence is not restricted to mere ethnic differences. One important example of gaining cultural competence to better minister to others comes from the ministry of a husband and wife, Lon and Brenda Solomon of McLean Bible Church in McLean, Virginia. Lon is the pastor of the church. The couple had a daughter, Jill, who was born with Dravet Syndrome, a rare seizure disorder.[41] Their child, just a few months old, began to have seizures, which ultimately challenged their perspectives on ministry. They saw the need for ministry to those with special needs, so they involved their church in a ministry to young people with special needs called Jill's House.[42] One of their aims is to provide a "safe, fun place full of adventure and activities made just for them."[43] In their own words, the ministry is "designed around the children, we adjust to them, not them to us. The activities are carefully and strategically planned to meet the child where they are, with the purpose of bringing normalcy to childhood. We provide cozy and comfortable sleeping areas for safe and secure overnight stays, with constant and watchful care."[44] An examination of their ministry showcases how taking seriously the roles of being welcoming and of cultural competence to another cultural group can be tremendously effective. And they literally built a home for those of a different cultural group–this is hospitality. Becoming a multicultural ministry is not merely about being intentional about reaching different ethnic groups, but about reaching all types of different cultural groups.

PENTECOSTAL HOSPITALITY: EMPOWERING PEOPLE OF ALL CULTURAL GROUPS

One of the key messages that arose from the Day of Pentecost in Act 2 is that all people can be filled with the Spirit for empowerment for ministry. On the Day of Pentecost, the believers who had come together in one

---

41. Solomon, "Hope!"
42. "Meet Jill."
43. "Celebrate!"
44. "Celebrate!"

place "were all filled with the Holy Spirit and began to speak in other tongues as the Spirit gave them utterance" (Acts 2:4, ESV). As hearers heard these believers speaking in tongues and they asked what was happening, Peter made an important announcement about this experience of the Spirit: "this is what was spoken through the prophet Joel: 'In the last days it will be, God declares, that I will pour out my Spirit upon all flesh, and your sons and your daughters shall prophesy, and your young men shall see visions, and your old men shall dream dreams. Even upon my slaves, both men and women, in those days I will pour out my Spirit; and they shall prophesy'" (Acts 2:16–18, NRSV). The experience of the Spirit that Peter and others believers had undergone, was not only reserved for them, but for all types of people: males, females, the young, the old, and slaves. The Spirit was being poured out on all people regardless of their background.

Continuing with the reception of the Spirit for all people, it is important to note that the reception of the Spirit in Acts 2, is based on the Christ's promise in Acts 1:8: "But you will receive power when the Holy Spirit has come upon you; and you will be my witnesses in Jerusalem, in all Judea and Samaria, and to the ends of the earth" (NRSV). Christ's promise includes the idea that the reception of the Spirit is not just an experience of the Spirit for one's own personal benefit, but for empowerment to be a witness for Jesus. Pentecostals have reiterated the idea throughout the years that Spirit baptism is for empowerment for ministry.[45] Regardless of whether one wants to argue that tongues or any of the gifts is the evidence of Spirit baptism—for this line of argumentation differs among Pentecostals around the world—Pentecostals can agree that people of all types of cultural backgrounds may be filled with the Spirit for the empowerment for ministry.[46] This is crucial for this discussion, for it affirms the dignity of all types of believers, regardless of cultural backgrounds, for effective ministry.

Seymour extended hospitality through his leadership at the Azusa Street Mission, for it was a place where people of various diverse cultural groups could be empowered for ministry. In the early 1900s, lawful discrimination and segregation permeated society. One important way Seymour attempted to overcome discrimination was along ethnic, gender, age, and socioeconomic distinctions related to ministry.

---

45. Klaus, "The Mission of the Church," 574–85.
46. Cf. Anderson, *Introduction to Pentecostalism*, 187–95; 1 Cor 12:7.

Before getting into some of the specific ways Seymour extended hospitality by empowering various cultural groups, it is important to understand that an experience of Spirit baptism provided the theological rationale for this expression of hospitality at Azusa. After people received an experience of Spirit baptism, this showed for Seymour that these people were empowered for ministry—regardless of their cultural background, which he linked to Joel 2:28–32. Seymour exclaimed, "praise our God, He is now given and being poured out upon all flesh. All races, nations, and tongues are receiving the baptism with the Holy Ghost and fire, according to the prophecy of Joel."[47] There are a few ways Seymour ensured that his ministry was hospitable to various cultural groups.

First, the leadership for the ministry at Azusa was diverse along the lines of gender, ethnic background, and age. Some of the key leaders at the Mission were men, women, blacks, and whites. Although Seymour was black himself, he did not merely include other black leaders in key roles—it may have been a temptation of his to at least choose a majority of black leaders. In a picture of the leaders from August 1906, of the 12 people in the picture, only three are blacks (which includes Seymour). The only other prominent black leaders within Seymour's inner circle of leaders in August 1906 were two other black women. One was Jennie Evans Moore, who provided leadership for music at the Mission; she eventually became Seymour's wife.[48] And the other black woman was Sister Prince, likely viewed as the church Mother of the Mission, who would be sought after for prayer and advice.[49] Seymour's willingness to include people who were not part of his own ethnic group shows his exemplary approach in making his ministry hospitable to those who were different than him.

Seymour also extended hospitality to young people, by not merely viewing them as young people in need of babysitting or even ministry at Azusa, but as children who could be empowered by the Spirit for ministry. In *The Apostolic Faith*, the writer explains how God does not need a great theological preacher that merely provides "theological chips and shavings to people."[50] By contrast, the article explains that God can effectively use young people who are baptized in the Spirit: "A young sister,

---

47. Seymour, "Receive Ye the Holy Ghost," 2.
48. Robeck, *The Azusa Street Mission and Revival*, 99.
49. Robeck, *The Azusa Street Mission and Revival*, 103.
50. "Back to Pentecost," 3.

fourteen years old, was saved, sanctified and baptized with the Holy Ghost, and went out, taking a band of workers with her, and led a revival in which one hundred and ninety souls were saved."[51] The experience of the Spirit, through Spirit baptism, provided leaders with an important impetus for hospitality related to diversity in leadership.

Second, the ministry at Azusa led by Seymour showed hospitality to other cultural groups by being willing to listen and be influenced by others outside their cultural confines. A clear expression of hospitality extended to others to listen and learn is exemplified through Azusa's connection with Pandita Sarasvati Ramabai and her ministry in India, the Mukti Mission. Ramabai's Mukiti Mission focused on young widows and orphans in Pune, India. In 1905, a two year-long revival began at this mission, which included speaking in tongues and other physical manifestations.[52] This revival is important for Azusa, and for this discussion on hospitality, because the leadership at Azusa was willing to learn from those at the Mukti Mission.

The leadership at Azusa did not view the Mukti Mission merely as a great mission field that those in the West—including the Azusa Mission itself—could reach and teach. Rather, the leadership at Azusa listened and learned from the ministry at Mukti, which helped inform and strengthen the ministry and beliefs found at Azusa. One example of this is how Azusa leaders looked to the Mukti Mission as a model for understanding how to deal with manifestations in corporate worship.[53] The experience of the Spirit at Mukti revealed to Azusa how the Spirit might likewise be experienced among them. Hospitality, then, is not restricted to ministering to diverse cultures, but extends to recognizing one's own limitations and humbly receiving and learning from diverse cultures. Hospitality eliminates a patriarchal approach to ministry, being willing to consider others as being able to equally contribute to the ministry.

The relationship between the Azusa Street Mission and their willingness to learn from the Mukti Mission in India shows that hospitality cannot just go one way. Hospitality cannot just be about leaders and members of churches becoming welcoming and becoming culturally competent with other cultural groups. The goal for multicultural ministry should be

---

51. *Apostolic Faith*, October 1906.

52. Anderson, *Introduction to Pentecostalism*, 36–37; Burgess, "Ramabai, Sarasvati Mary (Pandita)," 1016–18.

53. "Manifestations of the Spirit in India," 4; Samuel, "God is Really Among You!" 96.

hospitality that is reciprocated—we must be willing to learn from other cultural groups.[54] On the one hand, people should seek to be hosts, but on the other hand everyone should also be willing to assume the role of guests.[55] Theologically, this reciprocal love reflects the God revealed in Scripture, who is a triune God. The triune God includes reciprocal love, whereby the Father, Son, and Holy Spirit express love to one another, but also receive love from one another.[56] In order for genuine hospitality to exist, mutual understanding and edification is critical.

Amos Yong, one of the most prolific Pentecostal scholars today, brings attention to an often-neglected cultural group—people who are disabled—and provides a way forward so that they too can be empowered for ministry. People may experience disabilities in various ways, whether mentally, intellectually, or socially.[57] And far too often, they are merely cared for paternalistically, rather than consulted as people who can benefit a community.[58] While praying for those who are disabled may be something they may want and appreciate, that cannot be the only way the church interacts with those who may be disabled. In a Pentecostal context, where signs, wonders, and miracles have often been highlighted, seeing someone who is disabled healed may be deemed as a great opportunity for God's power to manifest. But what about those who have not been *healed* the way some expect? Are those who are disabled a reminder of some sort of failure on the part of the church to have enough faith for healing? Or can leaders believe that, just like all people who have limitations in life, those who are disabled are capable and even necessary for the benefit of the church and the world? Like all other believers, those who are disabled can also minister in the power of the Spirit and can be a resource for ministry that has likely not been included in many church contexts. What ministries do churches lack because they have not acknowledged the important ministry that those who are disabled can offer?

A number of years ago when this author attended a conference for Pentecostal leaders in Canada, I took along a friend of mine who was also a Christian leader. As we walked in, my friend was a bit shocked.

---

54. Yong has also pointed out the importance of reciprocal hospitality towards those of other religions. See "The Spirit of Hospitality," 64.

55. Cf., Yong, *Hospitality and the Other*, para 1, chapter 4, location 3383.

56. Bird, *Evangelical Theology*, 729.

57. Yong, *The Bible, Disability, and the Church*, 12.

58. Yong, *The Bible, Disability, and the Church*, 13.

He could not understand how at an event for Christian leaders, it appeared that both he and I were the only people in attendance who were not white. He was partially correct. There were other faces at the event that were not white—on the banners and slideshows exotic-looking faces were presented as people who were in need of the gospel. It appeared that the only reason that a person who was not white could be relevant for the conference—or the ministry in general—was to be recipients of Pentecostal ministry. Examining how those at Azusa were hospitable to other cultural groups by not only including them in official roles for leadership, but genuinely listening and learning from them, will make a positive difference in Pentecostal ministry today.

A RESPONSE TO FOUR MISGUIDED APPLICATIONS OF PENTECOSTAL HOSPITALITY

While the ideals of hospitality for effective multicultural ministry are appropriate for application in ministry, it is possible that the application of these themes could be misguided in at least four ways, which are addressed here. First, there is the misguided application of multicultural ministry that reflects the "melting pot" approach to cultures. This approach, popularised in the United States many years ago, encourages the various ethnic groups to come together into one melting pot, whereby the various distinctions are eliminated so that there is only one ethnic group that emerges from this pot.[59] On the one hand, this approach appears to be hospitable in that various ethnic groups are welcomed into this melting pot. On the other hand, the goal of coming into this melting pot is inhospitality, for the goal is the eradication of cultural distinctions for the sake of creating one culture. Aiming to eliminate cultural differences for the sake of one would be a form of violence to the cultural identities of each person. God's actions on the Day of Pentecost reveal that each culture must be valued. Yes, the various cultures must be welcomed; but the church is also called to value each culture by a willingness to be sensitive and competent in its ministry to each cultural group.

Another way that an emphasis on hospitality for multicultural ministry can become misguided is when each cultural group becomes something of a "cultural ghetto" within the wider church community. This approach is so sensitive to each culture, that cultural groups are

---

59. Breckenridge and Breckenridge, *What Color is Your God?* 65.

able to maintain their culture with little or no mutual interaction and integration into the wider church. While it may seem like a church is being hospitable by being sensitive to each cultural group by encouraging their unique identities, it ultimately fails to be hospitable by an inability to integrate people of various cultural groups. Being hospitable includes making people feel welcome into the wider community. However, different cultural groups should not only be able to maintain their cultural identities, but also genuinely express reciprocal love with those of different cultural groups.

A third misguided application of hospitality for effective multicultural ministry is the use of what is often referred to as "affirmative action" in ministry. Affirmative action is the practice of intentionally including people of various cultural groups who are often misrepresented in certain industries. Industries may set a quota indicating how many people—or a percentage of people—within each demographic they must integrate into their industry in order to meet the affirmative action goals. On the one hand, this practice may be viewed positively for multicultural ministry, since the assumption is that the cultural group who is in the "majority" is intentionally involving those who are not represented. On the other hand, this practice can become misguided when leaders include people belonging to different cultural groups without discretion—particularly when it comes to ministry roles. Including people solely because they are part of a minority cultural group is not sufficient for placement in ministry. In keeping with the Pentecostal emphasis on the Spirit, Scripture reveals that God has given various gifts of the Spirit for believers, which should align with their role in the Church—not necessarily dependent on their cultural identity. Further, including different cultural groups cannot get in the way of including people based on call and character.

Another reason why an approach that resembles affirmative action is deficient for multicultural ministry is because it fails to take seriously the Pentecostal emphasis on the Spirit's manifestation on all believers. The Apostle Paul, in his discussion on the gifts of the Spirit, explained that each believer "is given the manifestation of the Spirit for the common good" (1 Cor 12:7, NRSV). Thus, trying to place someone of a particular cultural group in a more public role merely to appear multicultural is unfaithful to the Spirit's work among believers. A believer from a minority cultural group may offer something within the church's ministry that may or may not be a public role; however, leaders must seek to discern what each believer's role may be rather than just trying to appear multicultural. Furthermore, one other related deficiency of the affirmative action approach is that it often relegates the inclusion of minority cultural groups to a particular percentage of people (e.g., ensuring 50 per cent of people involved in the community are from a minority cultural group). However, Paul's explanation of the Spirit's work in believers in 1 Cor 12:7 reminds leaders that they are not obligated just to get approximately 50 per cent of believers involved in ministry. Leaders must aim at getting 100 per cent of believers of all cultures involved in ministry, since every believer is "given the manifestation of the Spirit for the common good."

The last misguided application of hospitality for multicultural ministry is the idea that everything that belongs to another cultural group's identity and/or beliefs is worthy of including within the wider church community—often associated with pluralism. To say that not every aspect of one's cultural identity and/or beliefs should be included may appear to be inhospitable—particularly since hospitality, as explained above, should include welcoming the different cultural identities. The church is not a local community center, but rather, it is a body of believers who profess their faith in the triune God revealed in Scripture. Christianity is an exclusive religion, in that the triune God revealed in Scripture prohibits worship of any other object other than Him.[60] And out of that worship of the triune God, he prescribes a way of living for believers. Thus, all cultural identities and practices must come under the lordship of this triune God.

CONCLUSION

Picking up on the title of this essay, "Samosas at the Pentecostal Potluck," churches should continue to share and receive those samosas—alongside Korean BBQ, Jerk chicken, and even some Poutine at those Pentecostal potlucks. Cross-cultural communication while sharing a meal representative of different cultures can be a powerful opportunity for multicultural ministry. But leaders must not stop with the food. Believers must be willing to ensure that they are hospitable to all cultural groups, by receiving what those cultural groups can uniquely offer, while also sharing their lives with them as well. When there is a genuine, mutual sharing of lives—beyond just the cultural elements that can be seen—believers can

---

60. Cf., Breckenridge and Breckenridge, *What Color is Your God?* 69.

begin to experience the type of Trinitarian community that Jesus hoped for in the Church when he prayed to the Father that believers may "all be one" just as he and the Father are united (John 17:21). We can extrapolate a Pentecostal theology of multicultural ministry from the Pentecostal emphases both in Scripture and the early history of the Pentecostal movement. This Pentecostal theology of multicultural ministry should be one that includes hospitality that is extended to all cultural groups so that all might experience an encounter with the triune God and the reciprocal love between believers.

Finally, regardless of the cultural group to which a ministry is seeking to be hospitable, it will require the Spirit's leading and wisdom in a way that is appropriate for each particular context. The discussion here is not meant to create a model that should be used in every church like a McDonald's franchise. Each church might address different cultural groups in unique ways—but at the end of the day, the hope is that churches are intentionally hospitable to cultural groups unlike their own.

BIBLIOGRAPHY

Anderson, Allan. *An Introduction to Pentecostalism*. Cambridge: Cambridge University Press, 2004.

———. *Spreading Fires: The Missionary Nature of Early Pentecostalism*. Maryknoll, UK: Orbis, 2007.

The Apostolic Faith. "Back to Pentecost." October 1906.

———. "Manifestations of the Spirit in India." June–September 1907.

———. "The Old-Time Pentecost." September 1906.

Bartleman, Frank. *Azusa Street*. 2nd ed. Alachua, FL: Bridge-Logos, 1980.

Bird, Michael F. *Evangelical Theology: A Biblical and Systematic Introduction*. Grand Rapids: Zondervan, 2013.

Bock, Darrell L. *Acts*. Baker Exegetical Commentary on the New Testament. Grand Rapids: Baker, 2007.

Boersma, Hans. *Violence, Hospitality, and the Cross: Reappropriating the Atonement Tradition*. Grand Rapids: Baker, 2004.

Breckenridge, James, and Lillian Breckenridge. *What Color is Your God?: Multicultural Education in the Church*. Wheaton: BridgePoint, 1995.

Burgess, R. V. "Ramabai, Sarasvati Mary (Pandita)." In *The New International Dictionary of Pentecostal and Charismatic Movements*, edited by Stanley M. Burgess, 1016–18. Grand Rapids: Zondervan, 2003.

"Celebrate! Who, How & Why We Serve," [n.d.], online: http://jillshouse.org/who-how-why-we-serve/.

Collins, Gary R. *Christian Counseling: A Comprehensive Guide*. 3rd ed. Nashville: Thomas Nelson, 2006.

Cox, Harvey. *Fire From Heaven: The Rise of Pentecostal Spirituality and the Reshaping of Religion in the Twenty-First Century*. Cambridge: Da Capo, 1995.

Douara, Deena. "Meet the Heroes Who Are Helping Bring Syrian Refugees to Canada." *The Toronto Star*, 9 December 2015. Online: https://www.thestar.com/news/canada/2015/12/09/sponsorship-groups-are-quiet-heroes-in-helping-refugees-relocate.html.

ERDO. "Mission, Vision, Core Values & Milestones," [n.d.], online: http://www.erdo.ca/mission-vision-milestones.

———. "Syrian Refugee Crisis," [n.d.], online: http://www.erdo.ca/crisis-response-syria.

Faupel, D. William. *The Everlasting Gospel: The Significance of Eschatology in The Development of Pentecostal Thought*. Blandford Forum, UK: Deo, 2009.

Gane, Roy. *Leviticus, Numbers*. NIV Application Commentary. Grand Rapids: Zondervan, 2004.

Garr, Alfred, and Lillian Garr. "The Work in India." *The Apostolic Faith*. June–September 1907.

Goff, James R., Jr. *Fields White Unto Harvest: Charles F. Parham and the Missionary Origins of Pentecostalism*. Fayetteville, AR: University of Arkansas Press, 1988.

Government of Ontario, "Syrian Refugees: How You Can Help," [n.d.], online: https://www.ontario.ca/page/syrian-refugees-how-you-can-help.

Hartley, John E. *Leviticus*. Word Biblical Commentary. Dallas: Word, 1998.

Hollenweger, Walter J. "Pentecostals and the Charismatic Movement." In *The Study of Spirituality*, edited by Cheslyn Jones et al., 549–54. Oxford: Oxford University Press, 1986.

Hunsberger, George R. *Bearing Witness of the Spirit: Lesslie Newbigin's Theology of Cultural Plurality*. Grand Rapids: Eerdmans, 1998.

Keener, Craig S. *Acts: An Exegetical Commentary*. Vol. 1. Introduction and 1:1—2:47. Grand Rapids: Baker, 2012

Klaus, Byron D. "The Mission of the Church." *Systematic Theology*, revised edition, edited by Stanley M. Horton. Springfield, MO: Logion, 2013.

Land, Steven Jack. *Pentecostal Spirituality: A Passion for the Kingdom*. Cleveland, TN: CPT, 2010.

Livermore, David. A. *Cultural Intelligence: Improving Your CQ to Engage Our Multicultural World*. Grand Rapids: Baker, 2009.

"Meet Jill," [n.d.], online: http://jillshouse.org/meet-jill/.

Mittelstadt, Martin William. *Reading Luke-Acts in the Pentecostal Tradition*. Cleveland, TN: CPT, 2010.

Parham, Charles F. *The Everlasting Gospel*. Baxter Springs, KS: Apostolic Faith Bible College, 1930.

———. *A Voice Crying in the Wilderness*. Baxter Springs, KS: Apostolic Faith Bible College, 1902.

Powell, Kara, et al. "The Church Sticking Together: The Vital Role of Intergenerational Relationships in Fostering Sticky Faith." March 8, 2016. http://stickyfaith.org/articles/the-church-sticking-together.

Robeck, Cecil M., Jr. *The Azusa Street Mission and Revival: The Birth of the Global Pentecostal Movement*. Nashville: Thomas Nelson, 2006.

Rowlison, Bruce. *Creative Hospitality*. Alhambra, CA: Green Leaf, 1981.

Samuel, Josh P. S. "'God is Really Among You!': The Spirit's Immediacy in Pentecostal Corporate Worship." Ph.D. diss., McMaster Divinity College, 2014.

Seymour, William J. "Bro. Seymour's Call." *The Apostolic Faith*. September 1906.

———. "Receive Ye the Holy Ghost." *The Apostolic Faith*. January 1907.

Solivan, Samuel. *The Spirit, Pathos and Liberation: Toward an Hispanic Pentecostal Theology*. Sheffield: Sheffield Academic Press, 1998.

Solomon, Brenda. "Hope! A Message from Jill's Mom—Brenda Solomon, Co-Founder of Jill's House," [n.d.], online: http://jillshouse.org/a-message-from-jills-mom/#.

Wenham, Gordon. *Leviticus*. Grand Rapids: Eerdmans, 1979.

Yong, Amos. *The Bible, Disability, and the Church*. Grand Rapids: Eerdmans, 2011.

———. *Hospitality and the Other: Pentecost, Christian Practices, and the Neighbor*. Maryknoll, NY: Orbis, 2008. Kindle edition.

———. "The Spirit of Hospitality: Pentecostal Perspectives toward a Performative Theology of Interreligious Encounter." *Missiology: An International Review* 35 (2007) 55–73.

Zilio, Michelle. "Not Enough Resources for Syrian Refugees in Canada: Poll." *The Globe and Mail*, 9 May 2016. Online: http://www.theglobeandmail.com/news/politics/not-enough-resources-for-syrian-refugees-in-canada-poll/article29935148.

8

Spirit Baptism, Exclusion, and Emerging Adults
An Ecclesiological Approach to a Present Challenge

Peter D. Neumann

INTRODUCTION

EMERGING ADULTS PRESENT A unique challenge to classical Pentecostals in the Canadian context.[1] This is the case due to a tension in values held by both groups. For my own denomination, the Pentecostal Assemblies of Canada (PAOC), the doctrine of the experience of Spirit baptism with the accompanying initial evidence of tongues is held as a core belief and community identity marker.[2] Further, a derivative policy of this doctrine is that only those who have spoken in tongues are eligible for ministerial credentials. But such commitments are frequently viewed with suspicion by emerging adults, who highly value radical autonomy and, perhaps most of all, inclusivity. For this group, institutional beliefs and policies that appear unnecessarily exclusive are regarded with suspicion or rejected outright.

---

1. The Pentecostalism that is in view in this paper is of the narrower "classical" sort, historically linked to Pentecostal revivals in North America in the early 1900s.

2. Other Pentecostal denominations, such as the Pentecostal Assemblies of Newfoundland/Labrador (PAONL), Assemblies of God, USA (AG), Church of God (Cleveland), and the Church of God in Christ hold very similar views on this doctrine.

The purpose of what follows is twofold. First, it is an attempt to raise awareness to the current reality and challenge facing Pentecostalism in Canada with regard to emerging adults and their attitudes toward Pentecostal distinctive doctrines and related policies. Second, it is an effort to suggest possible theological ways forward for Pentecostal leaders in addressing this challenge. My proposal, in brief, is this: In light of emerging adult cultural realities, including their high valuation of relationships and inclusivity, a fresh look at the Pentecostal doctrines of Spirit baptism and initial evidence through a communal perspective (an ecclesial hermeneutic) may provide theological resources for helping overcome some challenges in traditioning Pentecostal spirituality among emerging adults within a Canadian context.

This proposal is not without risks. Any time we take a fresh look at core beliefs in light of cultural realities there is danger of simply acquiescing to current trends and losing essential values. But to ignore cultural realities is also unacceptable if the church is truly to exemplify its catholic (universal and contextual) nature.[3] So, Pentecostals as people of the Spirit need to accept this task with its inherent risks.

To accomplish this proposal, this chapter will begin by expounding the nature of the challenge facing Pentecostalism with regard to emerging adults. This will entail an exploration of emerging adulthood as a social-psychological life stage, along with a survey of the cultural realities shaping this age group in North America, and within a Pentecostal Bible college in particular. Following this, our exploration will move to theological issues, involving two steps. The first will be to identify some level of shared values between emerging adults and historical Pentecostalism with regard to attitudes towards personal autonomy, experience, and inclusion. The second step will be to suggest that the Pentecost story (Acts 2), from which the Pentecostal Spirit baptism doctrine is derived, may be viewed through a more communal, ecclesial (as opposed to individualistic) lens. The hopeful result is that these insights will enable fresh ways of speaking about Spirit baptism that may resonate more effectively with emerging adults.

---

3. Van Gelder, *The Essence of the Church*, 51.

PENTECOSTAL DOCTRINE AND THE CHALLENGE FROM WITHIN

The doctrine of Spirit baptism, combined with the requisite counterpart of the initial evidence of tongues has long been central to classical Pentecostal spirituality and self-understanding. Pentecostal denominations such as the PAOC and Assemblies of God, USA (AG) believe that this articulation of a two-stage view of conversion and Spirit baptism with the accompanying sign of tongues can be supported biblically, theologically, and pragmatically.[4] Despite sophisticated defenses, however, one longstanding critique against the classical Pentecostal understanding of Spirit baptism is that it creates a two-tiered Christianity—an elitist *haves* and the *have-nots* among Christian believers.[5] In short, the traditional Pentecostal doctrine of Spirit baptism and initial evidence may be viewed as introducing exclusion, inequality, and even disunity within the broader Christian community.[6]

These are charges that Pentecostals have, for better or worse, been willing to bear, since ecumenical harmony has often been low on their priority list (although, fortunately, this is changing).[7] But the challenge Pentecostals currently face when it comes to their Spirit baptism and initial evidence doctrine is one arising not from other traditions but from within its own ranks, namely from among 18 to 29-year-olds, the so-called "emerging adults." We will spend some time characterizing emerging adulthood shortly. For now it is sufficient to note that emerging adults bring a unique challenge to Pentecostalism in the form of a fresh and robust application of the old charge of elitism. Elitism, characterised by exclusion and inequality, appears incompatible with the highly relational and inclusive values held by emerging adults in North America, according to recent research conducted in both Canada and the USA.

---

4. Robert P. Menzies (AG) and Roger J. Stronstad (PAOC) are two such Pentecostal apologists who use redaction criticism to emphasize Luke's distinctive charismatic pneumatology. See Menzies, *Empowered for Witness*; William W. Menzies and Robert P. Menzies, *Spirit and Power*; Stronstad, *The Charismatic Theology of St. Luke*; and Stronstad, *The Prophethood of All Believers*.

5. See, for example, Fee, "Toward a Pauline Theology of Glossolalia," 105–20; Macchia, *Baptized in the Spirit*, 32, 78, 114; Spittler, "Maintaining Distinctives," 122–24; and Kaiser, "The Baptism of the Holy Spirit," 36, cf. 15–46.

6. Allan Anderson ("To All Points of the Compass," 154) identifies exclusivism and disunity as one of the greatest weaknesses within contemporary Pentecostalism.

7. See Neumann, *Pentecostal Experience*, 133–45.

Since the average Canadian (and American) emerging adult is socialized into a cultural ethos that strongly prioritizes values such as diversity and inclusivity, it is difficult for this group to accept rigid and apparently exclusivist doctrines, such as Pentecostal Spirit baptism and initial evidence. Further, closer to home and compounding the issue is a practical question often raised by my students, training for Pentecostal ministry at Master's College and Seminary: Why is eligibility for ministerial credentials within the PAOC limited to only those students who have spoken in tongues? In other words, despite graduating from a Pentecostal Bible College, and despite even seeking the experience of Spirit baptism and tongues for lengthy periods of time but not receiving, a student can be excluded from credentialed ministry.[8] This makes little sense in the Canadian (and American) emerging adult mind.

How, then, should Pentecostal denominations respond? There are at least three options. One is to simply choose to ignore this reality and pretend that opposition to Pentecostal doctrines comes only from the outside—that little if any questioning of core faith tenets exists among those associated with the institution. Another option is to choose to become more resolute about protecting classical Pentecostal faith statements and policies, downplaying emerging adult concerns. A third option, and what I am proposing, is to acknowledge some validity to the values held among emerging adults, and use this as an opportunity to think afresh about traditionally held doctrines and policies, to see whether or not there is need for re-articulation in a way that can preserve Pentecostal values while also addressing some of the legitimate concerns emerging adults bring to the table. To understand these concerns, we now turn to a character sketch of emerging adults and the current cultural realities in Canada (and the USA).

EMERGING ADULTS IN CANADA (AND NORTH AMERICA): AN OVERVIEW

Since Jeffrey Arnett proposed it as "a new conception of development for the period between the late teens and twenties,"[9] the term "emerging

---

8. The PAOC's *General Constitution and By-Laws*, section 10.2 states: "All applicants for credentials shall have a personal experience of salvation and shall have received the baptism in the Holy Spirit with the initial evidence of speaking in other tongues . . . " So, the experience of tongues is a prerequisite for credentials.

9. Arnett, "Emerging Adulthood," 469.

adulthood" has become a commonly-used and helpful way of describing the 18 to 29-year-old age group.[10] This term identifies a unique stage of life (relatively new, culturally),[11] markedly different from both adolescence and young adulthood.[12] It is a between time of sorts, enabled and shaped by cultural factors, particularly those of the western industrialized world. Arnett summarizes this stage as a "distinct period of the life course, characterized by change and exploration of possible directions."[13] It is a time of growing autonomy, with yet few adult responsibilities, and therefore a stage of considerable instability, experimentation, diversity, transition (in residences, jobs, and schools), and seemingly endless options and possibilities. Stabilization and restriction of possibilities occurs only in the movement into (young) adulthood in the later twenties.[14]

There are other cultural realities that need to be taken into account when attempting a portrayal of emerging adulthood in North America, and Canadian culture in particular. A helpful and concise sociological analysis is provided in the 2012 report, authored by James Penner et al, and commissioned by the Evangelical Fellowship of Canada's Youth and Young Adult Ministry Roundtable, *Hemorrhaging Faith: Why and When Canadian Young Adults are Leaving, Staying and Returning to Church*.[15] While other resources will be referenced, the *Hemorrhaging Faith* report will serve our purposes well here to outline some of the primary issues by providing a bird's-eye-view of the emerging adult cultural landscape,

---

10. Arnett was primarily concerned with describing 18 to 25-year-olds, but Christian Smith notes that academic literature now typically identifies emerging adults as consisting of those of ages 18–29, and so I have chosen to follow Smith's lead. See Smith and Snell, *Souls in Transition*, 6. "Emerging adult/hood" is now common terminology used in sociological studies for this age group. For example, see Setran and Kiesling, *Spiritual Formation in Emerging Adulthood*; Penner et al., *Hemorrhaging Faith*; and Hill, *Emerging Adulthood and Faith*.

11. Arnett, "Emerging Adulthood," 477–79.

12. Arnett, "Emerging Adulthood," 471, 476–77.

13. Arnett, "Emerging Adulthood," 469.

14. Arnett, "Emerging Adulthood," 471.

15. Penner et al., *Hemorrhaging Faith*. This research project involved extensive surveys and interviews with Canadian young people. Those considered to be in the "young adult" category are those aged 18–34, which includes those up to five years older than what is typically understood to be an "emerging adult" (118). For a sociological survey of the American emerging adult scene, see Smith and Snell, *Souls in Transition*; Kinnaman, *You Lost Me*; and Hill, *Emerging Adulthood and Faith*. For a Canadian analysis, although its focus is primarily teens, see Bibby, *The Emerging Millennials*.

and how in particular this might impact this generation's relationship to religious belief and activity.

Despite its negative-sounding title, and while acknowledging that the church in Canada is losing large numbers of emerging adults,[16] the *Hemorrhaging Faith* report is not ultimately pessimistic. Rather, it is intended to identify the factors that help keep emerging adults in the faith, as well as the ones that cause them to leave, with the goal of equipping the Canadian church to minister more effectively to youth and emerging adults.[17] In the report Penner et al identify seven cultural factors that challenge emerging adults' engagement in religious faith: postmodernism, radical autonomy, identity formation, religion, consumerism, time pressure, and the information explosion.[18] We will briefly review these in order, except for religion, which will be left until last.

The first cultural factor, *postmodernism*, is described as a "reaction to Modernism." But specifically it is some of postmodernism's "cynical outcomes" that are of concern to the *Hemorrhaging Faith* authors, in particular its impact on popular epistemology. In a postmodern view "the assertion of truth is reduced to an attempt to coerce, and religion—with its comprehensive doctrine of truth—is reduced to organized coercion."[19]

Radical autonomy, a second factor, describes the pervasive desire among emerging adults to be "free from the demands, power and control of others." This has a direct impact on how emerging adults view groups, religious or otherwise. "Groups make demands of its members, and if power is viewed with suspicion as an attempt to coerce then young adults are reluctant to participate in groups."[20] This, as we will examine shortly, has significant impact on how emerging adults view community and relationships, and of course organized religion. At this point it will suffice to note that Penner et al observe that it is not the case that emerging adults do not involve themselves in organized groups (religious or otherwise). Social relationships are paramount to emerging adults. It is just that due to the high value of radical autonomy, these groups cannot

---

16. Penner et al., *Hemorrhaging Faith*, 20–38. On religious attendance among youth in Canada, also see Bibby, *The Emerging Millennials*, 162–87. Confirming this is an issue needing to be addressed in the USA, see Kinnaman, *You Lost Me*, chapter 1.

17. Penner et al., *Hemorrhaging Faith*, 10, 114–15.

18. Penner et al., *Hemorrhaging Faith*, 12–15.

19. Penner et al., *Hemorrhaging Faith*, 12; also see Smith and Snell, *Souls in Transition*, 48–49, 101.

20. Penner et al., *Hemorrhaging Faith*, 12; Smith and Snell, *Souls in Transition*, 49.

"make restrictive demands of its members. Young adults move in and out of groups quite freely—as long as when they go in, the door stays wide open."[21]

A third cultural factor raised by *Hemorrhaging Faith* is *identity formation*. Citing Arnett's work on emerging adulthood, Penner et al highlight that this is a "normless, self-exploratory phase."[22] No longer is one's identity primarily dictated by one's nationality, race, religion, or gender. Rather, "Unlike in the past, identities are primarily formed rather than received."[23] But even as one's identity is shaped by experimenting with seemingly endless possibilities and options, there is reluctance to arrive at any one particular identity, lest it impede one's autonomy. For, "identities—if they are to be permanent—bind you to groups. So identities tend to be made and remade, and the materials [emerging adults] build these identities out of tend to flow from the will, i.e., what is inside me, rather than traditional sources."[24]

Consumerism and *time pressure* are two other cultural factors identified by Penner et al. Emerging adults have been socialized not only to believe that newer is better (and so what is old is disposable), but that life is based on exchange and consumption, and that they should have lots of choice.[25] For this reason, "Church may also be viewed as something to be consumed, a product or service to meet the needs of the consumer."[26] Perceived needs must be met in order for what organized religion offers to be considered worthwhile.[27] Constrained time to accomplish all that is expected during this life phase (e.g., school, new job, etc.) may leave emerging adults "especially prone to feeling overwhelmed,"[28] and, as we will see, makes participation in religious activities less of a priority in their schedule.

---

21. Penner et al., *Hemorrhaging Faith*, 12; Smith and Snell, *Souls in Transition*, 79–80.

22. Penner et al., *Hemorrhaging Faith*, 12.

23. Penner et al., *Hemorrhaging Faith*, 13.

24. Penner et al., *Hemorrhaging Faith*, 13. Christian Smith states that emerging adults want to keep their opportunities open (79–80).

25. Bibby, *The Emerging Millennials*, 29.

26. Penner et al., *Hemorrhaging Faith*, 13.

27. Penner et al., *Hemorrhaging Faith*, 14; also see Bibby, *The Emerging Millennials*, 181.

28. Penner et al., *Hemorrhaging Faith*, 14.

A sixth factor is the *information explosion*, but perhaps this is too narrow a way of identifying the issues raised under this heading in *Hemorrhaging Faith*.[29] The report states that the "amount and type of information available is ever-expanding and easier to access than ever before," in large part due to technology and the internet.[30] But the authors also suggest that exposure to "thoughts and ideas from around the globe . . . feed into pluralistic values and may lead to disengagement from faith or church."[31] The broader issue here, in my view, is pluralism and its effect on relationships and community, of which the information explosion is one contributing influence.[32]

Pluralism, as I am using it here, simply refers to the widespread receptivity among youth and emerging adults to diversity and inclusivity. Christian Smith identifies openness to diversity of persons, races, and religions as part of the American emerging adult cultural landscape. Since everyone is different, one must be accepting of others and of personal choices.[33] Cultures and their particularities are viewed as relative, and people are expected to be open-minded with regard to cultures, religion, morality, and ways of life in general.[34] If this is a reality in the USA, then it is even more so in Canada, where multiculturalism has been an official political policy since 1971. That the Canadian government's website describing this policy labels multiculturalism as "an inclusive citizenship," speaks volumes.[35]

---

29. Penner et al., *Hemorrhaging Faith*, 14–15.

30. On Canadian youth and information technology, see Bibby, *The Emerging Millennials*, 84–100.

31. Penner et al., *Hemorrhaging Faith*, 14, cf. 14–15.

32. Penner et al take up the issue of community later in their report, which may be why they do not list it specifically among the cultural influences affecting emerging adults (52–65).

33. Smith and Snell, *Souls in Transition*, 48–49.

34. Smith and Snell, *Souls in Transition*, 49–53.

35. Government of Canada, "Canadian Multiculturalism." The value of multiculturalism as policy is described as follows: [By adopting this policy] "Canada affirmed the value and dignity of all Canadian citizens regardless of their racial or ethnic origins, their language, *or their religious affiliation* . . . Canadian multiculturalism is fundamental to our belief that all citizens are equal. Multiculturalism ensures that all citizens can keep their identities, can take pride in their ancestry and have a sense of belonging. Acceptance gives Canadians a feeling of security and self-confidence, making them more open to, and accepting of, diverse cultures. The Canadian experience has shown that multiculturalism encourages racial and ethnic harmony and cross-cultural understanding. . . . Multiculturalism has led to higher rates of naturalization

Canadian sociologist, Reginald W. Bibby, summarizes how this policy has impacted Canadian culture: "What started out as an emphasis on languages and cultures has expanded to create *a psyche of diversity and inclusion*. We now have a Canada characterized not only by cultural and racial mosaic but also by a religious mosaic, a sexual mosaic, a family mosaic, and educational mosaic, a moral mosaic, a lifestyle mosaic, and so on."[36] One result of this pluralistic, multicultural influence has been the growing tendency among youth to see things "in relativistic terms."[37] For example, worldviews are pretty much held to be on equal terms, and one must not be judgmental toward other ways of life.[38]

So, what does this mean for relationships and community? As already noted, personal autonomy is a high value among emerging adults, serving to challenge group authority. But this does not mean that emerging adults are inclined to be loners; quite the opposite is in fact the case. Relationships and community are paramount—but with a paradoxical twist. As Bibby states, for this emerging generation, "nothing is more important to them than *friendship*." Yet at the same time, "The value teens place on friendship is matched only by the importance given to *freedom*."[39] Penner et al describe the community/independence tension as follows: "There is a strange paradox that arises when it comes to young adults and community. The emerging generation is fiercely independent and self-reliant. Yet its members say there's nothing more important to them than friendship. They crave relationship and long for a place of belonging."[40]

---

than ever before. With *no pressure to assimilate and give up their culture*, immigrants freely choose their new citizenship because they want to be Canadians. As Canadians, they share the basic values of democracy with all other Canadians who came before them. At the same time, *Canadians are free to choose for themselves, without penalty, whether they want to identify with their specific group or not. Their individual rights are fully protected and they need not fear group pressures*" (emphasis added).

36. Bibby, *The Emerging Millennials*, 6–7, cf. 103.

37. Bibby, *The Emerging Millennials*, 7.

38. See also Smith and Snell, *Souls in Transition*, 80. Christian Smith affirms this inclusive attitude for the American context.

39. Bibby, *The Emerging Millennials*, 24, cf. 21–41 (emphasis original).

40. Penner et al., *Hemorrhaging Faith*, 52. The scene south of the Canadian border is comparable among American emerging adults. David Kinnaman observes: "The Mosaic generation epitomizes a me-and-we contradiction. To generalize, they are extraordinarily relational and, at the same time, remarkably self-centered. We want to change the world! Look at me! Let's make a difference together! I want to be famous!" See Kinnaman, *You Lost Me*, chapter 1.

With this backdrop, the *Hemorrhaging Faith* report recommends that churches work to create an ethos of "Authenticity" and "Inclusivity."[41] With regard to the latter, "Canada's young adults have grown up in a world directed by pluralism and even relativism. They have been taught to include everyone and tolerate all beliefs. To many of them, acceptance and inclusion are top priorities, so they want to belong to a church that thinks the same way."[42] In light of this, Penner et al suggest that churches would be wise to be especially sensitive to the high aversion of emerging adults toward what they perceive as judgmentalism and exclusivity.[43] Since inclusivity is so highly valued, even the appearance of being exclusive erects a barrier to emerging adult acceptance. Further, this is not simply due to a feeling of being personally excluded—it is a communal, relational value.

> Young adults are "turned off" of church by people, programs and practices that notice and account for certain individuals to the exclusion of others. In fact, young adults are so committed to the values of inclusion and acceptance that they don't just get annoyed for their own sakes. Sometimes their "beef" with exclusive church members and practices is *motivated by empathy for others*.[44]

The seventh and final cultural factor we will review is *religion*, or more accurately, the way emerging adults have been socialized to view religion. Penner et al state that religion exists to "support and help the individual: Religion is therapeutic."[45] Operating here is a rather pragmatic view; organized religion is valued if it turns out to be useful or "worthwhile,"[46] and emerging adults believe this to be the case socially and personally (at least to a degree). Socially, religion is valued because it is assumed to provide a basic moral framework for life. But very often emerging adults simply view all religions as teaching the same, basic and generic moral values.[47] Christian Smith identifies this as "Moral Thera-

---

41. Penner et al., *Hemorrhaging Faith*, 57, cf. 57–61.
42. Penner et al., *Hemorrhaging Faith*, 60.
43. Penner et al., *Hemorrhaging Faith*, 61–64.
44. Penner et al., *Hemorrhaging Faith*, 64 (italics added).
45. Penner et al., *Hemorrhaging Faith*, 13.
46. See Bibby, *The Emerging Millennials*, 181.
47. Penner et al., *Hemorrhaging Faith*, 13; also see Smith and Snell, *Souls in Transition*, 148.

peutic Deism," which in short entails that "God wants people to be good, nice, and fair to each other, as taught in the Bible and by most major world religions."[48]

Applied personally, religion exists to help one be more or less happy and satisfied in life.[49] If a religion happens to advocate a moral view that is considered to be "unnecessarily restrictive," then, since religion is not "strictly necessary," it is easy for emerging adults to discount those religious moral views.[50] This approach to religion does not simply apply to moral values, but also to confessional aspects of religions. So, various beliefs from multiple religions may be assembled in piecemeal fashion, based on personal preference or the influence of friends.[51]

We now need to return to some previously discussed themes, namely those of radical autonomy and community, to see how these might apply to organized religion. Earlier we noted that emerging adults love community but are wary of allowing groups to dictate their behaviour or limit their options. Bibby's findings demonstrate the prevalence of this attitude among Canadian teenagers with regard to religion. Approximately 68 per cent of Canadian youth surveyed in 2008 self-identified with a particular religion, but only two in ten indicate that they attend a religious service weekly or more, and three in ten monthly or more.[52] The discrepancy between theory (mere identification) and practice (attendance) is notable here, and is likely tied to the fact that participation requires a higher level of commitment and investment of resources (time, money, energy), whereas mere identification does not.[53]

---

48. Smith and Snell, *Souls in Transition*, 154. Smith summarizes Moral Therapeutic Deism as follows: "First, a God exists who created and orders the world and watches over human life on earth. Second, God wants people to be good, nice, and fair to each other, as taught in the Bible and by most world religions. Third, the central goal of life is to be happy and feel good about oneself. Fourth, God does not need to be particularly involved in one's life except when God is needed to resolve a problem. Fifth, good people go to heaven when they die." Bibby (*The Emerging Millennials*, 182–83) for the most part sees these values as true also among Canadian youth, although he disagrees that deism is the primary view of God behind these values. Instead, he observes two polarized groups forming, based either in theism or atheism, and so suggests the existence of "Moral Therapeutic Theism," and "Moral Therapeutic Atheism."

49. Smith and Snell, *Souls in Transition*.

50. Penner et al., *Hemorrhaging Faith*, 13.

51. Penner et al., *Hemorrhaging Faith*, 13. Also see Smith and Snell, *Souls in Transition*, 136, cf. 34–38.

52. Bibby, *The Emerging Millennials*, 176, 78.

53. See Smith and Snell, *Souls in Transition*, 80.

When it comes to religious group commitment, then, it appears that some other concerns or distractions are taking precedence. Smith confirms, participation in religious life can easily be disrupted "by social, institutional, and geographical transitions."[54] Further, the "macro distraction from religious devotion" during emerging adulthood is simply the effort it takes in learning to stand on one's own, which includes learning to navigate school, a new job, and even basic life skills.[55] Add to this the time allocated for entertainment, and little room is left for religious activity.[56] So, radical autonomy factors strongly in placing religious group participation on the backburner for many emerging adults. Personal, individual concerns take precedence over that of the (religious) group. Perhaps it is no coincidence, then, that according to Bibby, in 2008 32 per cent of youth chose to identify themselves as "none" with regard to religious affiliation (an increase from 12 per cent in 1984).[57]

Thus is the cultural reality of the emerging adults in Canada (and North America). They value community, relationship, inclusivity, and options. They spurn that which smacks of exclusivity. What does this mean for religions with their particular values and (especially for our purposes) doctrines? Christian Smith summarizes the implications well. He states that while being highly accepting of different religions,

> none of what is distinctive about any given religious tradition, history, worldview, worship style, and so on matters all that much to emerging adults. They suspect these particularities might separate people of different religions, might bring into question the equal value of different cultures, might imply implicit judgments against others who are different. Emerging adults can easily see a religious particularity as carrying an implicit claim to being not merely somebody's personal preference but the right way, by conviction, to think about and do things religiously. *Such implication does not seem inclusive but rather*

---

54. Smith and Snell, *Souls in Transition*, 75, cf. 76.

55. Smith and Snell, *Souls in Transition*, 76, 77, cf. 34–38.

56. Smith and Snell, *Souls in Transition*, 78. Also see Penner et al., *Hemorrhaging Faith*, 15–17.

57. Bibby, *The Emerging Millennials*, 176; also see Smith and Snell, *Souls in Transition*, 104. According to Smith, 27 per cent of American 18- to 23-year-olds identified themselves as "Not religious." Confirming the trend of non-attendance among emerging adults in the USA, David Kinnaman (*You Lost Me*, chapter 1) states, "The ages eighteen to twenty-nine are the black hole of church attendance; this age segment is 'missing in action' from most congregations."

exclusive and judgmental and so does not sit well with the majority of emerging adults.[58]

While the extent to which these cultural values are applied among emerging adults will likely not sit well with many Pentecostals (and many Christians in general), this is the cultural reality in which Canadian (and North American) Pentecostals find themselves. Further, it would be surprising if these cultural factors did not influence the values of emerging adults within Pentecostalism, and so to that issue we now turn.

EMERGING ADULT PENTECOSTAL MINISTRY TRAINEES: A SNAPSHOT FROM MASTER'S COLLEGE AND SEMINARY

Master's College and Seminary (MCS) is a ministerial leadership training institution of the PAOC, serving eastern Canada.[59] In December 2013, I administered an anonymous, voluntary survey among the undergraduate stream of students in an effort to determine whether or not the current cultural realities affecting emerging adults in Canada in general were impacting students ages 18–29 at MCS. I designed the survey to focus on student beliefs concerning the most particular of Pentecostal doctrines—Spirit baptism as an experience subsequent to conversion and tongues as initial evidence—as well as the PAOC's denominational policy requiring evidence of tongues for eligibility for ministerial credentials. 162 of 166 completed surveys were accepted for analysis.[60] The scope and implications of such a survey are admittedly limited, but some of the results are worth mentioning here because they show some indication that Canadian Pentecostal emerging adults share similar cultural values with Canadian emerging adults in general. What follows are three tables summarizing the responses of three questions most pertinent to our interests, along with some brief commentary.

---

58. Smith and Snell, *Souls in Transition*, 81 (emphasis added).

59. See http://www.mcs.edu/. The undergraduate college stream of this institution is located in Peterborough, Ontario, and as of fall 2013 there were approximately 200 students (women and men) taking courses at the campus. MCS also offers online courses, but those students were not included in this study.

60. Four students were disqualified because they were over thirty years old. In some cases students did not respond to questions (or in a clear way), which is why some totals are below 162. The survey questions are available from the author upon request.

Table 1: Spirit baptism is an experience subsequent to conversion

Student Responses		
Options	Number	%
Strongly Disagree	1	1%
Somewhat Disagree	6	4%
Mostly Agree	26	17%
Agree	53	34%
Strongly Agree	68	44%
Total Responses	154	100%

A high percentage of students, almost eight in ten, advocated agreement or strong agreement with Spirit baptism as a subsequent experience to conversion, while a significant number agreed with reservations. Only 5 per cent identified themselves in overt disagreement. It is notable that the results here do not indicate any significant divergence with PAOC doctrine.

Table 2: Tongues is the initial evidence of Spirit baptism

Student Responses		
Options	Number	%
Strongly Disagree	8	5%
Somewhat Disagree	44	28%
Mostly Agree	45	29%
Agree	35	22%
Strongly Agree	25	16%
Total Responses	157	100%

Among the respondents, 38 per cent agreed or strongly agreed that the initial evidence of Spirit baptism is tongues. About one in three were less certain about this, but were willing to be identified as mostly agreeing. One third somewhat or strongly disagreed with this doctrine. There is, then, significant support for this belief, but less so than belief in a subsequent Spirit baptism experience. This is perhaps expected, since the tongues qualifier more narrowly delineates what qualifies as an authentic Spirit baptism experience. Students were not as confident in affirming this more restrictive conviction.

Table 3: Only those who have spoken in tongues should be eligible for PAOC ministerial credentials

Student Responses		
Options	Number	%
Strongly Disagree	63	39%
Somewhat Disagree	34	21%
Mostly Agree	25	16%
Agree	26	16%
Strongly Agree	12	8%
Total Responses	160	100%

Finally, we come to the most practical of all the questions in the survey, and admittedly the one that was of primary interest to me. It is one thing to say one adheres to PAOC doctrines of Spirit baptism and the initial evidence of tongues, but what if one has not spoken in tongues? Should that disqualify one from credentialed ministry? Among the emerging adult students surveyed, six in ten somewhat or strongly disagreed with this denominational policy of the PAOC (almost four in ten fell into the strongly disagree category). Only 24 per cent were confident or very confident of this policy, with 16 per cent agreeing but apparently with some doubts. So, the majority do not believe the PAOC has this one right. Despite general adherence to PAOC related doctrines, most of the students reject this policy that would restrict people from being credentialed leaders in the denomination. An important question is, *why?*

The answer to this is not reducible to any one factor, but likely falls into one or all of three broad categories: (1) biblical/theological, (2) philosophical, and/or (3) psychological/empathetic. In other words, students likely show disagreement with PAOC policy because (1) they are not confident in biblical/theological reasons provided, and/or (2) they disagree philosophically concerning the weight allocated to the initial evidence doctrine in the credentialing process, and/or (3) psychologically they empathize with someone else who might find themselves ineligible for credentials due to having not spoken in tongues (since it is not the respondent him/herself that faces credential ineligibility). Noteworthy in this regard, and not shown in Table 3, is that of those 97 who disagreed with the PAOC policy, 69 report having spoken in tongues and 27 do not (one left this answer blank). This means that about 72 per cent of those who disagreed with the policy are doing so for reasons other than that it would personally disqualify them from credentialed ministry.

The first two tables indicate that there is general support for the PAOC doctrines of Spirit baptism and initial evidence, so theological differentiation is less likely an option among the survey respondents when it comes to reasons why they disagree with PAOC credential policy concerning the tongues requisite. It is not unreasonable to conclude, then, that the primary reasons for disagreeing are predominantly philosophical and psychological/empathetic. In other words (and in keeping with the empathy predicted in the *Hemorrhaging Faith* report), there is strong reluctance to exclude when it is not entirely clear that such a move is necessary. This conclusion is supported by the reasons actually provided by students themselves as to why they responded to the questions the way they did. Among those students who offered reasons, the following themes are common among those who disagreed with the policy concerning tongues being necessary for credentials. Representative comments in the students' own words have also been provided.[61]

- God, not humans organizations, should be the judge of qualifications for ministry.

  "...How dare someone in authority make the judgment of whether or not someone should be allowed to be a pastor? ... They could have a wonderful heart and love God more than anything, but you will not allow them to become a pastor because of one gift that God gives?"

- Character is more important than speaking in tongues (or other spiritual gifts).

  "One who may speak in tongues but shows no bearing of the fruits of the Spirit should not be credentialed while one who shows that fruit, and other gifts of the Spirit, is denied those credentials."

- The doctrine is unscriptural, or, if Spirit baptism is affirmed, there are serious doubts about the initial evidence angle.

  "Since this doctrine has its weaknesses, I do not believe those who disagree should be barred from holding credentials."

61. All the comments selected here are from students who report having spoken in tongues, meaning that they are not personally disqualified from attaining credentials on the basis of the PAOC policy.

- Many good people will be excluded from ministry with this policy.

    "We are missing out on utilizing a large part of the body of Christians who clearly have been called to full-time vocational ministry. They embody Pentecostalism and hold the Holy Spirit in high esteem. This breaks my heart."

- It is unloving, unfair, or weird to exclude anyone from credentialed leadership just because they have not spoken tongues.

    "Completely an exclusive thought not freeing or loving at all."
    "That's a little weird. What if someone didn't speak in tongues until they were 50, does that mean they have to wait until then to be a credential holder?"
    "Oh goodness this thought is medieval."

- As long as someone is pursuing Spirit baptism, that ought to be sufficient.

    "As long as they believe in the doctrine and are pursuing the baptism I do not think they should be denied credentials."

In sum, the results of the survey are what we might have expected. Emerging adults training for Pentecostal ministry in Canada reflect the values of emerging adults in the broader culture, including values of community, inclusivity (openness to diversity and aversion to exclusion), and aspects of radical autonomy. Overall there is less confidence in doctrines that appear to be too exclusionary or limit options (note, for example, the greater acceptance in general of the Spirit baptism as subsequent doctrine as compared to the initial evidence doctrine). Cultural values are perhaps most evident, however, in the reluctance to see people excluded from ministerial credentials based on the lack of a particular spiritual experience. This means that the PAOC (and other North American Pentecostal denominations) are currently facing a challenge from within when it comes to their distinctive Pentecostal doctrines, and my hunch is that this will only become a more acute issue in the years ahead.

Pentecostal Preaching and Ministry

ASSESSING AND ADDRESSING THE CHALLENGE: A PROPOSAL

So how are Pentecostals to respond? Just because strongly-held values of inclusivity and high tolerance exist among emerging adults does not make them correct (or incorrect for that matter). And simply acquiescing to cultural values by changing doctrine and policy is not an appropriate means of preserving adherence among emerging adults, since doing so might undermine what are considered highly important (and biblically supportable) communal institutional values, central to Pentecostal identity. At the same time, if Pentecostals ignore or choose not to respond to the current cultural realities among emerging adults, the ongoing charge of elitism with regard to their doctrine and policy will remain uncontested, potentially compounding the issue, since emerging adults are far less apt than previous generations to accept ideas they perceive to be elitist or exclusionary. So, is there a way forward?

The challenge here is to take into consideration the cultural ethos of emerging adults in Canada, while attempting also to preserve Pentecostal values and beliefs concerning Spirit baptism and tongues.[62] This is no easy task, but one that needs to be undertaken if Canadian Pentecostals are to engage culturally in the days ahead with the younger generation of Pentecostals. In response I am proposing a way forward that is not so much innovative theologically, as it is pragmatic. I believe that if Pentecostals want to continue to pass on their values and beliefs to upcoming generations, then Pentecostals must take the current cultural reality among emerging adults seriously. This means being willing to consider that something might be learned from the current cultural values held by emerging adults, specifically with regard to inclusivity and community, and that what we might learn may provide impetus to take a second look at the core biblical text from which Pentecostals derive their theology surrounding Spirit baptism and initial evidence, namely Acts 2. Emerging adults should also be willing to learn from the wisdom of previous generations and perhaps question the extent to which cultural values should influence their Pentecostal beliefs and policies. But my main emphasis here will be to explore potential points of convergence between

---

62. Bradley Noel proposes that Pentecostals need to be more interested in preserving values than specific beliefs and doctrines; Noel, *Pentecostalism, Secularism, and Post Christendom*, chapter 9.

emerging adult values and Pentecostalism, rather than simply critiquing emerging adult culture.

I propose that two general steps be taken in response to the emerging adult cultural reality. First, Pentecostals need to do some self-reflection on their own tradition to see historically where exactly they might converge (or diverge) with emerging adult values. Just as emerging adults are influenced by broader culture, so too older and previous generations of Pentecostals were influenced and shaped by the cultural realities of earlier times—including influence upon the way doctrines were articulated and denominational policies developed.[63] Such self-reflection might demonstrate that Pentecostals and emerging adults actually share (to an extent) some values, such as radical autonomy and even inclusivity (albeit in different ways and for different reasons). Recognizing this will hopefully reduce some of the tension leading to impulsive rejection of values that appear to threaten institutional identity.

Step two is for Pentecostals to open themselves to the possibility that there may be more communal, ecclesiological ways of interpreting their core beliefs concerning Spirit baptism and tongues, and specifically how they read Acts 2. Here I will not propose anything new, but briefly highlight some recent Pentecostal approaches to reading Acts 2 that demonstrate a greater willingness to wrestle with the ecclesial elements evident in the passage. I do this in an effort to encourage Pentecostals toward taking a communal and ecclesiological approach more seriously as a means by which to reflect upon their doctrine of Spirit baptism and initial evidence, and related policies. These steps are not intended to be *the* solution to the emerging adult challenge, but they are, I believe, necessary ones for Pentecostals to take as a way of addressing it.

Step One: Self-Awareness and Pentecostal Doctrine of Spirit Baptism

We learned earlier that emerging adults in North America value personal autonomy, while at the same time valuing diversity, community, and inclusivity, so long as the group does not lord it over the individual too much or exclude someone except for very good reason. But did not early Pentecostals exemplify a comparable value with emerging adults

---

63. I have argued extensively elsewhere that Pentecostal experience of God needs to be understood as mediated through culture and tradition. See Neumann, *Pentecostal Experience*, especially chapter 2; also see Neumann, "Whither Pentecostal Experience?"

concerning the way they viewed institutions? The evidence is that Pentecostals have from the outset exhibited an uneasy relationship with institutional and traditional Christianity, and that they valued personal autonomy in ways similar to the emerging generation.[64] Institutions, along with their doctrines and policies, were generally viewed as being "man made,"[65] and so overly restrictive when it came to the work and leading of the Spirit.[66] Practical realities eventually determined that Pentecostals would form institutions like the PAOC, but they did not have to be happy about it. As Canadian Pentecostal theologian, Randall Holm, succinctly quips, "Pentecostals are not necessarily anti-institutional, they just do not like institutions."[67]

When it comes to theological reflection on corporate Christianity, then, Pentecostal ecclesiology is "underdeveloped."[68] Veli-Matti Kärkkäinen observes that Pentecostal ecclesiology is rather "ad hoc" to allow "much room for improvisation."[69] So, what tends to be valued are flexible institutional structures that allow the missional task of the church to be accomplished in an efficient and most of all effective way.[70] This is what has led to preference for congregational autonomy in such denominations as the PAOC.[71]

What is it that shaped this penchant for personal autonomy and individualism? Among early Pentecostals it was not postmodernism, since this philosophical movement did not yet exist.[72] More likely individualism and autonomy were values socialized from the modernistic culture in which Pentecostalism emerged.[73] Kenneth J. Archer has done excel-

64. Neumann, *Pentecostal Experience*, 133–60.

65. Faupel, "Whither Pentecostalism?" 21. This is readily seen in early Pentecostal literature. See for example, Spurling, *The Lost Link*; and Parham, *A Voice Crying in the Wilderness*, 22.

66. Althouse, "Ecclesiology," 69.

67. Holm, "A Paradigmatic Analysis."

68. Althouse, "Ecclesiology," 69.

69. Kärkkäinen, "Ecclesiology," 73.

70. Albrecht, *Rites in the Spirit*, 243.

71. Althouse, "Ecclesiology," 70.

72. We earlier noted that Penner et al seem to identify radical autonomy as emerging from postmodernism, for example. James K. A. Smith, however, argues that postmodernism, rightly understood, values community and history (Smith, *Who's Afraid of Postmodernism?* 109–46). Also see Noel, *Pentecostalism, Secularism, and Post Christendom*, 75–76.

73. Lewis, "Towards a Pentecostal Epistemology," 16.

lent work demonstrating the degree to which modernism affected early Pentecostalism, in particular with regard to the way they interpreted and used the Bible. Archer argues that while Pentecostals hardly shared all the assumptions of modernism, they were nevertheless influenced by aspects of cultural modernity, and thus might be best labelled "paramodern."[74]

Included among the aspects of modernism that did affect Pentecostals is the value of personal autonomy, so long as this did not violate explicit biblical norms. This value is one shared with emerging adults, although the latter perhaps exercise this in a more radical way. It should also not be forgotten, however, that early Pentecostals were quite radical in their attitude toward ecclesial policies and church creeds—such were viewed as sure ways to quench the Spirit's work.[75] The preference for autonomy also made the avoidance of schism much lower on the list of priorities for Pentecostals, to say the least. Pentecostals, while desiring the unity of the Spirit on the one hand, found it easy to break relationships with other churches, often over relatively minor differences.[76] Both emerging adults and earlier Pentecostals share an overly lax view of the importance of historical institution and community bonds.

This focus on personal autonomy can also be seen in what Pentecostals accent regarding their doctrines of Spirit baptism and tongues. Pentecostals tend to emphasize that Spirit baptism is a *personal experience for the individual believer*. Of course, it is an experience ultimately *for others*, in that the Spirit comes to empower one for more effective ministry and service.[77] Yet this remains a highly individualized experience,[78] and the ecclesiological dimensions are largely eclipsed in Pentecostal articulations of Spirit baptism and initial evidence doctrines.

When it comes to providing a biblical exposition of these beliefs, Pentecostals generally emphasize the *repeatability* of the experiences with the Spirit recorded in the book of Acts for believers today. What is less evident in traditional Pentecostal use of Acts, and sometimes missing

74. Archer, *A Pentecostal Hermeneutic*, 29–34.

75. Jacobsen, *Thinking in the Spirit*, 357–58.

76. Anderson states, "The legacy for Pentecostals is that they have been responsible for more divisions in the last 100 years than it has taken the rest of Christianity 2,000 years to produce. Ironically, the more Pentecostals divided, the more they multiplied. But this does not absolve guilt in bringing disunity to the body of Christ." See Anderson, "To All Points of the Compass."

77. See for example, Menzies, *Empowered for Witness*, 175.

78. Spittler, "Spirituality, Pentecostal and Charismatic," 1097.

altogether, is emphasis on the *non-repeatability* of the Pentecost event, in other words, its historicity—its embeddedness in time and space in God's salvation story. This latter emphasis is needed in order to understand Pentecostal experience within a more robust communal, ecclesial context.

The typical Pentecostal penchant for the Spirit baptism experience of Acts 2 as primarily being personal and repeatable is exemplified by AG theologian, Stanley M. Horton's (1916–2014) articulation of the classical Pentecostal position on this doctrine.[79] He emphasizes the experiential dimension, stating, "Please do not close your mind when I speak of experience. Spirit baptism is an observable and intensely personal experience, not just a doctrine."[80] More specifically, when it comes to supporting this doctrine using Acts 2, he highlights the following points. (1) Spirit baptism is a distinct experience from conversion. (2) Supporting this, Acts 2 was not the birthday of the church, but the empowering experience of its members.[81] (3) This was an experience for each and every believer: "No doubt, all 120, as well as the 3,000 who also believed that day, were filled with the Spirit. That is, they had, 'a full, satisfying experience.'"[82] (4) Concerning tongues speech, this was understood by the foreign Jews visiting Jerusalem on Pentecost, but was actually praise speech directed toward God.[83]

In sum, Horton's emphasis is that Spirit baptism is a personal empowering experience (although it happened simultaneously to many believers), made evident outwardly by tongues. That this experience is repeatable is stressed by his insistence that Pentecost is not the church's birthday (i.e., not the historical beginning of the church). While Horton makes some important observations, what is missing is that there is really no real mention of the communal or ecclesial significance of tongues,

---

79. Horton is a good representative of the classical Pentecostal position. He is one of the contributors to the discussion on the meaning of Spirit baptism in Brand, ed., *Perspectives on Spirit Baptism*, 47–94, cf. 94–104. Also see Mittelstadt, *Reading Luke-Acts*, 69. Mittelstadt says Horton's earlier book, *What the Bible Says about the Holy Spirit*, is arguably "the most influential defense of Spirit baptism toward the close of the twentieth century."

80. Horton, "Spirit Baptism," 48.

81. Horton, "Spirit Baptism," 56–57, cf. 56–71.

82. Horton, "Spirit Baptism," 59.

83. Horton, "Spirit Baptism," 71–72, cf. 71–78.

and the historical implications for the church are downplayed in the effort to accent individual repeatability.

In response to Horton, Ralph Del Colle (1954–2012) observes that this Pentecostal understanding of Spirit baptism "lacks ecclesial interpretation."[84] The experience, in other words, is not sufficiently integrated into the broader corporate life and history of the church. So, even though Horton uses the word "church," when he mentions that Pentecost is the church's empowering, in the rest of the discussion he does not address what Spirit baptism or tongues might *mean* for the corporate life of the church. The emphasis instead is on the repeatability of the experiences had by the disciples of Acts 2 for individual believers today.

Other scholars defending the traditional Pentecostal view of Spirit baptism and initial evidence have likewise tended to underplay the ecclesial and historical dimensions of the Acts 2 story while defending their view that the outpouring of the Spirit on Pentecost was a gift for empowering and not new spiritual life, and also a repeatable experience for believers of all ages.[85] Such an emphasis has biblical warrant, but the vigorous defence of this position is also due to its being tied to Pentecostal institutional identity.[86] The Spirit baptism and initial evidence doctrines, which distinguish Pentecostalism from other denominations and traditions, require an emphasis on repeatable individual experience. The ecclesial dimension of the Acts 2 story, however, is not immediately necessary to the defence of these doctrines, and this is perhaps why it too often receives insufficient attention.

When personal experience is emphasized without adequate reference to what this means for the church corporate, it is easy for *have* and *have not* categories to develop. And when categories become institutionalized, some may find themselves unintentionally but *officially* excluded rather than included. In light of the emerging adult reality, especially their desire for inclusivity and abhorrence of exclusion, a reading of the

84. Del Colle, "Response by Ralph Del Colle," 101–4.

85. Robert P. Menzies and Roger J. Stronstad are two such Pentecostal scholars. While at times Menzies and Stronstad do begin to explore the ecclesial implications of Acts 2, this element tends to be eclipsed by their accent on the repeatability of the Spirit baptism experience for the individual, as opposed to the communal implications. See Stronstad, *Charismatic Theology*; Stronstad, *Prophethood of All Believers*; Menzies, *Empowered for Witness*; Menzies, *Pentecost: This Story Is Our Story*; and Menzies and Menzies, *Spirit and Power*. For a review of their contributions see Mittelstadt, *Reading Luke-Acts*, 51–54, 58–59.

86. Noel, *Pentecostalism, Secularism, and Post Christendom*, 41.

Acts 2 narrative that pays attention to the historically non-repeatable, as well as communal (ecclesial) elements of the Pentecost experience with the Spirit may help to accentuate the inclusive dimensions of Spirit baptism and tongues. Such a re-reading holds the potential to challenge both traditional Pentecostals and emerging adults to loosen their fixation on autonomy and personal experiences with the Spirit, and to introduce a more inclusive ethos within institutional Pentecostalism. So, having taken the first step of self-awareness, we now move to the second step, a brief look at some Pentecostal attempts to draw out the ecclesial implications of Spirit baptism and tongues.

Step Two: Reading Acts 2 through an Ecclesial Lens

One important question worth asking when reading the Pentecost story in Acts 2 is this: Is the story primarily concerned with the experience of individual believers or with the corporate experience of the church? Applications for both can be inferred from the text, but what if a communal lens was applied to the reading, as opposed to a more modernistic lens of personal autonomy and individual experience? Might this help Pentecostals nuance the way in which they articulate their doctrines of Spirit baptism and initial evidence toward greater sensitivity to communal and ecclesial matters?

Above I suggested that the Pentecostal emphasis on personal experience and autonomy is possibly reflected in the emphasis on the *repeatability* of the Acts 2 story. While I believe this is an important element that Pentecostals must preserve, this does not entail ignoring the reality of the *non-repeatable* aspects of the Pentecost story. In fact, Assemblies of God, USA theologian Anthony D. Palma acknowledges exactly this in his book, *The Holy Spirit: A Pentecostal Perspective*: "The coming of the Holy Spirit upon the waiting disciples on the Day of Pentecost was unprecedented. In a very important sense, it was a unique, historic, unrepeatable event . . . It was a historical-redemptive event."[87] So, the repeatability/non-repeatability of Pentecost is not an either/or but a both/and issue. If both aspects are not given sufficient attention, our understanding of Spirit baptism and tongues will be deficient.

---

87. Palma, *The Holy Spirit*, 110. Elsewhere Palma states that the Spirit constitutes the church (60–64).

What might surface if we temporarily bracket out the repeatable and individual aspects of the Acts 2 story and focus on its non-repeatable, ecclesial dimensions? In other words, what if we read the text with an eye for the community-shaping elements of the story? Fortunately, a number of Pentecostal scholars have been giving attention to just this way of reading Acts 2. Here, referencing some of these scholars, I will highlight three ecclesial features that emerge when reading Acts 2 through a communal lens.

Pentecost as a Historical Community-Shaping Event

The first ecclesial feature to note is simply that *Pentecost is a historical community-shaping event*. This emphasis on history and event has been downplayed by Pentecostals in an effort to distance themselves from the idea that Pentecost is the church's birthday and to distinguish the disciples' conversion from their empowerment.[88] This does not mean, however, that we need to abandon the historicity and uniqueness of the event, and its permanent significance for the shaping of the church. In other words, regardless of whether the church did or did not begin on the day of Pentecost, the church was not the same after Pentecost; the outpouring of the Spirit changed things forever.

Perhaps no Pentecostal theologian better emphasizes this point than Simon K. H. Chan. Chan's contribution to Pentecostal theology is largely found in his work on ecclesiology, spirituality, and liturgy.[89] One of his main contentions is that in order for Pentecostals to pass on (tradition) their doctrines and experiences, they need to develop a more robust ecclesiology.[90] In fact, it is the Pentecostal tendency to view experience of the Spirit ahistorically (i.e., overly personal without reference to the Trinity's overall work in and through the church in history) that has made it weak in its traditioning abilities.[91] Pentecostals have too easily been willing to distance themselves from the broader church tradition,

---

88. The position that denies Pentecost as the church's birthday (held by Robert Menzies and Roger Stronstad) finds recent support in Twelftree, *People of the Spirit*, 75, cf. 21–22. Twelftree argues that the church began earlier at Jesus' calling of the twelve apostles (Luke 6:12–16).

89. On Chan's ecclesiology and pneumatology see Neumann, *Pentecostal Experience*, 218–49.

90. Chan, *Pentecostal Theology*, 35.

91. Chan, *Pentecostal Theology*, 11–23.

focusing instead on personal experiences with the Spirit. But in doing so they have failed to recognize that the Spirit and church go hand in hand—Spirit baptism is a communal event even more so than personal. States Chan:

> A basic problem in Pentecostalism is that it is hardly aware of this communal context of Spirit baptism. The Pentecostal reality has tended to be understood as individualized experiences. My relationship with God is primary, while my relationship with others is secondary. But the truth of the matter is that we cannot conceive of fellowship with God apart from fellowship in God through the Spirit. There is no question of priority. Our relationship with the triune God at once brings us into the fellowship with the saints, since no real communion with God as possible without our being baptized into the body of Christ, the church. Yet all too often Pentecostals are more concerned with their "personal Pentecost" than with the corporate reality of which each person has his share.[92]

For Chan, Spirit baptism and ecclesiology are inseparable. The way he arrives at this conclusion is in large part through the way he interprets the historical event of Pentecost. In short, Pentecost is the day on which Jesus, the "Spirit-baptizer," poured out the Spirit, thereby fully revealing the identity of the Spirit as the third Person of the Trinity. There would simply be no Trinitarian theology without the historical day of Pentecost.[93] Pentecost, then, is not simply an event in the life of the church, but also in the life of the Triune God.[94]

But how does this relate specifically to ecclesiology? In what sense is Pentecost a community-forming event? Chan explains:

> Now, the story of the Spirit is about his coming to the Church making the Church an inextricable part of the Spirit-event. The story of the Church is part of the story of the Spirit since the basic identity of the Spirit is spelled out in relation to his coming to the Church. We cannot talk about the Spirit without at the same time talking about the Church and vice versa. The Church, therefore, is part of the Trinitarian narrative because she is part of the story of the Spirit. The Church is thus more than an agent to carry out the mission of the Trinity; she is part

---

92. Chan, "Mother Church," 180–81.

93. Chan, "Jesus as Spirit-Baptizer," 141.

94. Chan, "The Church and the Development of Doctrine," 73; also see Chan, *Liturgical Theology*, 35.

of the Trinitarian mission itself. Mission is more than what the Church does but what the Church *is*.[95]

Chan thus advocates a "pneumatological ecclesiology,"[96] and reciprocally an "ecclesial pneumatology."[97] In other words, church and Spirit need to be understood as inseparable. The Spirit gives the church its unique essence (ontology),[98] and actually places the church into the story of the Trinity by indwelling the church, uniting it to Christ, and by forming it into the temple of the Spirit.[99]

The upshot is that Pentecostals need to seriously consider Chan's insistence that Pentecost is a unique non-repeatable event that permanently shapes the believing community. The historical church, with all its shortcomings, is the creation of the Spirit. Therefore belonging to the Spirit-community needs to be taken far more seriously than it often has been. Individual experiences of Spirit baptism, therefore, must be understood within this broader communal reality. In this perspective the church is elevated from being viewed as a group to which one might decide to belong (or not), to being the people of God, the body of Christ, and temple of the Spirit to which each believer is inexorably bound.

This communal view, derived from the Acts 2 story itself, surely should challenge Pentecostals of all generations—emerging adult or older—to rethink their willingness to treat the church as a body of people with whom fellowship is optional when certain personal preferences are not met. This should challenge traditional Pentecostalism's willingness to schism sometimes at the drop of a hat. It should also challenge emerging adults to realize that belonging to the global church in most cases means belonging to a denomination as a local, tangible expression. This reality also requires appreciating that at times there are necessarily larger and more complex institutional issues at play, and that commitment and patience are needed as part of belonging.

---

95. Chan, "Jesus as Spirit-Baptizer," 142 (emphasis original).
96. Chan, "Jesus as Spirit-Baptizer," 142.
97. Chan, *Pentecostal Theology*, 99.
98. Chan, *Liturgical Theology*, 22–23, 27.
99. Chan, "Jesus as Spirit-Baptizer," 142–48.

Pentecost Accents Diversity and Inclusivity

The second ecclesial feature to observe from looking at Acts 2 through a communal lens is that *Pentecost accents the simultaneously diverse and inclusive character of the church community*, and this is expressed primarily through the sign of tongues. It seems to me that an important question to ask about the Pentecost story is why God chose tongues to be the unique sign accompanying the church's Spirit baptism. When viewed through the lens of personal experience, the answers to this are woefully deficient because tongues is viewed as a mark or "evidence" that one has had a particular experience with the Spirit. Tongues, then, is reduced to an outward sign pointing to my personal experience. But why tongues and not some other sign? If an outward sign is needed simply to indicate that one has had a specific and personal experience with God, could not just about any marker do?[100]

Menzies suggests that tongues specifically "fits the bill" as evidence (for personal Spirit baptism) because it is not only proclamatory speech, but also identifiably supernatural, since the disciples spoke beyond their natural ability in unknown languages.[101] Still, however, this does not quite answer the question as to why it was tongues specifically. After all, presumably God could have caused the disciples to speak with prophetic, inspired speech in their own language, but of unusual high volume—supernaturally loud beyond human ability! Would this not have equally sufficed as evidence of Spirit baptism? Why not, if the point was simply to identify that one has had a personal spiritual experience?

Viewed through a communal lens perhaps things become clearer. An ecclesial approach to understanding the tongues of Acts 2 means asking: What would be the significance of having the community (not, for the moment, individuals) speak in the tongues of the nations? From this angle, tongues may be understood not simply as an indicator of a personal divine-human encounter, but more significantly, as a signpost pointing to the meaning of Spirit baptism for the church corporately. Personal evidence, then, would perhaps be relegated to a secondary issue. The tongues of Pentecost serve to identify the way in which God is shaping the community of God's people by the Spirit to bear witness to Christ.

---

100. I take up this question at a more popular level in Neumann, "Why Tongues and Not Purple Hair?" 18–19.

101. Menzies and Menzies, *Spirit and Power*, 127.

On this matter, Frank D. Macchia is an important contemporary Pentecostal theological voice. In his work he has attempted to revision Pentecostal theology by broadening an overly narrow understanding of Spirit baptism.[102] Macchia advocates that the church is structured charismatically (i.e., shaped by the Spirit) because the ecclesial community functions only as a direct result of Spirit baptism, and is thus the "*ecclesial Spirit.*"[103] Here, however, our attention will be given to a few of Macchia's observations concerning the theological significance of the tongues of Pentecost for the church community.

First, Macchia prefers the word "sign" to "evidence" when speaking of tongues, the former being a far richer term to describe the meaning of this experience for believers.[104] Second, with regard to its connection to Spirit baptism, "tongues occupies a privileged role because it signifies the meaning of this empowering experience."[105] As mentioned above, tongues serves as a visible signpost to reveal the meaning of the Spirit being poured into the church. Among Pentecostals, Macchia sees tongues as serving as a sacrament of sorts, "an audible means of making God present."[106] Through tongues God is encountered; he discloses himself, revealing his character and his will.[107] Thus the tongues of Pentecost are intended to reveal something of God's character, and how, by the Spirit, the church is being caught up into relationship with God and into the divine mission.

The fact that tongues occurred in the context of community on Pentecost is significant for Macchia. Experience of the Spirit cannot be fully appreciated alone but is more completely realized "in solidarity with others in koinonia."[108] As I summarize elsewhere, "In this way, tongues can function to restrain unbridled Pentecostal individualism, while simultaneously engendering appreciation for the necessity and blessing of structured elements of corporate liturgy, such as the Lord's Supper."[109] Re-

102. Macchia, *Baptized in the Spirit*; cf. Neumann, *Pentecostal Experience*, chapter 3.

103. Macchia, *Baptized in the Spirit*, 155, 56 (emphasis original).

104. Macchia, "Tongues as a Sign," 68.

105. Neumann, *Pentecostal Experience*, 189; cf. Macchia, *Baptized in the Spirit*, 172.

106. Macchia, "Tongues as a Sign," 62, cf. 61–76.

107. Macchia, "Sighs Too Deep for Words," 48, 54, 55, 57.

108. Macchia, "Sighs Too Deep for Words," 65.

109. Neumann, *Pentecostal Experience*, 191; Macchia, "Sighs Too Deep for Words," 67; and Macchia, "The Question of Tongues," 124.

lated to this, Macchia observes that tongues on Pentecost signify a "differentiated unity."[110] When the disciples spoke in unlearned but intelligible languages, it signified an invitation to people of "all languages, races, cultures, classes and genders"[111] that they are welcome to be participants in God's redemptive missional activity—it is a sign of inclusivity.[112] For this reason, Macchia believes that Pentecost may also be understood as both a fulfilment and reversal of the story of Babel (Gen 11), "rejecting its oppressive homogeneity, while affirming the diversity of all cultures and peoples in the fulfillment of the kingdom."[113] So, summarizes Macchia, "Spirit baptism thus implicitly undercuts any efforts to oppress or unjustly discriminate based on differences of gender, race, social class, or physical/mental capabilities. Spirit baptism intends to grace all of creation with the dignity of being accepted, called, and gifted of God."[114]

Macchia has more to say about tongues, but the above is sufficient to demonstrate that tongues is more than a sign that one has had an experience with the Spirit.[115] Viewed from a historical, communal perspective, tongues signifies how the Spirit was (and is) shaping the church. Also notable here is that on Pentecost, tongues definitely did not serve to exclude, but to accent the broad, inclusive scope of who was welcome to participate in God's in-breaking kingdom.[116]

Applied to the emerging adult challenge, might the fact that the Acts 2 story has a strongly inclusive emphasis at least cause Pentecostals to more strongly consider inclusivity as a primary value of the Spirit? Of course, any claims to truth are going to be exclusive to some degree—and this is not simply a challenge for Christians, but for any individual, group, religion, or movement that proposes to articulate a belief or value as *true*. It is naïve to think that everyone can be included in everything, so that no one will ever find themselves excluded. Nevertheless, the inclusive trajectory of Acts 2, the foundational Pentecostal story, should give

---

110. Macchia, *Baptized in the Spirit*, 212.

111. Neumann, *Pentecostal Experience*, 192.

112. Macchia, "Groans Too Deep for Words," 149–73.

113. Neumann, *Pentecostal Experience*, 192; Macchia, *Baptized in the Spirit*, 211–22; Macchia, "Babel and the Tongues of Pentecost," 36–47; and Macchia, "'I Belong to Christ,'" 5–7.

114. Macchia, *Baptized in the Spirit*, 219.

115. See Neumann, *Pentecostal Experience*, 192–94.

116. Similar observations concerning racial and cultural inclusivity have been made by Solivan, *The Spirit, Pathos and Liberation*, 166–78.

Pentecostals ample reason to pause and reflect. In light of the tongues of Acts 2 pointing to inclusivity, it does seem awkward that in Pentecostal denominations the initial evidence doctrine is applied in a way that practically excludes some believers. In short, it may be that the emerging adult penchant for inclusivity finds support in the Pentecost story itself.

Pentecost and the Goal of Koinonia

The third ecclesial feature to emerge from looking at Acts 2 through a communal lens is that *Pentecost accents the Spirit's goal of koinonia, forming and shaping loving relationships in the church*. Pentecostals typically highlight the first verses of Acts 2—the Spirit's outpouring and tongues. Perhaps less typical in Pentecostal discussion of Spirit baptism are the last few verses, Acts 2:42–47.[117] While Spirit baptism empowers for prophetic witness, the longer-term outcomes are portrayed in these verses. It is notable that Roger Stronstad believes these verses deserve more attention, as they reveal the "inner life of the prophetic community."[118]

Stronstad discusses this passage in *The Prophethood of All Believers*, and identifies four characteristics of the Spirit-empowered community's inner life: "(1) the apostles' teaching; (2) fellowship; (3) the breaking of bread; and (4) prayer."[119] Apostolic teaching revolved around explanation and interpretation of the words and works of Jesus' life. Fellowship is shown in concrete ways, such as "sharing property and possessions."[120] The breaking of bread refers to the specific receiving of the Lord's Supper with its focus on the crucifixion. And prayer, generally corporate, is emphasized throughout Luke and Acts as "the environment in which God acts."[121] Finally, Stronstad notes that the result of these activities is

---

117. "They devoted themselves to the apostles' teaching and fellowship, to the breaking of bread and the prayers. Awe came upon everyone, because many wonders and signs were being done by the apostles. All who believed were together and had all things in common; they would sell their possessions and goods and distribute the proceeds to all, as any had need. Day by day, as they spent much time together in the temple, they broke bread at home and ate their food with glad and generous hearts, praising God and having the goodwill of all the people. And day by day the Lord added to their number those who were being saved" (NRSV).

118. Stronstad, *Prophethood of All Believers*, 77, cf. 77–80.

119. Stronstad, *Prophethood of All Believers*, 77.

120. Stronstad, *Prophethood of All Believers*, 78.

121. Stronstad, *Prophethood of All Believers*, 79, cf. 80.

profound unity among believers.[122] What Stronstad begins to help us appreciate is the connection between the outpouring of the Spirit and the bonding of the disciples in fellowship (*koinonia*). This is a point that should not be missed, since it highlights that the Spirit's goals are largely, if not ultimately (as Chan would argue) ecclesial—the outpoured Spirit is building the community of prophets in loving relationship.

One other contemporary Pentecostal voice worth bringing into this discussion is Amos Yong. In his book, *Spirit of Love: A Trinitarian Theology of Grace*, he attempts to draw on resources from the Pentecostal tradition in the development of a theology of love. Among the significant biblical resources for Pentecostals are the twin volumes of Luke–Acts. Yong believes that a study of Lukan pneumatology can reveal "how the gift of the Spirit in Acts unveils divine love."[123] While the word "love" does not actually appear in Acts,[124] Yong points out that the Spirit in Acts is "nothing less than the gift of God," graciously and unconditionally bestowed on God's people.[125] It is true, he notes, that the "most immediate" reason for the giving of the Spirit in Acts is to "enable prophesying," but what needs to be kept in mind is the ultimate purpose of this ability, namely that God "desires to save all people, even the whole world." So, God gives the Spirit as gift, who brings power, but with the universal goal of redemption in view.[126]

In the Pentecost story, one of the less immediate effects of the "gift of the Spirit" can be seen in the offer of forgiveness made in Peter's first sermon (Acts 2:38). Here, Yong believes, the "divine gift of grace" may be seen "as the positive capacity to receive forgiveness."[127] Further, the universal scope of this offer is not just geographical but eschatological: "forgiveness of sins and the gift of the Spirit are not only available to the ends of the earth but also to the ends of time."[128] When it comes to Acts 2:42–47, which concerns the longer-term effects of the Spirit's outpouring, Yong makes two important observations. "First, the charismatic experience of the Spirit graciously empowers altruistic benevolence." Early

---

122. Stronstad, *Prophethood of All Believers*, 80.
123. Yong, *Spirit of Love*, 93.
124. Yong, *Spirit of Love*, 94.
125. Yong, *Spirit of Love*, 95.
126. Yong, *Spirit of Love*, 95.
127. Yong, *Spirit of Love*, 96.
128. Yong, *Spirit of Love*, 97.

believers selflessly gave of what they had in order to help and bless others. Second, Pentecost "formed a community of the Spirit, a fellowship . . . affectively united by joy, practically bound together by generosity, and spiritually-oriented worship." The initial outpouring of the Spirit was, then, "a baptism of love," resulting in "a gracious community of love."[129]

The contributions of Yong and Stronstad allow Pentecostals to expand the application of what might typically be considered a result of Spirit baptism. When the concluding verses of Acts 2 (vv. 42–47) are taken into account, we find a portrayal of Spirit baptism that emphasizes love, self-giving, and self-sacrifice as further evidences of the Spirit's presence and enabling. It should also not be missed that the commitment of the early church believers to one another was hardly one that was held lightly or easily abandoned. The community was not a commodity to be consumed and disposed of when fellowship became less convenient or raised demands on the individual. The Spirit-inspired *koinonia* of the early church involved a far deeper sense of obligation and responsibility to and for one another.

Applied to the emerging adult challenge, the above shows that the trajectory of Spirit baptism is associated with the shaping of a community that exemplifies *koinonia*—shared purpose, love, acceptance, unity, commitment, and inclusivity. But we also see that this Spirit-generated love within the ecclesial community was a love that created a willingness in individuals to give of themselves (self-sacrifice) for the sake of the community. Both of these emphases reinforce the observations made earlier, and can serve to encourage and challenge older Pentecostals and emerging adults to appreciate the importance of community, along with the sacrifice necessary to attain the unity of the Spirit.

CONCLUSION

This essay has argued that the emerging adult reality introduces unique challenges to classical Pentecostal articulations of Spirit baptism and tongues as initial evidence. The high value of personal autonomy, relationships, and inclusivity among this age group shapes them to readily identify aspects of Pentecostal doctrine and policy, especially with relation to tongues, as being unnecessarily exclusivist and elitist. This is a reality that Pentecostals in Canada (and North America) cannot ignore.

---

129. Yong, *Spirit of Love*, 97–98.

In response, I have not proposed that Pentecostals should simply acquiesce to cultural values by changing their doctrines in an effort to appease emerging adult sentiments. Instead, I have acknowledged that the situation is complex, but also urged that Pentecostals take a fresh look at the Pentecost story through a communal lens as a way forward in attempting to address the emerging adult challenge. Doing so provides theological resources to enable Pentecostals to speak not only about individual experience with the Spirit, but also the implications of Spirit baptism for the ecclesial community. An ecclesial look at Acts 2 identifies sometimes overlooked points of convergence with some emerging adult cultural values, namely inclusivity, love, and unity. At the same time Acts 2 contains resources to challenge the anemic view emerging adults, and even older Pentecostals, sometimes hold toward the church corporate. A greater awareness of the meaning of Spirit baptism through reading the Pentecost story through a communal lens can only serve to enhance Pentecostal understanding of the presence and activity of the Spirit in the world today, and may serve to help unify generations within the Pentecostal tradition. The Spirit of Pentecost is, after all, poured out for both "young" and "old" (Acts 2:17).

BIBLIOGRAPHY

Albrecht, Daniel E. *Rites in the Spirit: A Ritual Approach to Pentecostal/Charismatic Spirituality*. Journal of Pentecostal Theology Supplement Series. Sheffield: Sheffield Academic Press, 1999.

Althouse, Peter. "Ecclesiology." In *Handbook of Pentecostal Christianity*, edited by Adam Scott Stewart, 69–73. DeKalb, IL: Northern Illinois University Press, 2012.

Anderson, Allan H. "To All Points of the Compass: The Azusa Street Revival and Global Pentecostalism." *Enrichment Journal* (Spring 2006). No pages. Online: http://enrichmentjournal.ag.org/200602/200602_164_allpoints.cfm.

Archer, Kenneth J. *A Pentecostal Hermeneutic for the Twenty-First Century: Spirit, Scripture and Community*. Journal of Pentecostal Theology Supplement Series. New York: T. & T. Clark, 2004.

Arnett, Jeffrey Jensen. "Emerging Adulthood: A Theory of Development from Late Teens through the Twenties." *American Psychologist* 55 (2000) 469–80.

Augustine, Daniela C. "The Empowered Church: Ecclesiological Dimensions of the Event of Pentecost." In *Toward a Pentecostal Ecclesiology: The Church and the Fivefold Gospel*, edited by John Christopher Thomas, 157–80. Cleveland, TN: CPT, 2010.

Bibby, Reginald W. *The Emerging Millennials: How Canada's Newest Generation Is Responding to Change and Choice*. Lethbridge, AB: Project Canada, 2009.

Brand, Chad Owen, ed. *Perspectives on Spirit Baptism: Five Views*. Nashville, TN: Broadman & Holman, 2004.

Chan, Simon K. H. "Mother Church: Toward a Pentecostal Ecclesiology." *Pneuma* 22 (2000) 177–208.

———. *Pentecostal Theology and the Christian Spiritual Tradition.* Journal of Pentecostal Theology Supplement Series. Sheffield: Sheffield Academic Press, 2000.

———. "The Church and the Development of Doctrine." *Journal of Pentecostal Theology* 13 (2004) 57–77.

———. *Liturgical Theology: The Church as Worshiping Community.* Downers Grove, IL: IVP Academic, 2006.

———. "Jesus as Spirit-Baptizer: Its Significance for Pentecostal Ecclesiology." In *Toward a Pentecostal Ecclesiology: The Church and the Fivefold Gospel*, edited by John Christopher Thomas, 139–56. Cleveland, TN: CPT, 2010.

Del Colle, Ralph. "Response by Ralph Del Colle." In *Perspectives on Spirit Baptism: Five Views*, edited by Chad Owen Brand, 101–4. Nashville, TN: Broadman & Holman, 2004.

Faupel, D. William. "Whither Pentecostalism?" *Pneuma* 15 (1993) 9–27.

Fee, Gordon D. "Toward a Pauline Theology of Glossolalia." In *Listening to the Spirit in the Text*, 105–20. Grand Rapids: Eerdmans, 2000.

Government of Canada. "Canadian Multiculturalism: An Inclusive Citizenship." Accessed 14 January 2014. http://www.cic.gc.ca/english/multiculturalism/citizenship.asp.

Hill, Jonathan P. *Emerging Adulthood and Faith.* Calvin Shorts Series. Grand Rapids: Calvin College Press, 2015.

Holm, Randall. "A Paradigmatic Analysis of Authority within Pentecostalism." PhD diss., University of Laval, 1995.

Horton, Stanley M. "Spirit Baptism: A Pentecostal Perspective." In *Perspectives on Spirit Baptism: Five Views*, edited by Chad Owen Brand, 47–94. Nashville, TN: Broadman & Holman, 2004.

Jacobsen, Douglas G. *Thinking in the Spirit: Theologies of the Early Pentecostal Movement.* Bloomington: Indiana University Press, 2003.

Kaiser, Walter C. "The Baptism of the Holy Spirit as the Promise of the Father: A Reformed Perspective." In *Perspectives on Spirit Baptism: Five Views*, edited by Chad Owen Brand, 15–46. Nashville, TN: Broadman & Holman, 2004.

Kärkkäinen, Veli-Matti. "Ecclesiology." In *Global Dictionary of Theology: A Resource for the Worldwide Church*, edited by William A. Dyrness and Veli-Matti Kärkkäinen, 251–62. Downers Grove, IL: IVP Academic, 2008.

Kinnaman, David. *You Lost Me: Why Young Christians Are Leaving Church—and Rethinking Faith.* Grand Rapids: Baker, 2011.

Lewis, Paul W. "Towards a Pentecostal Epistemology: The Role of Experience in Pentecostal Hermeneutics." Paper presented at the Annual meeting for the Society for Pentecostal Studies, Church of God Theological Seminary, Cleveland, TN, March 12–14, 1998.

Macchia, Frank D. "Sighs Too Deep for Words: Toward a Theology of Glossolalia." *Journal of Pentecostal Theology* 1 (1992) 47–73.

———. "The Question of Tongues as Initial Evidence: A Review of *Initial Evidence*, edited by Gary B. Mcgee." *Journal of Pentecostal Theology* 1 (April 1993) 117–27.

———. "Tongues as a Sign: Towards a Sacramental Understanding of Pentecostal Experience." *Pneuma* 15 (1993) 61–76.

———. "Groans Too Deep for Words: Towards a Theology of Tongues as Initial Evidence." *Asian Journal of Pentecostal Studies* 1 (1998) 149–73. Online: http://www.apts.edu/ajps/98-2/98-2-macchia.htm.

———. "'I Belong to Christ': A Pentecostal Reflection on Paul's Passion for Unity." *Pneuma* 25 (2003) 1–6.

———. "Babel and the Tongues of Pentecost: Reversal or Fulfilment?—a Theological Perspective." In *Speaking in Tongues: Multi-Disciplinary Perspectives*, edited by Mark J. Cartledge, 34–51. Studies in Pentecostal and Charismatic Issues. Bletchley, UK: Paternoster, 2006.

———. *Baptized in the Spirit: A Global Pentecostal Theology*. Grand Rapids: Zondervan, 2006.

Menzies, Robert P. *Empowered for Witness: The Spirit in Luke–Acts*. Journal of Pentecostal Theology Supplement Series. Sheffield: Sheffield Academic Press, 1994.

———. *Pentecost: This Story Is Our Story*. Springfield: Gospel Publishing, 2013.

Menzies, William W., and Robert P. Menzies. *Spirit and Power: Foundations of Pentecostal Experience: A Call to Evangelical Dialogue*. Grand Rapids: Zondervan, 2000.

Mittelstadt, Martin William. *Reading Luke–Acts in the Pentecostal Tradition: Reflections on the History and Status of Research*. Cleveland, TN: CPT, 2010.

Neumann, Peter D. "Whither Pentecostal Experience? Mediated Experience of God in Pentecostal Theology." The 40th Annual Meeting of the Society for Pentecostal Studies, Memphis, TN, March 10–12, 2011.

———. *Pentecostal Experience: An Ecumenical Encounter*. Princeton Theological Monographs. Eugene, OR: Pickwick, 2012.

———. "Why Tongues and Not Purple Hair? Tongues and the Meaning of Pentecost." *Testimony* (June–July 2012).

Noel, Bradley Truman. *Pentecostalism, Secularism, and Post Christendom*. Eugene, OR: Wipf & Stock, 2015.

Palma, Anthony D. *The Holy Spirit: A Pentecostal Perspective*. Springfield, MO: Logion, 2001.

Parham, Charles F. *A Voice Crying in the Wilderness*. Baxter Spring, KS: Apostolic Faith Bible College, 1910.

Penner, James, et al. *Hemorrhaging Faith: Why and When Canadian Young Adults Are Leaving, Staying and Returning to Church*. N.p.: The EFC Youth and Young Adult Ministry Roundtable, 2012.

Pentecostal Assemblies of Canada. *General Constitution and by-Laws*. Mississauga, ON: Pentecostal Assemblies of Canada, 2010. No pages. Online: https://www.paoc.org/about/what-we-believe.

Setran, David P., and Chris A. Kiesling. *Spiritual Formation in Emerging Adulthood: A Practical Theology for College and Young Adult Ministry*. Grand Rapids: Baker, 2013.

Smith, Christian, and Patricia Snell. *Souls in Transition: The Religious and Spiritual Lives of Emerging Adults*. Oxford: Oxford University Press, 2009.

Smith, James K. A. *Who's Afraid of Postmodernism? Taking Derrida, Lyotard, and Foucault to Church*. The Church and Postmodern Culture. Grand Rapids: Baker Academic, 2006.

Solivan, Samuel. *The Spirit, Pathos and Liberation: Toward an Hispanic Pentecostal Theology*. Journal of Pentecostal Theology Supplement Series. Sheffield: Sheffield Academic Press, 1998.

Spittler, Russell P. "Maintaining Distinctives: The Future of Pentecostalism." In *Pentecostals from the Inside Out*, edited by Harold Smith, 121–34. The Christianity Today Series. Wheaton: Victor, 1990.

———. "Spirituality, Pentecostal and Charismatic." In *The New International Dictionary of Pentecostal and Charismatic Movements*, edited by Stanley M. Burgess, 1096-1102. Grand Rapids: Zondervan, 2002.

Spurling, Richard G. *The Lost Link*. 1920. Reprint, Middletown, DE: Bonilla, 2013.

Stronstad, Roger J. *The Charismatic Theology of St. Luke*. Peabody, MA: Hendrickson, 1984.

———. *The Prophethood of All Believers: A Study in Luke's Charismatic Theology*. Journal of Pentecostal Theology Supplement Series. Sheffield, UK: Sheffield Academic Press, 1999.

Twelftree, Graham H. *People of the Spirit: Exploring Luke's View of the Church*. Grand Rapids: Baker Academic, 2009.

Van Gelder, Craig. *The Essence of the Church: A Community Created by the Spirit*. Grand Rapids: Baker, 2000.

Yong, Amos. *Spirit of Love: A Trinitarian Theology of Grace*. Waco, TX: Baylor University Press, 2012.

9

Pentecostal Spirituality amidst Other Spiritualities
Religious and Secular

Lyman Kulathungam

Canada may be post-Christian or even post-religious, but she seems to be vibrantly spiritual. Amidst her consumerism, scientism, secularism, and agnostic atheism, she exhibits a spirituality that seeps through not only religious, but also secular sectors of society. Religion is often identified with spirituality; yet, one may be spiritual without being religious. One may be meticulously involved in religious ritualism without manifesting any expressions of spirituality. Hence, spirituality may be taken in a broader sense; encompassing religion for some, while able to stand alone for others without any religious affiliations. Spirituality taken in this broader sense is applicable to the Canadian populace.

During the past century, despite the demise of organized religion, there has been a significant global resurgence of religiosity at the grassroots level. My book, *The Quest*, explores how various religious communities are involved in a search to be freed from the predicament in which they perceive themselves: a salvific quest.[1] Significantly, such a salvific quest exhibits a pronounced spiritual overtone. The contemporary Canadian multicultural mosaic provides an ideal arena for people of various religious persuasions to be actively involved in different modes of spiritual expression.

1. Kulathungam, *The Quest*, xiii–xv.

Spirituality also finds its way into the most unexpected sectors of Canadian secular society: scientific, literary, medical, and ecological quarters. Adherence to spiritual practices outside the ambit of religion may be taken as "Secular Spirituality." The volume *Spirituality and the Secular Quest* in the World Series on Spirituality shows the academic world's acknowledgement of such a brand of spirituality.[2] As Roger Housden observes, we as humans "live on the edge of a fullness of life that, while constantly available, seems all too often to be just out of reach. A lack, or sense of incompleteness that gives rise to a longing for something beyond the known, and that cannot be spoken."[3] He identifies this as an expression of spirituality, unbound by any religion.

Canadian Pentecostal Spirituality figures amidst such a multifarious mix of spiritualities. The question arises as to how Pentecostals relate to spiritualities outside their domain. Some Pentecostals ignore the question and live in splendid isolation. Some brand it as demonic and feel it needs to be exorcised. Some accommodate it articulating a pluralistic stance, very much in line with the pluralistic Christology that John Hicks propagates,[4] while some attempt to present Pentecost condescendingly as a superior spirituality.

Our proposal points out that Pentecostal Spirituality is not only relevant to these spiritualities, but could also productively relate to the aspirations of those involved in them. But for this to be articulated, we need to show that the very character of Pentecostal Spirituality facilitates such a task. We intend to explore avenues that would enable it to fulfill such a role and thereby exhibit its relevance and positive impact in the contemporary Canadian world of vibrant spirituality. In the context of this alternative proposal, the above-mentioned stances seem either inappropriate or inadequate.

Spirituality, in whatever mode it shows itself, seems to be a universal human phenomenon that arises out of a search—a leap beyond the material and the mundane. It appears to stem from the very makeup of human personhood. From a Christian perspective, the ontological basis for such spirituality is the fact that God is Spirit and we as humans are created in His image (Gen 1:27). This provides the rationale to claim that we humans have a spiritual component in our very makeup. As God's image,

---

2. Van Ness, ed., *Spirituality and the Secular Quest*.
3. Housden, "Secular Spirituality," para. 2.
4. For example, see Hick, *God Has Many Names* and *Religious Pluralism*.

we reflect a spirituality, however damaged it may be. Just like an image is geared to reflect the original, we strive to be spiritual whether we believe in God or not. This seems to be the motivating factor for all expressions of human spirituality. It is what makes Pentecostal spirituality relevant to other spiritualities. After all, Pentecostals are also human! Such relevance will never become outdated so long as humans are humans with a spiritual component.

Moreover, Pentecostal Spirituality has the potential to fulfill the core spiritual aspirations of all people. In relating Christ to the salvific aspirations of faith communities, *The Quest* presents him as the one who could meet such aspirations on account of his unique personhood.[5] Similarly, Pentecostal Spirituality could fulfill the spiritual aspirations of people, both religious and secular, due to its unique character. In order to articulate this, we need to first identify the aspirations of these spiritualities. Then we need to find out what in Pentecostal Spirituality renders it capable to fulfill such aspirations.

SPIRITUALITY IN THE RELIGIOUS CONTEXT

The predicament from which Christ frees humanity is at its core due to spiritual default. Hence, God's salvific quest accommodates the spiritual. Christology and Pneumatology may be demarcated disciplines in theological academics, but in God's economy they are two facets of the same quest. His spiritual quest, which is manifested in the ministry of the Holy Spirit, is intertwined with His salvific quest orchestrated through Christ.

Various religious communities orchestrate their salvific strategies, adopting different spiritual modes. Hinduism, Sikhism, Buddhism, Taoism, and Islam, which are popular in Canada, exhibit certain significant features. These spiritualities commence with the human being, viewed as one with a spiritual component. Hinduism and Sikhism identify this as Soul (*athma*). *Tao*, the "God" of Taoism is both transcendent and immanent. The human being, as a part of the immanent *Tao*, figures as the soul in Taoism.[6] For Islam, the human soul that Allah created out of a single soul (Quran 4:1),[7] will be spiritually fulfilled when it achieves peace

---

5. Kulathungam, *The Quest*, 19–37.
6. Kulathungam, *The Quest*, 74–79.
7. All quotations from the Quran are from Ali's *The Holy Quran: Text, Translation and Commentary*.

through submission to Allah (Quran 5:105). Though Buddhism denies the soul as a permanent entity, it acknowledges the human being as a dynamic stream of consciousness which figures as the reference point of its spirituality. Commencing from the human being, these communities orchestrate their salvific strategy adopting various spiritual modes such as the Hindu *Margas*, the Buddhist Eightfold Path, the Taoist *Tai-Chi* and the Islamic Five Pillars, along with Sufi mysticism and Jihadist aggressive maneuvers.

Hindu Spirituality

The Hindu ways of devotion (*Bhakti Marga*), spiritual knowledge (*Jnana Marga*), and selfless actions (*Karma Marga*), all working within the ambit of the Law of Karma, have a pronounced spiritual undertone. They attempt to free one from the cycle of rebirths (*samsara*) in order to attain "salvation" (*moksha*). Hindus are reputed for their devotion enacted through prolonged fasting sessions, pujas, pilgrimages, devotional self-tortures, and worship in temples. They strive to do good works as a means to elevate their status in the next birth. They believe that ignorance of one's true identity is that which keeps them in bondage. *Maya* causes such spiritual blindness. Hence, true spiritual knowledge is the way out. Transcendental Meditation provides one such way.

Transcendental Meditation, based on Vedanta Hinduism, takes God as Cosmic Consciousness (*Brahman*), which includes the human soul (*athma*). Deceived by *Maya,* we are not aware of who we really are, as part of the Divine, causing spiritual blindness. Transcendental Meditation frees us from such a predicament by enabling us to realize our true divine identity. The following diagram presents its strategy.

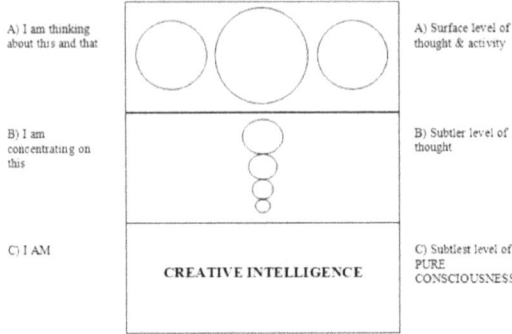

Figure 1

The circles in the first level indicate our restless preoccupation with this and that, but concentrating on one thing amidst several takes us to the next level. When concentrating, we gradually lose awareness of even that one thing too. The shrinking size of the single circle in the second level shows this. Finally, we end up in a state of being fully conscious, but not of anything in particular; the subtlest level of Pure Consciousness. The absence of circles in the third level indicates this. When we reach this "I Am" stage, we become aware of our identity as part of the Divine Cosmic Consciousness, and this frees us from bondage. Hence, Transcendental Meditation, though popular as a practice to reduce health problems, is essentially a meditational mode to gain spiritual knowledge that liberates.[8] Through such ways, Hinduism presents a salvific spirituality geared to free one from bondage.

Buddhist Spirituality

Buddha's first sermon on *The Four Noble Truths* presents a way of liberation. The first three truths describe human existence as suffering (*dukka*) that the transitory nature of all phenomena (*anicca*) generates. What causes human bondage is craving (*tanha*) that arises out of a warped view of who the craver is and what is being craved. The craver thinks that a permanent soul is at his or her core, and things craved are everlasting. Buddha, however, taught that soul has no permanent identity (*anatta*) and the world is transitory (*anicca*). The tragedy is that humans crave, unaware that both the craver and the things craved are transitory.

---

8. Kulathungam, "Christian Meditation," 22–37; and Kulathungam, *The Quest*, 158–59.

Buddhism came out of Hinduism, so some of the core concepts of Hinduism are also found in Buddhism. One such concept is *Maya*, or deceptive nature. It is *Maya* that causes people to be deceived about their identity and about the world.

As a way out, Buddha presents the Eightfold Path as his fourth truth: right views, right intention, right speech, right action, right livelihood, right effort, right mindfulness, and right concentration.[9] These steps fall into three activities—gaining knowledge (*prajna*), moral conduct (*sila*), and meditation (*samadhi*)—providing the steps by which a seeker attains enlightenment (*Nirvana*). One starts with understanding one's true self that seeks and the world that is sought. This knowledge enables proper moral conduct, which leads one to meditate. Since craving is embedded in one's mental state, it needs to be rectified through meditation (*Bhavana*) that generates wisdom (*prajna*). "Wisdom" here is experiential and spiritual at its core, enabling enlightenment: a personal intuitive moment in which one sees the "nothingness" of all that appears to be real, the *Nirvanic Moment*.[10] Based on Buddha's sermon, early Buddhism presented a salvific way that articulated a meditative spirituality; a non-theistic way dependent on self-effort. But subsequent developments in Buddhism, such as the deification of Buddha and resort to *Bodhisattvas* (savior-figures), highlight the inadequacy of self-effort.

Taoist Spirituality

The Taoist *Tai-Chi* is a salvific mode that is more than mere physical exercise. The Way (*Tao*) of Taoism, taken both as transcendent and immanent, is a dynamic way like a flowing river. The human being is part of *Tao* and needs to flow with it. The way out of human bondage was to stop resisting *Tao*. In order to flow with it, they presented *Tai-Chi*.

Tai-Chi is a slow-moving meditative exercise that enables one to flow with *Tao* and reach a state of tranquility (*Wu-Wei*). It is a way directed by the dynamics of *Yin-Yang*. *Yin* and *Yang*, though opposites, are also complementary to each other. The following diagram shows how they relate to each other.

---

9. Radhakrishnan and Moore, eds., *A Source Book of Indian Philosophy*, 275.
10. Kulathungam, *The Quest*, 125.

Figure 2

Yin and *Yang* bulge into each other. There is a dark *Yin* circle in the *Yang* area and vice versa, showing that there is nothing that is totally *Yin* or *Yang*. Taoism sees every facet of life through the lens of *Yin-Yang*.[11]

To flow with *Tao*, one has to first know it, but knowledge based on the Laws of Non-Contradiction and Excluded Middle will not help, since the interplay of *Yin-Yang* challenges the logical foundations of traditional knowledge. For, how could one accommodate these laws and at the same time claim that contradictions are complementary? *Tai-Chi* enables one to cultivate an illuminative insight (*ming*) to flow with *Tao*; such insight is not intellectual but spiritual.[12] Thus *Tai-Chi* exemplifies a spiritually-oriented salvific way based on human effort.

Islamic Spirituality

Associating spirituality with Islam seems strange in a world that links Islam with terrorism. But one can decipher in Islam—both in its orthodox version, its subsequent developments, and even in its militant manoeuvres—a spirituality that makes Pentecost relevant to Muslims.

Islam's five pillars provide a spiritually-oriented salvific way, founded on the dictum: "Submission to God (*Allah*) yields peace (*salam*)." The first pillar *Shahada* declares: "There is no god, but God (*Allah*), and Muhammad is His Messenger." A believer should believe and declare it until death. Acknowledging Muhammad as God's final prophet entails adherence to the other four pillars: Daily prayers performed at least five times daily (*Salat*), tithing (*Zakat*), fasting (*Sawm*), and pilgrimage to Mecca (*Hajj*). When practised with sincerity they exhibit a mode of ritualistic spirituality. But in the course of time rituals tend to become mere formalities. The formalistic practice of the Five Pillars led to religious legalism.

11. Kulathungam, *The Quest*, 76–77.
12. Kulathungam, *The Quest*, 78.

Shi'ites reacting to such legalism introduced certain practices that entailed experiential involvement and had a spiritual overtone. One such practice is Karbala. Shi'ites, who are followers of Ali, Muhammad's son-in-law, revere and remember the tragedy when his son, Hussayn, was brutally killed at Karbala. Shi'ites gather every year to mourn Hussayn's martyrdom, hoping that such mourning will help to rid them of their sins. In the Shi'ite context, Karbala turns out to be a significant spiritual occasion having a transformational impact on its participants.[13]

Sufism is another reaction to Islamic legalism.[14] Sufis strive to submit to Allah experientially, which they claim is more spiritually satisfying. Trance-oriented dances and chants are popular modes of Sufi spirituality. Members of each group are mentored by a guru on a distinctive spiritual path. When they reach the peak point, they claim to become almost one with Allah. No doubt this conflicts with the Islamic view of a transcendent God. Controversial though it may be, the Sufi striving to experience the Divine shows how Muslims want a personal relationship with God.

Quite in contrast with peaceful Sufism, there is Jihadist Spirituality. Jihad's role is both salvific and apocalyptic. In its salvific role it enables the participants to get rid of their sins and enter Paradise without facing the Day of Judgment (Quran 9:111). Traditional Islam interprets *Jihad* as an internal peaceful striving. But the Wahhabis (a branch of Sunni Islam) and their followers highlight verses from the Quran and the Hadith to claim that believers should aggressively fight against infidels (*kafirs*) (Quran Surah 9:29; 8:13–17; 4:101–102; 4:89). They seem convinced that fighting in the cause of Allah will give them direct entry to Paradise.[15]

In its apocalyptic role, Jihad prepares the world for *Mahdi*, the twelfth Imam, now in hiding, to appear and along with Jesus (*Isa*) establish Allah's kingdom (Quran 8:39–40). Surah 8:39 commands believers to fight against anti-Allah forces in order to facilitate total annihilation of evil. The instructions given to jihadist participants highlight Jihad's salvific and apocalyptic roles. The directives given to the 9/11 attackers were meant to assure them that they were involved in a sacrificial spiritual moment in their lives, one that would have lasting consequences in their

---

13. Kulathungam, *The Quest*, 223.
14. Kulathungam, *The Quest*, 199.
15. Kulathungam, *The Quest*, 217–19.

own lives, as well as globally.[16] However controversial Islam is, it exhibits a spirituality that is salvific at its core.

Adopting various modes, these spiritualities articulate a salvific way through human effort. But there lingers a doubt as to whether or not one has arrived. However committed one is to devotional practices, good works, and exhilarating spiritual highs, can they provide the assurance that one is liberated? For instance, the final stage of Transcendental Meditation may give a sense of one's divine identity, a *Moksha* moment, but when the excitement of the moment passes away how does one continue to be assured of one's divine identity? The Taoist tranquility of *Wu-Wei* depends on the balance between *Yin* and *Yang*, which may fall out of balance at any time. In Islam, one can be sure of entrance to Paradise only after death.[17] These ways based on human effort, indicate a need for "assurance of salvation." Pentecostal Spirituality meets that need for it is founded on God's grace rather than on human effort, and the Holy Spirit provides that assurance that "we are the children of God" (Rom 8:16; 1 John 3:24).

Through various methods, these communities strive for a personal relationship with the Divine. Sankara's articulation of Transcendental Meditation, though providing awareness of one's divine identity, lacks the personal relationship with the Divine that seekers crave. This is why his disciple Ramanuja envisioned "Cosmic Consciousness," as a deity to which they could relate.[18] The move from early non-theistic to later theistic Buddhism shows that Buddhists want to relate to a deified Buddha rather than be guided through mere doctrine. Reacting to Islamic legalism, Sufism presents an intimate union with Allah. Pentecostal Spirituality renders a personal relationship with God, which is what these communities desire.

SPIRITUALITY IN THE SECULAR CONTEXT

As noted earlier, Secular Spirituality goes beyond the religious. Peter Van Ness makes a case for the legitimacy of Secular Spirituality, on two grounds. He observes that some portray their practices as spiritual while

---

16. Kulathungam, *The Quest*, 217–18.
17. Kulathungam, *The Quest*, 229–30.
18. Kulathungam, *The Quest*, 146.

not bonding themselves to any religion. Further, he claims that being religious is not a necessary condition for being spiritual.[19]

The World Spirituality Series' inclusion of a volume on secular spirituality under the title "Spirituality and the Secular Quest,"[20] highlights spirituality's relevance to the secular world, particularly in the context of its quest. Those involved in it attempt to get out of the predicament in which they perceive themselves to be by operating outside the framework of religion. Locating such an authentic expression of the human spirit unbound by any religion, Roger Housden concludes that "Secular Spirituality" is not an oxymoron; that one could be secular and yet be spiritual.[21]

Such spirituality finds expression through avenues such as music, art, film, and environmental ethics. In an interview prior to his death, David Bowie, the popular songwriter, made a confession about his career that highlights how spirituality seeps into the realm of music. When asked, "Why do you do what you do?" he responded, "I guess taking away all the theatrics or the costuming and all the outer layers of what I do, I'm a writer . . . I started examining the subject matter that I write about, and it really only boils down to a few songs based around loneliness, to a certain extent couple[d] with isolation, some kind of spiritual search, and a looking for a way into communicating with other people."[22] Music of the *Blues* illustrates how the quest of secular spirituality of African-Americans finds expression through music. The Blues may be taken as secular spirituals. They affirm the bodily expression of the black soul and the quest for Black Identity amidst a culture that obscures even the presence of black people.[23]

The science fiction film, *The Matrix*, excited theologians because of its spiritual overtone. Its central theme is that humans live in a world that is an illusion, manipulated by forces beyond their control. The salvific theme of the film becomes evident with the introduction of Neo as the Christ figure, the one who brings freedom to the people. But the filmmakers swerve away from the gospel when they make this Christ figure a liberator who uses excessive violence to achieve his goals. The directors are unable to go beyond the myth of redemptive violence, a recurring

19. Van Ness, *Spirituality and the Secular Quest*, 68–79.
20. Van Ness, *Spirituality and the Secular Quest*, 68–79.
21. Housden, "Secular Spirituality," 2.
22. Bowie, "Bowie."
23. Cone, "The Spirituals and the Blues," 127.

message of several Hollywood movies. Starting with *Dances with Wolves*, a number of films and television series such as *Avatar*, *Life of Pi*, and *Legends of Tomorrow* contain glimpses of salvific-spirituality.

Ecological Ideology is another area where spirituality seeps both into religious and secular realms. Deep Ecology affirms the intrinsic sacredness of nature, claiming that there is no gap between humans, nature, and the Divine.[24] This generates a pantheistic spirituality. On the other hand, some activists are united in articulating a secular strategy to solve the ecological crisis based on a view of the natural world. Borrowing the name of the Greek earth god *Gaia*, scientist James Lovelock formulated a hypothesis that has almost become the official ideology of various Green Parties. The *Gaia* hypothesis takes biosphere to be a self-regulating entity, capable of keeping our planet healthy by controlling the physical and chemical environment.[25] People are called upon to appreciate and align with the dynamics of nature rather than exploit it. Such a hypothesis exhibits a spiritually-oriented secular strategy to solve the ecological crisis. Similarly, Holistic Medicine views the human being as a living system whose parts are interconnected, which has resources for healing itself. Release from a false sense of self enables cooperating with this living system; orchestrated through psycho-spiritual medical practice. Such expressions of secular spirituality arise from the fact that humans, whether religious or not, have a spiritual component. This motivates them to go beyond the material and mundane.

SPIRITUALITY IN THE PENTECOSTAL CONTEXT

Pentecostal Spirituality figures amidst such a mix of spiritualities. How can it relate to such expressions in a productive manner? A reputed Persian Sufi mystic, Bayazef Al-Bastami (804–874 CE), commented on his spiritual journey, "For thirty years I sought God until I recognized that God was the seeker and I the one sought."[26] Pentecostal Spirituality is just that. It points out that God is the seeker and humans are the sought. God's quest to fulfill humanity's spiritual aspirations is orchestrated through the person of the Holy Spirit.

---

24. Barnhill and Gothlieb, eds., *Deep Ecology and World Religions*, 3.
25. Lovelock, "Gaia," xii.
26. Schwartz, *The Other Islam*, 44.

The pivotal historical moment of such a quest is the Day of Pentecost (Acts 2). It ideally epitomizes God's quest to meet humanity's spiritual aspirations through the ages. The Day of Pentecost did not take the Judeo-Christian community by surprise. Joel, Isaiah, Ezekiel, and Zechariah of the Old Testament era and John the Baptist of the New Testament era prophesied about it.[27] Jesus not only made definitive statements about the Holy Spirit's personhood and mission, but also commanded the disciples to wait for his advent. These anticipatory pronouncements indicate that the Day of Pentecost was not a historical accident but the climax of God's involvement with human spirituality. Such a day sets the precedence for subsequent enactments of Pentecost and provides the parameters for Pentecostal Spirituality.

Since time began, God's quest has been evident. The Creation narrative portrays the Spirit of God hovering over the face of chaotic waters (Gen 1:2). Deuteronomy 32:11 portrays God protecting his people like an eagle hovering over its young. Genesis 6:3 depicts God's Spirit striving with men, indicating the Spirit's redemptive involvement with humanity's cancer of sin. These portrayals point out the creative and redemptive facets of God's quest that, as Steve Studebaker observes, are distinguishable though inseparable.[28]

Even though the term Holy Spirit occurs only three times in the Old Testament (Ps 51:11; Isa 63:10–14), it does not mean that he was absent before the Day of Pentecost. Frequently-used terms like Spirit of God, Spirit of the Lord, My Spirit, the Spirit of Judgment, Spirit of Fire, or Spirit of Justice could refer to the Holy Spirit. In fact, the New Testament references to the Holy Spirit's work in the Old Testament (Matt 22:43; Mark 12:36; Acts 1:16; 4:25; 7:51; Heb 3:7; 2 Pet 1:21) confirm that that these Old Testament expressions refer to the Holy Spirit.

But why did God wait until the Day of Pentecost to reveal Holy Spirit's identity? God, who had brought the children of Israel out of a polytheistic world, naturally wanted them to first become committed to monotheism; to acknowledge him and only him. Despite his repeated warnings, they drifted into worshipping other gods. For instance, even after Gideon had a personal encounter with God, the Israelites Gideon led ended up following other gods. He made a golden ephod, or idol, and the Israelites worshipped it (Judg 8:27). Moreover, even after they

---

27. See Joel 2:28–29; Isa 44:3; Ezek 36:25–28; Zech 4:6–9; Jer 31:31–32, as referred to in Heb 10:15; and John 1:32–33; Matt 3:11–12.

28. Studebaker, *From Pentecost to the Triune God*, 67–78.

had lived through the plagues in Egypt, including the Passover, and had experienced the miracle of the Red Sea, heard God's voice, and seen his presence, within the forty days that Moses was on the mountain they had created another god; a golden calf (Exod 24; 32). Hence, in a context where Israelites were prone to deviate, terms like "Spirit of God" were less confusing than a term like "Holy Spirit," which would have encouraged them to deviate into polytheism. The Old Testament expressions were more conducive to understanding God as one.

In *The Quest*, I have presented a revelatory model that God seems to employ; an object lesson mode when revealing himself as the triune God.[29] Just as the second person of the triune God becomes evident with Jesus' Incarnation, the third person of the triune God becomes evident with the Holy Spirit's descent on the Day of Pentecost. Rodney Stark proposes that God's revelations are always limited to the current capacity of humans to comprehend them—the strategy of "Divine Accommodation."[30] The Holy Spirit's advent facilitated the Judeo-Christian community to comprehend and appreciate a spirituality that exhibits certain unique features.

Such spirituality highlights God the Spirit seeking humans. First and foremost, the Day of Pentecost enacts a spirituality that commences with God seeking humanity. The Day of Pentecost puts a 'Dead End' sign on all who strive to ascend to spiritual heights, following the Babel way (Gen 11:1–9). God the Spirit had to take the initiative since humans on their own are unable to fulfill their spiritual aspirations. Sin makes humans spiritually dead (Eph 2:4). At salvation the Spirit enlivens the dead (Eph 2:5). From then on, the spiritual journey continues, enabled by the Spirit rather than through human effort.

Such spirituality facilitates personal relationship. The spiritual journey of several faith communities shows a striving for personal relationship with the Divine. Pentecost fulfills such a quest. What happened on that eventful day goes beyond an exhilarating experience. It was the Holy Spirit's entrance into the lives of those who waited for him. He is neither a formula to be mastered nor a power to be manipulated, but rather a person, a Divine Person. Baptism in the Spirit comes as a gift of a person who wants to fellowship with those who receive him. Just before his departure, Jesus comforted his disciples that they need not panic since he would send a person like himself, another Counsellor to be with them,

29. Kulathungam, *The Quest*, 21–25.
30. Stark, *Discovering God*, 6.

empowering and guiding them (John 14:15–17). This is what makes Pentecostal Spirituality so unique. It is a spirituality that ushers one into a life of fellowship with the Holy Spirit. In addition, the Spirit makes the departed Jesus real. The Spirit enables one to confess Jesus (1 John 4:2–3), testify about him (John 15:26), glorify him (John 16:4), and acclaim him as Lord (1 Cor 12:3). Living in the Spirit involves personal relationship with the triune God. As Jesus indicated to his disciples (John 14:1), such relationship is both ongoing and abiding.

Such spirituality enables an empowering transformation. As we have noted, people, whether religious or not, aim for a better quality of life through their spiritual practices. Pentecostal Spirituality is essentially transformational. The Spirit that abides also regenerates and empowers, changing the heart of stone into a heart of flesh (Ezek 36:26–28). Jesus commanded his disciples to wait for the Holy Spirit to be endowed with power. The witness of those who were Spirit-baptized on the Day of Pentecost and thereafter exhibits the Spirit's empowerment in their personal life and in the witness of their new-found faith.

Such spirituality encompasses all. Significantly, the Day of Pentecost marks the beginning of the extension of such spirituality to encompass all people. Previously, the Spirit had empowered only certain individuals and only for a specific time and purpose. On this day, however, not only the 120, but also as many as 3,000 people who responded to Peter's sermon, received the Holy Spirit (Acts 2:38). The book of Acts records several Pentecostal occasions that followed that Day (4:31; 8:14–17; 9:1–19; 10:45; 19:1–6). God lavished his Spirit on everyone, regardless of gender, culture, nationality, or ethnicity. This was what Peter alluded to in his sermon (Acts 2:15–21) as fulfillment of Joel's prophecy (Joel 2:8–32). Moreover, the Baptism of the Holy Spirit comes with an extended warranty. Peter told people who inquired about the baptism that the promise was for them, their children, and for those who were far off (Acts 2:39). Since then, the world has seen a multifarious variety of spiritual expressions claiming to be 'Pentecostal.' But in order to identify those that are authentic, we need to find out whether they fall in line with the core features of the Spirituality that the Day of Pentecost, as well as various Pentecostal occasions recorded in the Bible, exhibit.

Such spirituality involves the triune God. The Day of Pentecost highlights God's quest to fulfill people's spiritual aspirations by orchestrating a relationship with them, enhanced through the Baptism in the Spirit. It is God the Father's promise (Acts 1:4), orchestrated by God the

Son, gifting God the Holy Spirit. The triune God—Father, Son, and Spirit are involved in it. Studebaker highlights the vital connection between the Pentecostal experience and the Trinity.[31] For such involvement to become a reality experientially, the sought has to yield to the Seeker. The Baptism in the Holy Spirit is a significant step in this journey of further yielding to the Spirit after salvation. Speaking in tongues plays a vital role in such yielding.

Why Tongues?

The Bible characterizes tongues both in a literal sense as a physical organ (Mark 7:33; Jas 3:5) and in a figurative sense as language. As such, it is an integral part of human personhood. Linguist Noam Chomsky claims language to be an integral part of human nature, which enters into every aspect of human life, thought, and interaction—a species property.[32] Charles Taylor stresses that language is more constitutive than expressive, in that it does not merely describe but constitutes meaning and fundamentally shapes human experience.[33] Though language unites communities, it has a divisive impact, even among those speaking the same language. There has been concerted effort by linguistic philosophers to search for a generative grammar, a syntactical structure that underlies all languages. Chomsky takes 'Babel' metaphorically, depicting the multiplicity of languages that occurred with the demise of a 'universal syntax' that led to not only dividing the human populace, but also depriving language of its core communicative efficacy. With the hope that a common language would unify humanity, the search for the "unknown syntax" figures in the world of linguistics. What is actually needed is a fundamental change in human nature, and this is where Pentecostal Spirituality fits in.

God recognized the corrosive effect of perverted human nature orchestrating a universal language. He saw their vain attempt to build a city with a tower to reach the heavens, to make a name for themselves, and avoid being scattered (Gen 11:5–6). People united by language, enthused by a parochial sense of security, striving to reach the impossible, and hoping to become world-renowned. In fact, God's dispersal through multiplying languages was a redemptive act to prevent such a catastrophic

---

31. Studebaker, *From Pentecost to the Triune God*, 2.
32. Chomsky, *New Horizons*, 3.
33. Taylor, *The Language Animal*, 41–45.

blunder. The Day of Pentecost is God's response to Babel's blunder. On that day he did not offer people a universal language but changed them at their core by providing them a mode of linguistic articulation that united them, edified them, and empowered them to be his witnesses, not only in Jerusalem their comfort zone, but in challenging parts of the world (Acts 1:7, 8; 2:11).

Speaking in an unknown tongue is not the same as *glossolalia*, which is vocalizing of speech-like syllables that lack meaning. For instance, the Hindu Mantras like *aum* are effective in meditation because of their tonal repetition. Unintelligible word combinations are very different from Pentecost's unknown tongue that, though unknown to the speaker, qualifies as a language on the grounds of its intelligibility. The "tongues of men" were intelligible to some of those gathered on the Day of Pentecost (1 Cor 13:1). On the other hand, there are some tongues that only angels understand (1 Cor 13:1), while there is a "tongue" uttering mysteries that is intelligible to only God (1 Cor 14:2). An "unknown tongue" can be interpreted, which implies that it is not meaningless babbling (1 Cor 14:4–5). It should be noted that while "tongues of men" may be interpreted using the rules of language of a particular language, "tongues of angels" and "tongue spoken only to God" do not fall under rules of human language. That does not mean that they are meaningless. Downplaying tongues makes us miss the point of Pentecost. An 'unknown tongue' is not mere gift-wrap to be discarded after Spirit Baptism, but is very much a part of the gift.[34] Moreover, even though speaking in tongues is primarily vocal, that does not exclude sign language as a tongue. Deaf people, too, have legitimate Spirit baptisms, where unknown sign languages figure. Receiving such a gift of the Holy Spirit involves yielding to him; and speaking in tongues, whether vocal or through sign language, is very much part of yielding. Speaking in tongues is a response to the plea of the Spirit, rather than a reaction to the power of the Spirit, like falling or shivering. As James Smith points out "glossolothic prayer expresses a depth of dependency upon God, and thus humility before the divine."[35] On the other hand, being a voluntary act, one may even speak hypocritically in an unknown tongue (1 Cor 13:1). Hence, there could be pseudo spirit baptisms and encounters!

---

34. Kulathungam, "Why Tongues?" 22–37.
35. Smith, *Thinking in Tongues*, 144.

Tongues play a vital role even after Spirit Baptism. As a mode of self-edification, speaking in tongues enriches one's prayer life, making the fruit of the Spirit evident in one's life. Praying in the Spirit fulfills Jesus' prophetic word to the Samaritan woman that a time was coming when true worshippers would worship God, who is Spirit, "in the Spirit and in truth" (John 4:21–24). We should note that the phrases "in the Spirit" and "in truth" are not exclusive but rather inclusive. When one worships in the Spirit it is based on truth and vice versa. Praying "in the Spirit," whether in a known or unknown tongue, whether individually or on a corporate basis, also fulfills the guidelines Jesus gives in the Lord's Prayer.[36] According to Paul, tongues could serve as an avenue for edifying the congregation, provided it is done in an orderly way without disturbing worship, and it is accompanied by interpretation (1 Cor 14:5, 6). When done in that fashion, speaking in tongues encourages both the speaker/s and the hearers in their faith and to become more open to the miraculous.[37]

Speaking in tongues, because of its novelty, also provides evangelistic occasions. If the 120 disciples had just held a traditional prayer meeting without any occurrence of speaking in tongues, people would not have been perplexed. In fact, Peter's sermon was a response to the query about speaking in tongues, "What does this mean?" Three thousand would not have been saved if Peter had not responded to this query!

Pentecostal Spirituality works within the framework of the triune God's quest to fulfill the salvific-spiritual aspirations of humans. Such spirituality is inseparably connected with a personal relationship with the Holy Spirit. One has to voluntarily partner in such a relationship, which entails yielding to the Spirit, and it is here that tongues plays a vital role. How best can such spirituality fulfill aspirations of the contemporary Canadian populace whether religious or secular?

RELATING PENTECOST TO OTHER SPIRITUALITIES

A popular trend in Contemporary Spirituality is its post-modernistic emphasis that subjective experiential knowledge is what renders spiritual

---

36. Jesus introduces the "Lord's Prayer" (Luke 11:2–4; Matt 6:9–13) so as to provide some guidelines for effective prayer. Significantly "praying in the Spirit and in truth," which includes tongues (Rom 8:26; 1 Cor 14:1–4; Jude 20), seems to be very much in line with Jesus' guidelines.

37. Smith, *Thinking in Tongues*, 144, 145.

attainment valid. In a world of religious pluralism and relativism, a subjective experiential criterion for spiritual validity naturally becomes acceptable. Even Pentecostals could be prone to adopt such a stance. Paul's warning to the Corinthian Church seems relevant. Corinth was part of a revival of Greek spiritualism that advocated recourse to multiple intermediaries, the main one being *Logos* (Divine Word), in order to experience a *gnosis*, an intuitive insight. Such illumination renders subjective experiential knowledge to validate spiritual attainment. Paul warns the Corinthian Christians not to get entangled with such spirituality and deviate from the Spirit that they had received on the Day of Pentecost (2 Cor 11:1–4). The common denominator in all Pentecostal experiences is the involvement of the Holy Spirit. Spirituality without the Holy Spirit, however exhilarating the experience may be, is not Pentecostal Spirituality. *Keep Pentecost on track!*

Spirituality involving fellowship with the Holy Spirit, though personal, needs to stay clear of the individualism that looms large in a secular humanistic world; one that often breeds self-importance, self-reliance, and self-arrogance. The Pentecostal journey runs counter to the direction of individualism. A believer's life story is: "I must decrease and He must increase" (John 3:30). But this does not mean that the believer is dehumanized in the hands of an autocratic God. Such a relationship really ushers one into an intimate relationship with a loving God. Moreover, it leads one into authentic relationships with both believers and nonbelievers. This would naturally unite the church as well as make Christian witness more effective.[38] *Keep Pentecost personal, but not individualistic.*

The move to change the church into a theatre and worship into performance is perhaps due to Hollywood showmanship that finds its way into the North American social fabric. Worship geared to performance may meet the rigorous standards of classical or contemporary musicality, fulfill the requirements of artistic production, entertain congregations, and attract crowds: but is it Pentecostal worship? Performance-oriented worship tends to encourage showmanship and separate the platform from the pew, making the congregants onlookers rather than participants. Mega church, super-scripted, digitally timed multiple services naturally put pressure on both pastors and participants. No doubt worship does need to be at its best musically, but it is much more than that. It involves participation of all worshippers as seen on the Day of Pentecost and

---

38. Hazzard and McKenzie, "The Heresy of Individualism," 14.

provides occasion for the ministry of the gifts of the Spirit. The New Testament fellowship of believers (Acts 2:42–47) confirms how spirituality articulated within corporate contours enables church growth. Chandelier acrobatics, prophetic interruptions, altar ministries, exuberant prayer sessions, and congregational tongue talking exhibit participation even though some of them do not meet the stipulations of orderly Pentecostal worship. Nevertheless, if worship "in Spirit and in Truth" is to have a real impact on the congregants, it needs to encourage participation rather than performance. *Keep Pentecost participatory, not performative.*

Warnings about the disaster confronting the earth are loud and clear—a disaster that is traced to human exploitation. Such exploitation calls for change in human ethical behavior. Hence, there is a resort to religions since their value systems tend to mobilize people to preserve the environment.[39] How should Pentecostals respond to such a crisis? Perhaps prompted by hyper-spirituality, Pentecostals tend to denounce earthly existence, claiming, "we are not of this world." Their apocalyptic eschatology may encourage them to adopt an escapist mindset: "What we do to the earth does not matter since we will leave it one day (death or rapture)." They could also become fatalistically indifferent: "Since the present earth is to be replaced by the New Earth (2 Pet 3:6–10), we need not be responsible for the environment now; God will fix it all in the future." In their evangelistic fervour, some tend to concentrate on individual salvation forgetting that individuals need the earth to survive. On the grounds that Christ's redemption and the Spirit's care encompass both humanity and the world, Pentecostals need to be actively involved in solving the ecological crisis. While observing that Pentecostals are underrepresented at the "ecological table," mainly because of their eschatological focus, A. J. Swoboda emphasizes that both ecological justice and ethics need to be part of eschatological witness in the twenty-first century.[40] Such an approach needs to stay clear of both anthropocentric and biocentric approaches. The former assumes that earth and its resources exist only for the benefit of humans and hence may be exploited to satisfy human greed. Preposterous though it may sound, God's mandate to the first humans to have 'dominion' sometimes warrants sacred exploitation! On the other hand, the Deep Ecology biocentric approach affirms the intrinsic sacredness of earth, claiming that there is no gap between

---

39. Tucker and Grim, *Overview of World Religions and Ecology*, 1.
40. Swoboda, *Tongues and Trees*, 227.

humans, nature, and the Divine; a pantheistic spirituality. No doubt the earth is sacred, not because it is divine but because it is God's creation. Since both humanity and the cosmos are flawed and desperately need help, they cannot solve the problem—patients cannot be doctors! We need a strategy that is neither human nor earth centered but Christocentric and Spirit hovered,[41] one that is grounded on the belief that Christ came to save both humans and the world. Adopting such an approach calls on humans to go beyond stewardship, which portrays God to be an absentee landlord, delegating the responsibility of caring for the earth to humans. He is very much involved in the redemptive process and calls on humans to partner with him. Pentecostal spirituality needs to partner in such a venture. *Keep Pentecost down to earth.*

We noted that both religious and secular spiritualties aim to be transformational. They strive through their spiritual practices to free themselves from the predicament in which they perceive themselves. If Pentecostal Spirituality is to meet such aspirations it needs to be connected with its salvific foundations. That is why Paul warns the Corinthians not to deviate from Jesus, the Spirit, and the gospel (2 Cor 11:1–4). The partnership of Pneumatology, Soteriology, and Christology is that which would render Pentecostal Spirituality relevant to the Canadian context. *Keep Pentecost on its salvific foundations.*

In the context of such a mix of vibrant spiritualities offering various strategies, we need to set borders to preserve our identity. But sometimes we make such borders into boundaries, which tend to exclude those striving for a more satisfying spirituality. We need to remember that the Holy Spirit is not only at work within the church, but also outside it, wooing people to Christ. Let us not domesticate Christ and quench the Holy Spirit's universal quest. *Keep Pentecost within borders, not boundaries.*

Canada may be post-Christian, but is far from being post-spiritual. As we have already noted, spirituality is an integral facet of human personhood. As long as humans are humans, one expects from them expressions of some sort of spirituality, either religious or secular. This accounts for the prevalence of spirituality among Canadians. After all, they are humans! In such a context Pentecostal Spirituality could become relevant to them, but for it to adequately meet their spiritual aspirations, it has to be on track. The way the believers lived and witnessed after being baptised in the Holy Spirit, as described in Acts 2:42–47, provides an ideal example

41. Kulathungam, "A Christocentric Anthropocosmic Approach," 1–3.

of how Pentecostal spirituality turned out to be relevant at that time. The Bible records that people came to Pentecost daily. The preaching, execution of various ministries, and the practice of prayer and worship all fell into the ambit of the lifestyle of these Pentecostals. The way they lived revolved around how they ordered their priorities. It was God first, then others, and then the individual. Interestingly, the God they worshipped would have been the triune God, who was very much involved in their baptismal experience. It was the Father's promise, the Son the baptizer, and the Holy Spirit the gift. Hence, they praised and worshipped the triune God. But that did not make them closeted within themselves. They regularly experienced fellowship with their fellow believers. Unselfishly, they shared what they owned with others. In our modern consumerist culture, where satisfying the needs and wants of the individual is all that matters, our priorities seem to be "Me, Myself, and Mine"! The spirituality of Pentecost runs counter to such a culture, but it is precisely this that makes Pentecost relevant to it. Pentecostal spirituality has the potential to slip into performance and showmanship, especially in the orchestration of ministerial gifts such as healing and prophecy and when preaching becomes televised propaganda. Then, however sensational Pentecostal performance could be, it would not be able to meet the spiritual aspirations of Canadians. If spirituality works within the parameters of the Day of Pentecost and does not deviate from the priorities of the early Pentecostals, then it will not become outmoded in Canada. So long as humans are spiritual, Pentecostal Spirituality will remain relevant. Moreover, it will be relatable to the spiritual aspirations of both the religious and secular sectors of the Canadian populace, provided Pentecostals are true to their identity and remain both spiritual and Pentecostal.

BIBLIOGRAPHY

Ali, Abdullah Yusuf, trans. *The Holy Qur'an Text, Translation and Commentary.* Brentwood, MD: Amana, 1989.

Bowie, David, interviewed by Peter Klein. "Bowie on what his songs were all about." CBS 60 Minutes Overtime unaired video, 1:32, 2003. Online: http://www.cbsnews.com/news/david-bowies-unaired-60-minutes-interviews/

Barnhill, David L., and Roger S. Gottlieb, eds. *Deep Ecology and World Religions: New Essays on Sacred Ground.* New York: State University of New York Press, 2001.

Chomsky, Noam. *Language and Mind.* New York: Harcourt Brace Jovanovich, 1972.

———. *New Horizons in the Study of Language and Mind.* Cambridge: Cambridge University Press, 2000.

Cone, James H. *The Spirituals and the Blues: An Interpretation*. New York: Seabury, 1972.

Hazzard, David, and Stacey McKenzie. "The Heresy of Individualism." *Enrich: The Leadership Magazine* (2014) 13–16.

Hick, John. *God Has Many Names*. Philadelphia: Westminster, 1980.

———. "Religious Pluralism and Salvation." In *The Philosophical Challenge of Religious Diversity*, edited by Philip L. Quinn and Kevin Meeker, 54–66. New York: Oxford University Press, 1999.

Housden, Roger. "Secular Spirituality: Oxymoron?" *The Huffington Post Religion Blog*, January 19, 2012. Online: http://www.huffingtonpost.com/roger-housden/secular-spirituality-an-oxymoron_b_1211837.html

Kulathungam, Lyman C. D. "A Christocentric Anthropocosmic Approach to the Ecological Crisis." Presented at the special Religion and Ecology joint panel, convened at the Conference of the Canadian Theological Society and the Canadian Society for the Study of Religion, in conjunction with the Congress of Humanities and the Social Sciences, Brock University, St. Catharines, Ontario, May 26, 2014.

———. "Christian Meditation: Doubts and Hopes." In *Eastern Journal of Practical Theology* 6 (Fall 1992) 22–37.

———. *The Quest: Christ Amidst the Quest*. Eugene, OR: Wipf & Stock, 2012.

———. "Why Tongues?" In *Eastern Journal of Practical Theology* 6 (1992) 22–37.

Lovelock, J. E. *Gaia: A New Look at Life on Earth*. Oxford: Oxford University Press, 1987.

Radhakrishnan, Sarvepalli, and Charles A. Moore, eds. *A Source Book of Indian Philosophy*. Princeton: Princeton University Press, 1957.

Schwartz, Stephen. *The Other Islam, Sufism and the Road to Globalization*. New York: Doubleday, 2008.

Smith, James K. A. *Thinking in Tongues: Pentecostal Contributions to Christian Philosophy*. Grand Rapids: Eerdmans, 2010.

Stark, Rodney. *Discovering God: The Origins of Great Religions and the Evolution of Belief*. New York: Harper Collins, 2001.

Studebaker, Steven M. *From Pentecost to the Triune God: A Pentecostal Trinitarian Theology*. Grand Rapids: Eerdmans, 2012.

Swoboda, A. J. *Tongues and Trees: Toward a Pentecostal Ecology*. Dorchester, UK: Deo, 2013.

Taylor, Charles. *The Language Animal: The Full Shape of the Human Linguistic Capacity*. Cambridge, MA: Harvard University Press, 2016.

Tucker, Mary Evelyn, and John Grim. "Overview of World Religions and Ecology." Presented at the Forum of Religion and Ecology, Yale University, September 15, 2009. Online: http://fore.yale.edu/religion/

Van Ness, Peter H., ed. *Spirituality and the Secular Quest*. World Spirituality Series 22. New York: The Crossroad, 1996.

Index of Subjects

Anglican Church of Canada, 10, 11, 14, 16, 17
Apostolic Messenger, The (newspaper), 112–16
Assemblies of God, USA, 13, 21, 151, 170
Azusa Street, 57, 109, 112, 117n36, 131–32, 136, 140–41, 143

Baptism of the Spirit, 111, 113, 115, 118, 120, 136–37, 140, 149–82, 198, 201
Buddhism, 11, 12, 188–89, 190–91

Canada, Church in, 10–27
Catholicism, 2, 10–11, 15, 16, 58, 81, 82–83, 85, 92–93, 98
Charismata, 58, 112, 144
Christ and Culture, 19–22
Church of God, 86
"Churchianity," 35
Clapham Sect, 95
Classical Pentecostalism, 57, 58, 92
Clergy, 11–12
Congregationalists, 13

Dispensationalism, 115, 120–21
Divinity of Christ, 24

Eastern Orthodox, 58, 92
Ecumenism, 151
Emerging adults, 150–82
Enlightenment, 23–24, 80
Eschatology, 103–23
European Social Survey, 80–81

Evangelical Fellowship of Canada, 153
Evangelicalism, 11, 51–52, 76, 89, 90, 95, 97

Full Gospel, 103, 113–14, 116–17

Globalization, 87
Glossolalia, 56–57, 58, 69n36, 201
Good Report, The (newspaper), 116–20
Great Tribulation, 116n34

Hebden Mission, 13
Hemorrhaging Faith, 153–56, 158, 164
Hinduism, 11, 12, 137, 188–90
Holy Spirit, 4, 12, 26, 33, 35, 37, 39–40, 42, 43–46, 48–52, 54, 57, 58, 59, 61–62, 63–65, 67, 68–76, 103, 107–8, 111, 119, 138–39, 141, 144, 177, 188, 196–206

Immigration, 12, 93, 97
Islam, 11, 12, 87, 96–98, 188–89, 192–94

Joint Declaration on the Doctrine of Justification, 92n54
Judaism, 12, 83
Just war, 96n69

Kingdom of God, 22, 23, 25, 43, 63–65, 89, 106

Latter Rain, 113–15, 122
Liberalization, 15

Index of Subjects

Local church, 47, 49
Lordship of Christ, 19, 23
Lutheranism, 83

Master's College and Seminary, 152, 161–65
Methodists, 13, 15
Missio Dei, 59
Missional, 32–52, 54–76
Missional Pentecostalism, 58–76
Moral relativism, 38, 40
Moralistic therapeutic deism, 47–48
Multiculturalism, 16, 126–46, 156n35, 157

National Study of Youth and Religion, 37–38, 46–48
Neo-Pentecostalism, 55n3, 58
New Testament, 33–34, 60, 70, 121
Nominal Pentecostalism, 56–57
"Nones," 11, 12, 18, 160

Old Testament, 33, 60, 129, 198

Pacifism, 96n69
Pentecost, 128–46, 169–82, 197–206
Pentecostal Assemblies of Canada, 8, 10, 11–13, 15, 85, 104–5, 118–19, 121n48, 132–33, 149, 151–52, 161–65
Pew Research Center, 3n11, 3n12, 96
Pneumatological realism, 32–52, 56n4, 69
Polarization, 16–18,
Post-Christianity in Canada, 3–4, 21, 22–27, 186, 205
Presbyterians, 13
Promise, The (newspaper), 109–11, 115

Prophecy, 59
Prophetic literature, 106–7
Protestantism, 2, 10, 11, 14–15, 46, 58, 81, 83, 85–86, 93, 98

Quiet Revolution, 14

Rapture, 114, 118
Redeemed Church of God, 93–94
Refugees, 132

Scripture, Authority of, 24
Second coming, 105, 107–8, 114, 117–18, 120–22
Secularization, 10–11, 16–18, 79–81, 82, 87
Sikhism, 11, 12, 188
Social justice, 95
Sovereignty of God, 47
Speaking in tongues, 103, 110, 114–16, 136, 163–82, 200–202
Statistics Canada, 11n1

Taoism, 188–89, 191–92
Trinity, 50, 54, 55, 142, 145, 146, 173–74, 199, 200, 206

United Church of Canada, 10, 11, 13–14, 15, 16, 17

Vatican II, 92
Vineyard, 58n11

Wesleyan, 95,
World War II, 15

Youth ministry, 134

Index of Modern Authors

Adedibu, B. A., 94
Airhart, P., 13n13
Alberts, W., 84n25
Allen, R., 67n33
Althouse, P., 168n66
Anderson, A., 151n6, 169n76
Anderson, R., 103n1, 131n15, 136n35, 136n37, 139n46, 141n52
Arblaster, P., 85n29
Archer, K. J., 168–69
Argue, A. H., 112
Arnett, J., 152–53

Bade, K., 93n57
Barnhill, D., 196n24
Bartleman, F., 132n22
Beach, L., 82
Beaman, L., 12n5
Berger, P., 80
Beyer, P., 12n5, 14n15
Bibby, R., 1n1, 2, 15n18, 16, 17n23, 18n30, 24, 81n13, 154n16, 155n21, 156n30, 157, 158n46, 159–60
Bilezikian, G., 49
Billiet, J., 81n11
Bird, M. F., 142n56
Bock, D. L., 130n12, 130n13
Boddy, A., 13
Boersma, H., 130n14
Boeve, L., 83n22
Bonhoeffer, D., 90–91
Boren, M. S., 43n22, 62n21, 63n23
Bosch, D. J., 93n55
Bowen, K., 1n1, 2n4, 17

Bowie, D., 195n22
Bramadat, P., 1n1, 16n21
Breckenridge, J., 143n59, 145n60
Breckenridge, L., 143n59, 145n60
Burgess, R. V., 141n52
Burgoyne, S., 3n9
Butler, E. H., 15n19
Byrne, B., 92n52

Carson, D. A., 20
Carter, C., 21
Chan, S. K. H., 173–75
Chomsky, N., 200
Choquette, R., 14n14
Christians, L., 83n23
Clifford, N. K., 14n16
Collins, A. Y., 106n10
Collins, G. R., 137n39
Collins, J. J., 106n11
Comte, A., 80,
Cone, J. H., 195n23
Courey, D., 79n2, 92n51
Cox, H., 132n20
Creemers, J., 86n30, 92n53

Dawson, L. L., 17n26
Dayton, D., 115n33
de Saint-Simon, H., 80
Del Colle, H., 171
Demart, S., 86,
Di Giacomo, M., 13n10
Dittes, J. L., 91n50
Douara, D., 132n26
Duncan, K., 21
Durham, W., 112

Index of Modern Authors

Eagle, D. E., 2, 81n13

Faupel, D. W., 103n1, 131n15, 168n65
Fee, G. D., 151n5
Ferguson, J., 65–66
Finke, R., 24, 80
Flatt, K., 2n9, 13n13
Flower, J. R., 21
Forde, G. O., 92n51
Foulkes, F., 72n43
Fredrickson, K., 90n46
Freston, P., 94,
Friesen, A. T., 55n3
Fulford, R., 120,
Fung, R. Y. K., 72n42

Gabriel, A., 105
Gane, R., 128n8, 128n9, 128n10, 133n29
Garr, A., 137n38
Garr, L., 137n38
Godwin, C., 86–87, 94n61
Goff, P., 95n66, 131n16, 131n17, 131n18
Gottlieb, R. S., 196n24
Gorski, P. S., 80n4
Grant, J. W., 26
Grim, J., 204n39
Grounds, V., 89
Guder, D., 43n22, 64n26, 64n27

Habermas, J., 84,
Handy, Robert T., 95n66
Hanson, P., 106n11
Hartley, J. E., 129n11
Hartropp, A., 95–96
Haskell, D. M., 2n9,
Hauerwas, S., 82, 88–89, 91
Hazzard, J., 203n38
Hebden, E., 12, 109–11
Hebden, J., 109–11
Hick, J., 187n4
Hodgson, M. G. S., 87n39
Hollenweger, W. J., 131n15
Holm, R., 168
Horton, S. M., 170–71
Housden, R., 187, 195
Hunsberger, G. R., 127n6

Jacobsen, D., 103n1, 169n75
James, W., 89
Jenkins, P., 3, 79, 93
Johnson, V., 103n3
Jones, M. W., 50n32

Kärkkäinen, V. M., 168
Keener, C., 129n11
Kinnaman, D., 36, 153n15, 157n40, 160n57
Klaus, B. D., 139n45
Kulathungam, L., 186, 188, 190n8, 191n10, 192n11, 192n12, 193n13, 193n14, 193n15, 194n16, 194n17, 194n18, 198n29, 201n34, 205n41

Land, S. J., 131n15
Lawler, H., 117
Laws, F., 118
Lee, C., 90n46
Lewis, P. W., 168n73
Linahan, J. E., 97n73
Lindsay, H., 105
Lipka, M., 81n13
Liushi, Z., 3n13
Livermore, D. A., 137n40
Lovelock, J., 196
Lupton, L., 112, 113n25
Luther, M., 113

Macchia, F., 126, 177–78
Manchin, R., 81n12
McAlister, R. E., 117–20
McCracken, V., 96
McKenzie, S., 203n38
Menzies, R. P., 151n4, 169n77, 171n85, 173n88, 176n101
Menzies, W., 151n4, 176n101
Meuleman, B., 81n11
Mills, C. W., 80
Mittelstadt, M. W., 126n3, 170n79
Moltmann, J., 92n51, 95
Moore, C. A., 191n9
Murphy, F., 106n11
Murphy, J. A., 118
Murray, S., 22, 24–27, 82

Index of Modern Authors

Netland, H., 66
Neumann, P. D., 151n7, 167n63, 168n64, 176n100, 178n111, 178n113, 178n115
Newberg, E. N., 57n6, 57n7
Newbigin, L., 23, 24-25, 42n21, 43n22, 63-65
Niebuhr, H. R., 19-22
Noel, B. T., 22n41, 166n62, 171n86
Norman, L., 105

Olena, L. E., 57n6, 57n7
Outka, G., 97n72

Palma, A. D., 172
Parham, C., 103n1, 114-15, 126, 131
Payette, J., 1n3
Penner, J., 153-56, 157n40, 158
Pfister, R., 86n33
Philips, T., 3n13
Pohl, C. D., 92n52
Powell, K., 133n30, 134n31, 134n32

Radhakrishnan, S., 191n9
Ramji, R., 12n5
Randall, H. E., 117, 118
Reimer, S., 2, 11n3, 11n4
Richard, L., 92n52
Robeck Jr, C. M., 132n21, 140n48, 140n49
Roxburgh, A. J., 43n22, 63n23

Samuel, J. P. S., 141n53
Schwartz, S., 196n26
Schweitzer, D., 13n13
Seljak, D., 1n1, 16n21
Seymour, W. J., 131, 139-40
Simms, S., 22-23
Simpson, A. B., 113, 114n32, 122
Slomp, H., 84n26
Sloos, W., 109n16
Smart, T., 116
Smith, C., 37-38, 46n28, 46n29, 47n30, 155n21, 156n33, 156n34, 157n38, 158-60, 161n58
Smith, J. K. A., 168n72, 201n35, 202n37

Snell, P., 155n21, 156n33, 156n34, 157n38, 161n58
Solivan, S., 135n34, 178n116
Solomon, B., 138n41
Spittler, R. P., 169n78
Stan, L., 83n24
Stark, R., 17, 24, 80, 198n30
Steensland, B., 95n66
Stewart, A., 12n7, 105
Stott, J., 72n40
Stronstad, R., 66, 151n4, 171n85, 173n88, 179-81
Studebaker, S. M., 4n14, 197n28, 200n31
Sutherland, A., 92n52
Swoboda, A. J., 204

Taylor, C., 80, 200
Tennent, T. C., 46n26, 46n27
Thiessen, J., 1n2, 12n6, 17n26, 18
Tucker, M. E., 204n39
Turcescu, L., 83n24
Tyra, G., 34n2, 34n3, 35n4, 35n5, 39n14, 39n15, 40n17, 41n18, 42n21, 44n24, 45n25, 55n1, 59n12, 59n13, 59n15, 60n16, 60n17, 60n18, 60n19, 60n20, 60n22, 62n22, 65n28, 67n34, 68n35, 71n38, 71n39, 73n45, 74n46, 74n47

Van de Poll, E., 83n122
Van Gelder, C., 150n3
Van Ness, P., 187n2, 194-95
Vondey, W., 55n2

Wakefield, G., 13n9
Warner, R., 80
Wattier, S., 83n23
Way-Way, D., 94
Weigel, G., 88
Weiler, J., 84, 88
Wells, H. G., 89n44
Wenham, G., 128n7, 129n11
Wesley, J., 113
Westfall, W., 15n17
Wilkinson, M., 2, 11n3, 11n4, 13n8, 16n22

Index of Modern Authors

Willimon, W., 88–91
Wood, L. S., 1n3

Yoder, J. H., 89

Yong, A., 55n3, 58n10, 126n5, 135n34, 142, 180–81

Zilio, M., 132n25

Index of Ancient Sources

GENESIS

1:2	197
1:27	187
6:3	197
11	178
11:5–6	200

EXODUS

23:16	128
24	198
32	198
34:22	128

LEVITICUS

23:15–21	128
23:15	128
23:16–17	128
23:18–19	128
23:22	129, 132

NUMBERS

11:25–29	59n14
28:26	128
28:27–31	128

DEUTERONOMY

7:9	32
16:10	128
32:11	197

JOSHUA

24:14	32

JUDGES

8:27	197

1 SAMUEL

10:6–11	59n14
19:19–24	59n14

1 CHRONICLES

12:18	59n14

2 CHRONICLES

24:20	59n14

Index of Ancient Sources

PSALMS

34:8	31
51:11	197
78:32–37	33
89:8	32
25:8–10	33

PROVERBS

1:5	31n1
2	39
15:30	116
19:21	43
20:12	31n1

ECCLESIASTES

7:18	66

ISAIAH

44:3	197n27
63:10–14	197

JEREMIAH

31:31–32	197n27

EZEKIEL

36:26–28	197n27, 199

HOSEA

4:1	32

JOEL

2	106

2:9–32	199
2:28–29	59n14, 197n27

ZECHARIAH

4:6–9	197n27

MATTHEW

3:11–12	197n27
5:7	36
6:9–13	202n36
8	31
9:10–13	36
10:19–20	35n4
12:7	36
18:21–25	36
22:43	197
23:1–36	36
23:23	36
25:21	91

MARK

7:33	200
12:36	197

LUKE

1:2	121
1:41–45	59n14
1:67	59n14
2:25–28	59n14
5:38	106
6:36	36
7:29–35	36
7:36–39	36
10:25–37	28
11:2–4	202n36
12:1	36
18:9	36
21:14–15	35n4
22:20	33, 106
24:49	110

Index of Ancient Sources

JOHN

1:32–33	197n27
3:3–8	71
3:8	75
3:30	203
4:21–24	202
5:39	36
9:16	36
9:24–34	36
14–16	35
14	35
14:6	66
14:15–18	35
14:15–17	199
14:26	35
15	35
15:1–8	34
15:26	199
16	35
16:7–11	71
16:12–15	71
16:13	35
17:14–15	20
20:21	93

ACTS

1:4	110, 199
1:7	201
1:8	71, 76, 108, 110, 139, 201
1:16	197
2	110, 126, 129, 135, 138, 139, 150, 166–67, 170–82, 197–206
2:1–11	127–28
2:4	59n14, 139
2:9–11	130
2:11	135, 201
2:15–21	199
2:16–18	139
2:17	106, 182
2:38	180, 199
2:39	110, 199
2:42–47	179, 181, 203, 205
4:8	59n14
4:12	66
4:25	197
4:31	199
7:51	70, 197
Acts 8:4–19	59n14
8:14–17	199
9	74
9:1–19	199
9:10–22	60, 74
9:17–18	59n14
10:44–46	59n14
10:45	199
13:9	59n14
16:6–10	71
16:7	72n41
17:6	67
17:22–23	66
19:1–6	199
19:6	59n14

ROMANS

5:12–21	107
8:1–4	71
8:5–13	72
8:9	72n41
8:15–16	71
8:16	194
8:26–27	71
8:26	69n36, 202n36
15:13	71

1 CORINTHIANS

4:2	91
7	121
9:20–22	42
11:25	33
12	112, 114
12:3	199
12:4–8	71
12:7	139n46, 144–45
13:1	201
14:1–4	202n36
14:2	201
14:4–5	201
14:5	202
14:6	202

217

1 CORINTHIANS
(continued)

14:13–15	69n36
14:18	59n14
14:24–25	71
14:39–40	75

2 CORINTHIANS

1:22	71
5:5	71
6:14–18	66
11:1–4	203, 205

GALATIANS

3:14	110
4:6–7	71
4:6	71, 72n41
5:16–21	71
5:22–25	71
5:24–25	72
5:25	71

EPHESIANS

1:13–14	64, 71
2:18	71
2:22	71
3:6	110
3:16–17	71
4:30	70, 71
5–6	121
5:1–17	66
5:18–20	59n14, 71
5:18	72
6:10–18	71
6:18	69n36

PHILIPPIANS

1:19	72n41

COLOSSIANS

1:21–23	33
2:6	33
3	121

1 THESSALONIANS

4:8	70
5:19	70

1 TIMOTHY

1:12	91
2:4	66
2:5–6	66

2 TIMOTHY

1:7	4
2:25	66

TITUS

1:1	66

HEBREWS

3:1–6	33
3:7	197
3:12–14	33
8:6–13	33
9:15–28	33
10:15	197n27
10:19–39	33
10:26	66
10:29	70

JAMES

3:5	200

Index of Ancient Sources

1 PETER

1:11	72n41

2 PETER

1:21	197
3:6–10	204

1 JOHN

2:20–21	66
3:24	194
4:2–3	199

2 JOHN

1:1–4	66

JUDE

3	42
20	69n36, 202n36

REVELATION

13:10	32

QURAN

4:1	188
4:89	193
4:101–102	193
5:105	189
8:13–17	193
8:39–40	193
9:29	193
9:111	193

www.ingramcontent.com/pod-product-compliance
Lightning Source LLC
Chambersburg PA
CBHW062024220426
43662CB00010B/1463